WHAT PEOPLE ARE SAYING

"I was thoroughly pleased with the format, contents, and layout of the book. It provided me with many proven tips that can be useful in preparing for entry into the work force. The example copies of how to complete various applications were easy to understand and not complicated. What really stands out is the Voyage everyone is on and how they overcame obstacles while seeking employment. I would recommend this book to anyone seeking employment in the civilian or government sector."

JEFFERY DENT, *Veteran Service Representative Staff Sergeant/E6, U.S. Army (Retired)*

"I strongly recommend *Voyager/Veteran* to veterans seeking full time meaningful employment. The author addresses each step that a veteran must negotiate to gain employment. He also provides a nine-step strategy for veterans to follow enabling them to develop the right mindset and thought process required to be creative in searching for employment."

JAMES A. CUPP, *Disabled Veterans Outreach Program Specialist Major, U.S. Army (Retired)*

"P.D. Pritchard has written an all-encompassing, easily understood resource for today's veterans voyaging through our contemporary employment environment. Especially for veterans just transitioning out of military service for that first real-world career opportunity, seeking a federal government position or preparing for a great opportunity in private employment field. *Voyager/Veteran* is a must-read for anyone wanting to understand the hiring process, inclusive of insightful tips that often result in offers of employment."

JOE FERGUSON, *Local Veterans Employment Representative Sergeant, 2nd Marine Division, U.S. Marine Corps*

"I worked with the author, who assisted me in the job search process, especially interviews, found in chapter 8 of *Voyager/Veteran*, which ultimately led to my being successfully employed in a very rewarding career."

SHANE HICKS, *E3, U.S. Navy, Honorably Discharged*

"P.D. Pritchard is an absolute wordsmith. He makes personal growth through career betterment an exciting topic. His utilization of short stories that any veteran can relate to adds significant value and allows his audience to connect immediately to each chapter. Additionally, he makes the job search task relatable by demonstrating clearly that veterans have already gained the necessary proficiencies to succeed through their training and experience. I cannot recommend this resource more highly for every veteran."

JIMMIE SIMPSON, *Local Veterans Employment Representative SSG USA, former ET2 (SS) U.S. Navy*

"While reading *Voyager/Veteran* found it to be a well-directed instructional map providing compassionate support while maintaining a real world view of the needs of veterans conducting job search. A special thanks to the author for his commitment to serving military personnel and his efforts to assist them in securing a promising future for both themselves and their families."

LAWRENCE A. LUCK, *Director of Academics Master Sergeant/ E7, U.S. Air Force (Retired) Operation Iraqi Freedom, Operation Enduring Freedom U.S. Army, 300th MASH Unit Desert Storm, Desert Shield, Vietnam*

"I thoroughly enjoyed *Voyager/Veteran* and, as a believer in face-to-face networking I especially enjoyed that section. By including anecdotes involving veterans seeking employment, the author provides a touch of the human aspect towards job searching, interviewing, and the follow-up after the interview, just to name a few of the features. As a veteran, I found the book to be engaging an informative. This book is squared away!"

JOYCE NORTON, *Veteran's Service Representative (LVER/DVOP)*
E4, U.S. Army, Honorably Discharged

"*Voyager/Veteran* a book designed to help veterans already in the civilian sector and those recently separated vets find work in today's competitive job market. It has much to offer, it's a relatable and rational journey through the entire process of seeking employment. Veterans and nonveterans alike will greatly benefit from the wisdom and lessons within. Soak in the essence of the anecdotal scenarios presented to get the bigpicture of what really takes place during the job search process: networking, developing an elevator pitch, writing a cover letter and resume, completing an application, interviewing and simply building bridges to your next career. It's a wonderful and enlightening read, one I would fully recommend to anyone seriously seeking to succeed in finding meaningful employment."

THOMAS STOQUERT, *Senior Fraud Investigator,*
MBA, CFE, CFI, Notary Sergeant, ES,
Counter Intelligence Special Agent, U.S. Army

VOYAGER/VETERAN

THE JOURNEY TO A SUCCESSFUL
JOB SEARCH MINDSET

VOYAGER/VETERAN

THE JOURNEY TO A SUCCESSFUL JOB SEARCH MINDSET

P.D. PRITCHARD, DVOP, GCDF, MS

Carpenter's Son Publishing

Voyager/Veteran: The Journey to a Successful Job Search Mindset

©2021 by P. D. Pritchard

Published by Carpenter's Son Publishing, Franklin, TN.

Edited by Ann Tatlock

Interior Design by Suzanne Lawing

Cover Design by Joyce Dierschke

Printed in the United States of America

ISBN: 978-1-950892-80-8

VOYAGER/VETERAN is designed to provide a paradigm (that is, a model) for conducting an exceptional and meaningful job search for veterans. This book embodies a combination of traditional and unconventional tools and simple universal truths. The material presented here includes anecdotal examples, formal/informal training, and educational disciplines, as well as cultural and social values. The focus is most certainly one of compassion, inquiry, and self-discovery. The goal is to foster a productive mindset that results in the development and realization of the veteran's true career and employment potential. The desired outcome is a journey toward self-sufficiency and sustainability.

Like mission-driven voyagers of the past, veterans today are best characterized by their commitment, comradeship, and goal orientation as they move forward into unknown territory—that of transitioning into and competing in the civilian sector of employment. Their exploring, pioneering, and sharing of successes and failures becomes a learning and personal growth process exemplified through the exhortation, "The journey never ends!"

> *"Success is not final, failure is not fatal;*
> *it is the courage to continue that counts."*
> WINSTON CHURCHILL

> *"Before you speak, listen. Before you criticize, wait.*
> *Before you pray, forgive. Before you quit, try.*
> *Before you retire, save. Before you die, give."*
> WILLIAM ARTHUR WARD, AN OFTEN QUOTED
> WRITER OF INSPIRATIONAL MAXIMS

"The mission is, 'To explore strange new worlds; to seek out new life and new civilizations; to boldly go where no man has gone before.'"
JAMES T. KIRK, CAPTAIN, STARSHIP USS ENTERPRISE
GENE RODDENBERRY, NEXT GENERATION AUTHOR AND FUTURIST

"If your mind carries a heavy burden of negative past,
you will experience more of the same. The past
perpetuates itself through lack of presence. The quality
of your consciousness at this moment is what shapes the future—
which, of course, can only be experienced as the Now."
ECKHART TOLLE, AUTHOR OF *THE POWER OF NOW*

To my brother Voyager Lee Hall, DVOP, an extraordinary individual who gallantly, gently, unceremoniously, and without apology moved on from a life of helping other veterans. Challenged by devastating circumstances, he was suddenly catapulted into a universe of complete acceptance, brightness, and love, destined to explore it endlessly. It is to him that VOYAGER/VETERAN is dedicated.

Contents

PREFACE

The passing of veterans like Lee Hall, DVOP (to whom this book is dedicated), serves to remind us that fundamental characteristics such as dignity, productivity, and self-sufficiency have now become the objectives of veteran services programs provided at local American Job Centers (AJCs) throughout this country. Back in the day, they were called the unemployment offices—where a person out of work registered for unemployment benefits and waited hopefully for the next job opportunity to emerge.

Today, American Job Centers aim to offer veterans a sense of empowerment while identifying meaningful job and career opportunities, especially for those veterans with specific barriers to employment. It's a place where a vast array of viable options and qualified staff are made available to all those who have served their country honorably—turning military and life experiences into promising futures.

To assist veterans as they seek out potential employment and career opportunities are the National Veterans Training Institute (NVTI), professionally trained and devoted individuals known as Disabled Veteran Outreach Program specialists (DVOPs), Local Veteran Employment Representatives (LVERs), and Veterans Administration (VA) Veteran Services Officers (VSOs)—all more commonly referred to as "Vet Reps." Generally, they are military veterans who have served their country and continue to serve other veterans and their families exclusively.

But there are also those independent of the military who are vet-oriented life coaches and counselors to whom we owe a debt of gratitude for assisting veterans in need. To these giving individuals VOYAGER/VETERAN is also dedicated.

INTRODUCTION

What began as respectable exchange of ideas became a contentious debate with Chris, a fellow Vet Rep. We were discussing the purpose and use of what might be considered an unconventional method for writing a resume that I have used successfully for years. The method was designed to introduce contemporary but very effective job search options to the general public, college students, and military veteran clients.

I was taken by surprise when Chris emphatically and boisterously declared, "Adding a few extra underlines or graphics in a resume just to be unconventional is nothing but a lot of BS! You don't need that crap. All you need to do is put down on paper a little bit about who you are and what you can do. Adding lines in bold across the face of a resume just takes up space and does nothing to convince an employer that an applicant has what he is looking for!"

Our conversation came to a convenient end when Chris responded to the insistent ringing of his phone, and I silently disappeared into my office to give him time to cool off. Shaking my head in disbelief and feeling totally mystified by my friend's outburst, I said to myself, "He just doesn't get it!"

Later, when Chris appeared a little more receptive, I explained, "That line of bold type, when utilized correctly, can become an effective employer attention-getting tool. It's a subtle but dynamic principle of effective communications that should be included in every resume written and submitted to an employer. Yes, admittedly, it is a concept not normally considered by experienced employment coaches, resume writers, and astute applicants doing a job search these days. Yet, similar ideas have been successfully utilized in the business world for several decades."

I went on to suggest, "Chris, a job search is all about going into business and marketing yourself in an innovative way to a potential client or customer. In this case, it's the employer!"

"I'm not sure how a job search is like going into business for yourself," he replied. "Where's the connection between writing a resume and starting a business?"

I suggested to Chris that the process of conducting a contemporary job search is in fact similar to going into business for yourself for this reason: A job search (including resume, cover letter, and interview) offers a product or service to a prospective client or customer (in this case the employer) using developed marketing, advertising, and salesmanship skills. So, think about it this way:

- **THE PRODUCT** is your general background, experience, and personal characteristics and accomplishments.

- **THE SERVICE** is your knowledge skills, abilities (KSAs), education, and training.

- **THE COVER LETTER** is your marketing strategy directed at a specific target or particular type of customer—the employer. As part of the business model, it introduces the who, what, why, where, when, and how of your product or service.

- **THE RESUME** is your personal advertisement. It addresses in specific detail the benefits to be gained by the client/customer (employer) through the utilization of your KSAs (knowledge skills and abilities), education, and training that match the job criteria. The resume identifies what the employer is getting for their investment in you. It is a personal advertisement designed to leave the employer wanting to learn more about the product or service you offer through further inquiry/sampling (the interview).

- **THE INTERVIEW** is your sales presentation. This is the where, when, and how. You meet the client/customer (employer) face-to-face, establishing rapport (a connection and common ground of interests, goals, and similarities) through intellectual and verbal persuasion. It's your opportunity to convincingly answer and ask questions indicating how your product or service qualifications have the capability of matching or filling the employer's needs."

"Chris, does this make any sense to you?" I asked.

"Yeah," he admitted. "I guess it does when you look at it the way you present it. Hey man, I apologize for losing my cool the other day. Sometimes I get fed up with all these ideas about job search, and whose model for a resume and cover letter works best. All that is needed with most of the vets we serve is something simple, something very basic."

In hindsight, if I had initially not allowed myself to be overcome by my friend's emotional response, and if he had been open to listening, I would have explained that a line in bold, centered, and running from left to right across the top of the resume page was there for a reason, and not merely inserted as window dressing as he had claimed. Yes, a reasonable explanation would have provided some clarity to my suggestion. But then again, a lot of us fall victim to living in a "could-a, would-a, should-a" world—most of the time, one of our own making.

I went on to explain to Chris, "The bold line I referred to is what I call the Center of Attention Line (CAL)." It's there because for me, as years of experience, experimentation, training, and research have demonstrated, it works! It is the art of accentuating the branding message of an applicant, drawing attention to and illustrating what they have to offer an employer. Simply stated, "branding" is what you say or do so your reader (the employer) will recall a certain image when you come to mind.

For example, the Center Line is located near the top of the resume page, one space below the heading. The heading itself usually consists of the applicant's name, address, city, state, zip code, phone number, and email address. Most of the time I use, and recommend, two Center Lines, or a double Center Line. I do this so that it can't be mistaken for a typographical error. Consider the following:

MARIE MCDOUGAL
1422 Bridge Road
Old Orchard Beach, ME04064
(207) 934-2221 / jmcd@yahoo.com

<u>EMPLOYMENT FOCUS</u>
(Some applicants prefer the term OBJECTIVE
or other creative descriptor)

The purpose of the Center Line is to subtly cue the reader, drawing their eyes and attention down and to the center of the page, to the title of each main topic heading of the resume where the applicant wants the employer to notice essential qualifying information.

This topic section should contain a statement (two very short sentences or a sentence of not more than from 15–21 words) addressing the applicant's general qualification that is employer needs-focused.

Restricting the number of words in a descriptive sentence has to do with (1) using words to attract the reader's attention and (2) facilitating brand retention. Again, brand retention is the means by which you use a unique combination of words to help an employer remember how you are best qualified to meet their needs. It's like painting a word picture or offering an image that the employer can easily call to mind. This is a method common to the advertising industry to attract the attention of potential customers to a product or service.

Consider a recently discharged female Unit Supply Specialist (92Y MOS) looking for a foot-in-the-door entry to a mid-level employment opportunity. She is applying to a nationally recognized warehouse and distribution corporation. Part of the employer's job announcement indicates a need for a person who can provide leadership and the handling of complex customer shipping problems. The following branding message might be used:

EMPLOYMENT FOCUS

Accomplished, outgoing, experienced team-builder and leader, with proven logistical operations troubleshooting skills, guarantees top-quality services to your customers.

It's important to understand that what is initiated here is the creation of a prompting impulse that heightens the employer's interest in fully reviewing an applicant's resume. This descriptive sentence is specific to focusing on the employer's needs, not the applicant's.

Why?

Because, as contemporary research indicates, the longer it takes an employer to locate interesting, attention-getting, or otherwise qualifying information about the applicant's qualifications, the quicker that employer tires of the search. He soon loses any desire to read further.

Thus, the employer in our example is subtly directed to critical information that immediately creates an interest in the applicant. This initial favorable impression leads the employer to want to sit down with the applicant and further discuss his or her potential. The next step is the interview.

Again, such an impression takes place within a few seconds. It all begins with a few simple lines strategically placed and centered at the beginning of a resume, and supported by enticing personal brand information.

HR professionals, recruiters, psychologists studying human behavior, and those who specialize in career development estimate that if an applicant's resume has not captured the employer's attention within the first 7–12 seconds (and some say 5–7 seconds), it will most likely be discarded. The first few seconds that a resume is in an employer's hand are critical. The applicant must engage in "mental directing" and "subliminal seed-planting" to create a favorable impression.

So if there's a point to be made here, it's this: There are a certain number of hidden or very subtle (subliminal) impression-making factors that we are exposed to in our everyday lives, most often through the medium known as marketing and advertising. Generally, we are not aware of their significance and influence unless we've been trained to look for them.

Similarly, in the job search process (e.g. during the crafting and submission of a resume and cover letter), we are actually performing a major role within the marketing and advertising function. Whether we realize it or not, applicants initially are and should be in control of determining the nature and delivery method of their message to the employer. They need to develop and apply the same creative and interest-generating material as that used in today's business world in order to attract the customer or client to a person, service, or product.

Surprisingly, the more applicants practice this technique, the better they become at doing it, and are able to intuitively recognize when it's being applied to them. This creative focus, once developed, becomes second nature to the applicant's thinking and communication skills.

We call this gift our Basic Intuitive Influential Factor. Some call it Creating a Favorable First Impression. As such, it needs to happen long before an applicant ever meets the employer face-to-face. And the most likely place for it to occur is through the branding statement at the very beginning of a resume.

Every serious veteran job applicant or candidate should consider and explore any and every ethical tool available to them, whether it is unconventional or not. The competitiveness and sophistication of today's job market demands it!

Today, all veterans currently involved in the job search process must master a reasonable amount of creativity and intuitive awareness —the ability to consciously generate those subtle but very effective communications links, or subliminal cues, favorable to influencing employer interviewing decisions. Following the path presented here in the job search guide, VOYAGER/VETERAN destroys any notion, illusion, and popular belief that the purpose of a resume is to get a job, because it is not!

So ask yourself, "What is the true purpose of a resume?" If you don't know, then do the research and/or … continue reading. Just know that creating and writing an effective resume is but only one of the many important building blocks/strategies needed to construct a basic job search foundation.

VOYAGER/VETERAN, your guide to identifying and developing those key building blocks, puts YOU in charge of how they are utilized. Similarly, this guide captures the all-encompassing essence of an effective job search found in the Rudyard Kipling poem:

> *"I keep six honest serving-men*
> *(They taught me all I knew);*
> *Their names are What and Why and When*
> *And How and Where and Who."*

VOYAGER/VETERAN has as its primary goal the development of the mindset or mental disciplines of creativity, adaptability, and flexibility needed to conduct a contemporary and effective job search.

Yes, important subjects like resumes, cover letters, networking and interviews are covered. But the crucial factor to mastering the non-technical aspect of the job search function—the number one all-important element—is keeping an open mind to all that you can learn and accomplish. Remember, once the pursuit of effective communications and learning stops, so does the realization of a dream job.

VOYAGER/VETERAN is designed to foster a malleable mindset adaptable to changing life circumstances. All your energy and effort needs be focused on developing and implementing your own winning strategy—unique to you. To succeed, you will need to be creative and develop independent thinking.

Adaptability and creative thinking are clearly seen in the story of Nan-in, a Japanese master during the Meiji era (1868–1912). One day he received an arrogant university professor who came to inquire about the discipline Zen. As Nan-in served tea, he poured his visitor's cup full, and then kept on pouring. The professor watched the tea cup overflow until he no longer could restrain himself.

"It is overfull. No more will go in!" the professor loudly exclaimed.

"Like this cup," Nan-in said, "you are full of your own opinions and ideas. How can I show you Zen unless your cup is empty?"

VOYAGER/VETERAN provides a cautionary reminder that we need to guard against falling into mental malaise, an unwillingness to be open to new ways of thinking. Sometimes, like the professor in the story, we need to let go of certain ideas we stubbornly cling to as true, and open ourselves up to new ideas.

VOYAGER/VETERAN is designed to activate the creative genius within. It consists of the following:

1. *Dealing with the Past*

2. *Shortcuts*

3. *Preparing for the Future by Accepting Change*

4. *The Value of Learning to Network*

5. *The Application Challenge*

6. *The Federal Application Process*

7. *The Reality of Resumes and Cover Letters*

8. *Preparing for and Participating in the Interview*

9. *The Necessity, Value, and Method of Saying Thank You*

10. *Epilogue, Manifesting Success—A Never-ending Journey*

1

DEALING WITH THE PAST

"The Path to Enlightenment"

At fifty-five, Roger had now achieved what society called senior citizen status. He had also achieved another milestone. He was a surviving veteran of the Vietnam War. As a former Marine helicopter pilot, he was bitter about the fact that those who served during that time were never really recognized for their sacrifices by their country. "Especially those," he often recalled, "who were left lying dead and rotting in those killing fields."

Day by day his every thought was shadowed by the fact that his service was never validated. He had not come home feeling victorious. Instead, he thought of the Spartan mother whose son marched off with his comrades to defend the Pass at Thermopylae against the Persian Hoard. As she watched him go, she said, "Son, come home victorious or on your shield." Roger felt as though he had neither come home victorious nor on his shield.

Years later, while at the public library, Roger happened across an article about the Spartans and their warrior code in a history magazine. As he read, his mind went back to his time in Vietnam. On 29 April, 1975, in the waters off South Vietnam, Roger got a last-minute assignment to the 7th Fleet. His job was to ferry personnel from installations in South Vietnam as the Viet Cong (VC) began overrunning two-thirds of the country. It was called "Operation Frequent Wind."

Roger's CH-53 Heavy Marine Chopper was like a mythological dragon dying and snorting its last breath of fire and fumes. The side of his machine was riddled with bullet holes, and a nauseating acrid smell of burning aviation fuel snaked its way along a tired exhaust system, venting gray puffs of noxious fumes.

The heavy laboring wop, wop, wop of those huge blades cut through the humid Southeast Asian air that day as the engine accelerated in the lift mode. The big bird rose slowly above the turmoil continuing to take place below.

The Khmer Rouge was advancing on the city of Saigon, and Big Bird had picked up its last load of frenzied civilians, U.S. Government personnel, and the last departing U.S. Marine Embassy Guard, MGy/Sgt John J. Valdez.

Roger flew out to sea toward the 7th Fleet. As he approached, he was waved off the decks of the *Coral Sea, Hancock,* and *Enterprise.* They were already filled with hot and smoking Hueys and assorted aircraft. Finally, Roger found landing room and his anxious load of survivors was deposited onto the deck of the U.S. Carrier *Midway,* already crammed with UH-1 Huey helicopters. They were safe for now out at sea, but for Roger there was the lingering recollection of those who would never make it back. Left in-country, they would never experience any safe ground.

All those who made the ultimate sacrifice just added fuel to the fire burning within Roger's soul. All those men were expendable, all collateral damage—and for what? Too, what consideration was given to the POWs left behind, and those unable to be airlifted out because his chopper was filled to the max?

When Roger considered the exception made for some Vietnamese bigwig named Buang-Ly, the senselessness of the war became all the more apparent to him. Major Buang-Ly was a Vietnamese Air Force major who loaded his wife and five children into a two-seat Cessna

O-1 Bird Dog and took off from Con Son Island. After evading enemy ground fire, Major Buang-Ly headed out to sea and spotted the *Midway*.

Midway's crew attempted to contact the aircraft on emergency frequencies while the pilot continued to circle overhead with his landing lights on.

So when a spotter from the *Midway* reported that there were at least four people in the two-seater aircraft, all thoughts of forcing the pilot to ditch alongside were abandoned. It was unlikely that the passengers of that overloaded Bird Dog could survive the ditching and safely get out of the plane before it sank.

After three flyovers, Major Buang-Ly managed to drop a note from a low pass over the deck: "Can you move the helicopter to the other side? I can land on your runway. I can fly for one hour more. You have enough time to move. Please rescue me! Major Buang-Ly, wife and five children."

The ship's commanding officer responded and ordered the arresting wires be removed from the helicopter. Furthermore, any helicopters that could not be safely and quickly relocated should be pushed over the side.

He called for volunteers, and soon every available seaman, regardless of rank or duty, was on deck to provide the manpower to get the job done. Millions of U.S. dollars worth of UH-1 Huey helicopters were pushed overboard into the South China Sea.

With a 500-foot ceiling, five miles of visibility, a light rain, and 15 knots of surface wind, the captain ordered the ship to make 25 knots into the wind. Warnings about the dangerous downdrafts created behind a steaming carrier were transmitted in both Vietnamese and English. To make matters worse, five additional UH-1 helicopters landed and cluttered up the deck. Without hesitation, the captain ordered them scuttled as well.

The captain later recalled, in an article in the fall, 1993 issue of the National Museum of Aviation History's *Foundation* magazine, "The aircraft cleared the ramp and touched down on the center line at the normal touchdown point. Had he been equipped with a tail hook he could have bagged a number 3 wire. The plane bounced once and came stopped abeam of the island, amidships, with a wildly cheering, arms-waving flight deck crew."

Major Buang-Ly was escorted to the bridge, where the captain congratulated him on his outstanding airmanship and his bravery in risking everything without knowing for certain a carrier would be where he needed it. The crew of the *Midway* was so impressed that they established a fund to help him and his family get settled in the United States.

The O-1 that Major Buang-Ly landed is now on display at the Naval Aviation Museum in Pensacola, Florida. Having witnessed the whole event, Roger had to admit to himself that the major's move was a gutsy one, but why so much attention to one person, when so many others who exhibited equal bravery were somehow overlooked?

Over the years, Roger's painful memories continued to fester like an open wound. He remembered the number of times he had been ordered to return to base with those he had rescued, while leaving others behind.

He remembered too the games they played with enemy body-count. They would wipe out whole villages, and list all inhabitants— civilian or otherwise—as the enemy to justify claims of military success. Roger wondered, "Who was keeping score on the body count of U.S. troops left behind?" This was in spite of the often repeated phrase by unit commanders, "No soldier left behind!"

Then Roger had returned home, neither victorious nor on his shield. A few jobless years later, Roger finally found helicopter work flying fat cat executives and oil rig workers around the Alaskan North Slope oil fields. The pay was good and the hours weren't too bad either, but he found the oil company executives arrogant. Their indifference toward the cultural norms of others, especially Alaskan Natives, just didn't sit well with him. Always demanding, oil execs triggered in Roger the memory of the aberrant behavior of those in military command. Sometimes such behavior resulted in fragging—that is, soldiers turning on their superiors.

It was an issue that he couldn't or wouldn't deal with in an acceptable manner. The anger always surfaced like a dead, bloated body of a warrior floating to the top of the Mekong River near the Cambodian Boarder—the result of engaging an overwhelming number of VC with tragic and predictable outcomes.

The flying job in Alaska was only one of Roger's attempts at steady work. He held numerous jobs over the years. After only a few months, he'd either walk off the job in disgust, without explanation, or he would just never show up to work again. His last paycheck would arrive at his P.O. Box, and that was it. Eventually, the anger from his past would subside for a while, and then he would find another job and it would begin all over again. Somewhere in this pitiful journey he convinced himself that his past had now become his future.

But occasionally there was that little respite, a white-hot dot of thought that sometimes glowed for a few seconds, illuminating that priceless piece of information he had received from Bong-Tow, a Vietnamese monk he had spent time with between in-country ops. Bong-Tow was fond of saying, "Roger, my son, what you think about all the time expands."

After a few years, the word was out that Roger, although a technical genius at the controls of a helicopter, didn't have much staying power. His dependability was always in question by those who did hire him.

At one point while he was working in Arctic Alaska, ferrying oil workers to exploratory drilling well rigs in the Chukchi Sea, he had given some thought to just losing himself in the vast wilderness of the Brooks Range, like so many of his buddies had done in the lower forty-eight.

They lived in the bush because they still had that in-country mentality about themselves, always living in a solitary survivalist mode only a Vietnam vet could relate to, answering to no one, always alert for intruders, ready for the next camp to be overrun by the enemy. The locals in adjacent towns, while out camping or hunting, occasionally came upon these vets face-to-face and saw that wild Neanderthal re-flection in their eyes: "Like they were on something, just a bunch of nut cases, those spooky dudes living in the woods."

But Roger didn't exactly feel shunned like some of his Nam coun-terparts. Part of him still lived in the past while the other half at-tempted to exist in the reality of the present. No day had ever been the same since he left Nam. But the past was about to reveal itself in a way he never anticipated, and his life would change in a way he never expected ...

Roger's friend Sam, now a Vet Rep with the State Department of Labor, talked him into attending a local Vietnam Veterans of America (VVA) meeting. As he entered the meeting hall, Roger thought he rec-ognized a few faces from his past, but he wasn't sure. He didn't bother to make a move to connect with anyone; he just sat there, quickly scan-ning the room, then looking down at the floor. Suddenly, something in his peripheral vision caught his attention for just a nanosecond— the color of burnt yellow. The synapse (the point at which a nervous impulse passes from one neuron to another) in his brain triggered something. Roger couldn't make the connection and he let it go.

Sam knew all too well the emotional roller coaster ride Roger con-tinued to experience. The two men had shared an apartment before and after Roger worked has a helicopter pilot in Alaska.

One day Sam came home and found Roger sitting on the living room floor, staring at the wall. He looked like he was drunk out of his gourd. Tears ran down his face, and he kept licking the salty teardrops from his lips.

"What's going on, Roger?" Sam carefully inquired.

"I'm fed up with everything," Roger said, "and I don't know how to explain what's happening to me or what my next move is. I'm really out of it."

To Sam, Roger looked and acted worse now than before he left for Alaska. He decided it was time to take Roger in hand. He thought ex-posing Roger to fellow vets at the local VVA might help him re-engage.

The VVA Post Commander stood up and introduced himself, then asked that new persons in attendance go around the room and introduce themselves. When it came to Roger, he signaled a firm "No!" by shaking his head from side to side.

He sat subdued and hunched over, remembering the sounds and smells of warriors in a group together—the familiar odor of sweat and mustiness, of ground-in earth coming off their clothes. He slowly leaned toward Sam and mumbled the words, "I gotta go, Sam. This ain't for me!"

Just as Roger started to stand up, he heard the guy at the head of the room announce, "Fellow veterans, today we are indeed privileged to have with us a visitor from Vietnam. Please join me in welcoming our friend Bong-Tow. The Reverend Tow has been visiting several of our VVA organizations throughout the country on a spiritual mission and will be available for questions and healing consultations for the next few months before returning home to Vietnam."

Now Roger understood the previously dismissed color of burnt yellow. Time stood still as he recognized ... Bong-Tow, his Vietnamese mentor. There he stood before the gathering of warriors in his *Haiqing* (Buddhist monk's robe).

He was shorter than Roger recalled, and childlike in size, weighing no more than 100 pounds soaking wet. But the freshly shaved, suntanned head and those large pointed ears were the same, and the wide smile of wonderment hadn't changed. His face emanated compassion and was free of judgment. In that regard, Bong-Tow was as Roger remembered him.

Roger found himself the only one standing and locked onto Bong-Tow's gaze. The reflection of recognition was in both their eyes. Simultaneously, they placed their hands together as in prayer, and bowed slightly toward each other—the older teacher and lost student in unison—as the rest of the group welcomed the visitor with applause.

After the meeting was over, Roger and Bong-Tow remained behind after everyone, including Sam, had left the meeting room. They stood there for a few moments staring at one another while the mist cleared from their eyes.

There was no man hug or fist bump given—they just grabbed each other's arms in a respectful manly embrace and shook each other, then sat down facing one another.

Bong-Tow spoke first; his English had improved considerably. Now he articulated his words as though he were a British-sounding scholar. "How have you been, Roger? The last thing you told me when you left, the last time we were together, was that you had some errands to do and we should meet later for our weekly talk."

Roger, still reeling from the shock of seeing his mentor, wiped his eyes and nose with a napkin from the table next to him. Somewhat at a loss for words, he said almost in a whisper, "When I left that day and went back to my hootch, the whole world came undone. All I remember is a last-minute change of orders to assist the 7th Fleet. They were getting ready to begin evacuation of all military and civilian personnel from the embassy in Saigon."

Roger and Bong-Tow talked for the next several hours, with Roger monopolizing most of the conversation, spewing out the festering discontentment he had held in over the years.

"Look, Bong," he said finally, "I'm running out of things to say right now. You showing up like this had blown my mind."

Bong-Tow instinctively placed his hand on Roger's shoulder to quiet his wild river of words and energy. "We will talk next week, my son."

In the weeks that followed, Bong-Tow returned to the VVA meetings. During one meeting, he explained to the members, "Continually harboring feelings of anger, distrust, and hostility negatively impacts and weakens the body. Recalling past painful experiences, especially feelings of guilt, renders the body, physically and spiritually, incapable of generating the energy necessary to make it through the day, often leaving a person feeling exhausted and depressed."

An anonymous voice from the back of the room asked, "So, what do you mean by *weakens the body*?"

Without hesitation, Bong-Tow responded, "Could I have a volunteer come to the front of the room?"

The room fell silent, with the exception of a few dry coughs and some territorial sniffs and snorts that signified, "Brother, you're invading my space. Back off!" This was not Bong-Tow's first experience with veterans who were reluctant to participate openly in a group setting; it was expected.

His next move took Roger by surprise. "We have a friend here who I know is willing to assist us with a demonstration. It is known as the Hard-Soft-Arm Awakening. Its use and results, as you will see, require little explanation. Just remember that what you think about intensely expands!" Bong-Tow paused, then extended his arm toward Roger. "Roger, my son, would you please come to the front of the room?"

Before Roger could respond, Bong-Tow went on to explain, "Roger is a dear friend and former student of mine. We met in my country during a tragic time of human discord. The conflict broke off our relationship before he could learn the value and meaning of the Hard-Soft-Arm Awakening. So, we will continue that lesson tonight."

Unaware of how he got from his chair in the back to the front of the room, Roger now stood at Bong-Tow's side.

It was puzzling. He was just suddenly there, standing and looking out over the gathering of fellow vets. The cacophony of mumbling, low voices, and whispering drifted off as Bong-Tow raised his hand to signal for quiet. The vets now sat in stone silence.

"Roger," Bong-Tow asked, "will you please close your eyes and listen to my words? Please relax and let your hands hang at your sides."

Roger let his arms hang at his sides and took several deep breaths and submitted to the limpness of his body as Bong-Tow gave instructions.

"Continue to keep your eyes closed," Bong-Tow instructed. "Now think back to a time in your life when something or someone made you very happy and hold onto that thought. Do not say what it is." There was a pause of a few seconds. "Are you remembering what it was, Roger?"

Roger, with a wide grin on his face, said, "Yeah, man, I got it!"

Bong-Tow continued, "Raise your dominant hand out from your side to shoulder level and make a fist." Roger raised his right arm out from his side and squeezed his hand into a muscular fist. Bong-Tow continued, "Roger, you may resist any pressure you feel as I push down on your arm and please continue with that happy thought from the past."

Bong-Tow gently grabbed Roger's wrist with one hand and attempted to pull the arm down. Having no success with one hand, he grabbed the arm with both hands. Roger's arm was unyielding. Finally, in an amusing conclusion, Bong-Tow lifted his feet off the floor and hung, like a playful monkey, from Roger's extended right arm for a few seconds. The room suddenly erupted into uncontrollable laughter. After a moment, Bong-Tow lowered his feet to the floor. The room paused in silence.

Bong-Tow said, "Roger, you may open your eyes and lower your arm to your side and relax."

To the gathering before him, Bong-Tow announced, "As you can see, Roger is an extremely powerful man." As Roger began to walk back to his seat, Bong-Tow said, "Roger, we are not finished. Please come back and stand with me again."

As Roger returned to the spot next to his mentor, it was clear to him that this scene was getting a little weird. It was something he felt, but couldn't explain. He had, from the beginning of his relationship with Bong-Tow, found him to be somewhat mystical, secretive and somehow, very magical. But, he always was at ease with him and trusted him. Time spent with him in that Vietnam temple left Roger feeling at peace with himself. And yet, a number of questions always lingered.

"Roger," Bong-Tow asked, "will you please raise your arm as you did before and make that big fist?"

Roger raised his right arm up to shoulder height and squeezed his hand and fingers into a huge knotted ball of bone and muscle, the knuckles turning white from the pressure.

Bong-Tow continued, "Roger, please close your eyes. Now I want you to think of a time in your life when you were sad about someone or something or when you felt guilty. Think of some event in the past you could not control that continues to plague your memory today, something that might bring you great feelings of regret, or pain, or anger. Do not tell me what it is, but when I touch you I want you to resist."

Roger closed his eyes once again and continued to extend his right arm.

"Are you still squeezing your fist?" Bong-Tow asked. "Can you see the event, Roger?"

Roger nodded as his face contorted slightly in pain. The anger he had harbored for years came out in a mix of sweat and tears that slowly streamed down his cheeks.

Not so much as a cough or a whisper was heard in the room. The silence was deafening.

Bong-Tow slowly stepped to Roger's right side. So that everyone gathered could see, he raised his arm and extended his index finger up in the air. Then he laid his finger on the wrist of Roger's extended arm, gently pushing his student's arm down to his right side.

A huge, collective gasp filled the room, followed by complete silence.

"What happened?" Roger asked. He opened his eyes, and a look of disbelief crossed his face. "How did you make my arm go down to my side so easily? I was squeezing my fist like you asked. I don't understand it. Did you hypnotize me?"

The slight smile on Bong-Tow's face was one of amusement, and yet it signified a secret which he unceremoniously revealed.

"When one thinks about peaceful, joyous, and pleasant experiences, the mind and the body are as one. They are in a positive state of Universal Energy to which all men are connected and therefore allow them to function always from a position of power and strength. As you have observed, Roger is capable of great strength. It also means that my student is capable of great joy when he opens his heart to learning and forgiving."

After a moment, Bong-Tow continued, "However, as you have also observed, Roger is capable of remembering unpleasantness in his life. And, in the privacy of his thoughts, as you have witnessed, it had become a negative and controlling influence, reducing and disconnecting him from his Universal Energy source, therefore rendering him weak and powerless. The mind and the body were separated, and once divided, they lost their strength."

By the following week, word had gotten out in the vet community that a little monk named Bong-Tow was doing some amazing works in helping veterans to heal old wounds and to move forward with their lives.

At the next meeting there were no empty chairs—it was wall-to-wall vets. There he was, this little guy in the burnt-yellow robe standing quietly before that sea of broken warriors. To those who had been attending these meeting for the past several weeks, the faint sound of lightly tinkling bells signaled that the meeting was about to start. The room quickly fell silent.

"Welcome to you all," Bong-Tow began. "I see that we have new faces among us tonight. We are happy that you are here."

During the session that followed, Bong-Tow reminded the group, "Our experience of the previous week demonstrates the destructive nature of carrying the burden of past discontent on our shoulders, thereby depriving us of the energy needed to continue our journey through this life.

"The past is like a ship's anchor that has hooked itself to a huge rock below and will not break free. Eventually, a storm will come and the waves will rise, filling the ship with water. It will be pulled to the bottom of the sea, and all who are aboard will perish.

"The burden of continuing to carry the past is unnecessary and blinds us all to man's true nature of helping others to help themselves, for we all have in common the need to simplify the same journey."

Bong-Tow continued, "Once two Zen monks were walking together along a muddy road. A heavy rain was still falling. Rounding a bend on their path, they met an attractive young woman in fine silk clothes.

Unable to cross the intersecting stream that was now rising into a small muddy river, the woman asked if one of them could lift her up and carry her across. The younger one said, 'Certainly not. My vows do not permit me to touch a woman!'

"The older monk simply picked her up and carried her across the river. The two monks walked on in silence for some time. Finally, the younger monk spoke. 'I cannot get over the fact that you carried that woman across the river. Have you no sense of propriety, no self-discipline?'

"The two of them continued up the mountainside, with the younger one constantly complaining about breaking vows, and falling farther behind."

"Master, stop,' he said. 'I grow weary and cannot go on. I do not understand. I am young and you are old, and yet I cannot keep up with you!"

"The older one asked, 'What did I do when I reached the other side of the river?"

"The younger one answered, 'You put her down.'"

"Exactly,' said the older monk, 'And you are still carrying her, and now you are exhausted!"

In closing, Bong-Tow remarked, "We have all shared and gained great knowledge of what we are and the ultimate path of bringing light and hope to others, but most especially to ourselves. We are all connected to and are part of the same Universal Energy source. The positive or negative energy we reflect with thought affects us all. And, any perceived transgression among ourselves must be forgiven if we are to realize and advance to our true purpose in this life, and that which comes after."

Like a teacher following the Socratic principle of inquiry, as a means of providing instruction and directing the student toward the answer, Bong-Tow asked, "Was it not the Christ of your Great Book who cautioned you to forgive your enemy? 'Judge not, and you will not be judged; condemn not, and you will not be condemned; forgive, and you will be forgiven' (Luke 6:37, ESV)."

He went on, "What of the enemy within? Does it not seem reasonable to forgive yourself as well as to forgive another? For how can you forgive another if you don't first set the example within? What is it that keeps us from joyfully moving forward with our lives? Is this not the constant hostile energy we spoke of earlier that weakens the body and keeps us a prisoner of our negative thoughts? Is it not a truth to say, *what we think about intensely all the time expands*?"

The question came from the back of the room, "How do we know what's in the back of our minds that we might not be aware of, but that might surface and get in the way of our being happy?"

Bong-Tow smiled, bowed slightly, nodded his head and said, "Whatever you need to know about the unconscious past in you, the challenges of the present will bring them out."

As the meeting came to a close, another younger monk in a burnt yellow robe approached Bong-Tow from the side of the room and handed him a piece of paper.

After a few seconds of looking at the paper, Bong-Tow made a brief announcement. "I will not be able to continue with our weekly sessions as I had planned. I have an urgent request to return to my country immediately. A student of mine is dying, and spiritual matters must be attended to. Please excuse me, as I need to prepare for my flight back to Vietnam in the morning."

All the vets shook hands with Bong-Tow and said their good-byes. When everyone else had left, Bong-Tow and Roger sat facing each other once more in silence, nodding to one another, acknowledging each other's presence and feeling the flow of mutual energy between them.

In a final gesture of mutual respect, teacher to student and student to teacher, they bowed to each other. Then, in a surprise move, Bong-Tow curled Roger's outstretched hand into a fist and fist-bumped it with his own, saying, "See, Buddha is mainstream too!"

They walked out the door together. Bong-Tow and his young assistant moved on to the waiting taxi in front of the building. Roger saluted the taxi as it left the curb. He walked to the parking lot where his friend Sam stood leaning up against the front fender of his pickup.

Sam asked, "So, how'd it go, pal?"

Roger thought a minute and said, "I really hated to see him leave. I think I was finally finding some direction in my life. For the past several weeks, I haven't had that knot in my gut whenever I think about Vietnam. Don't exactly know why, but it feels good and I just want to move on with my life. I think I'm going back to Vietnam so I can hook up with Bong-Tow and finish the healing. Maybe one of these days I'll be able to help other vets do the same thing ..."

VOYAGER BASICS

Veterans conducting a job search generally recognize and accept that we all have trials and tribulations, some to a lesser or greater degree than others. Often, we are motivated to push through our trials, and our efforts are rewarded with success.

However, there are those of us who find that, for some inexplicable reason, we aren't getting the anticipated response to our job search.

For many veterans, it's because of unresolved personal issues, resistance to change, or internalized conflicts, especially those from the past that just won't go away. You know, those little dramas that play out in the movie theater of our heads every waking hour of every day, with matinees on Saturday and Sunday when we are supposed to be relaxing. They continually plague us for months, and sometimes years —undermining whatever level of motivation we have at the time.

Unfortunately, none of us consciously realizes that we sometimes sabotage our best efforts to find a job. Yeah, we hear the dialogue and visualize the exchange between ourselves and an imaginary adversary. We play out our part in the scenes, dropping in and out of the drama, even as we make a conscious effort to do a job search. As the day ends we are exhausted, but it doesn't stop there. Sometimes we take it to bed with us and wake up completely wiped out by the next morning.

"Good morning sunshine! Welcome to a new day!"

"What sun? There's nothing but dark clouds hanging overhead!"

The day's outcome is predictably assured.

Mental battles tend to become mental barriers to successful outcomes. The achievement of personal goals, like finding suitable employment and moving forward with our life, continually eludes us.

So, before you go charging into the pages that follow, you might want to consider some of the inner distractions that could be impeding your ability to focus. Mental barriers like these may be keeping you from devoting sufficient time and energy to the task of doing a productive job search:

- "My boss just fired me for no reason, and I will even the score at the first chance I get!"

- "I've been out of work for six months now, and the wife is constantly nagging me to get a job!"

- "I don't know, lately it seems like I'm out on patrol again and it's like employers are trying to ambush me with all their stupid questions and demands."

- "I don't have PTSD. My Humvee never took a hit from an IED, and I came back in one piece."

- "The VA never took care of me like they were supposed to."

- "All this talk about employers giving vets a job is a lot BS."

- "It doesn't seem fair. Just because I'm a female vet, I'm not getting the same consideration as the guys do from employers."

- "Me and my mate split the sheets last year and nothing is going right for me since then. I can't even find a job."

- "I had a professional write my resume. It cost me a hundred fifty bucks and it hasn't gotten me a job yet. I really got ripped off and I'm pissed!"

There's no doubt that, given more time and space, we could come up with hundreds of variations beyond the few examples provided here.

So, consider this: if we don't understand what may be interfering with our attempts to secure employment, we need to ask ourselves, "Could my attitude about past negative events have any impact on my job search efforts? Even more critically, could my attitude keep me from holding a job, once I get one?"

It is always in our best interest to face our demons than to retreat into denial. And this may be one of the greatest benefits of engaging in a job search.

"How is that so?" you might ask.

Well, because we just opened the door to self-examination. We become willing to look at what may be holding us back. Recognizing our negative attitudes is a first step in doing something about them. A move toward self-discovery is a move toward self-sufficiency. It signifies that we do have the ability to make mature and insightful decisions.

As mentioned earlier, a job search is more of an intuitive and mental journey than it is a logistical or technical one. What's problematic is the dichotomy involved. (Dichotomy is the sharp division of things or ideas, coming from one source into two contradictory/opposite parts.)

It's important to realize that our source of pain can do one of two things: it can create a barrier that prevents us from moving forward, or it can lead us to create a solution to the problem we are facing.

This is best illustrated in the following story of two old Navy vets who are longtime friends. They are sitting in a row boat fishing on their favorite lake. One of them has been talking nonstop, and so the banter—and the hubris—begins:

1st Vet: "Say, Al, why don't you stop talking so much? You'll scare the fish away. If I have to, I'll put you in another boat and let you fish by yourself!"

2nd Vet: "Yeah, Mike, and I'll get my battleship and run over and crush your little row boat!"

1st Vet: "Okay, I'll get my submarine and torpedo your battleship, and put you at the bottom of this lake!"

At this point the conversation stops. After about an hour of silence, and with several fish now lying in the bottom of the boat, the banter resumes:

2nd Vet: "Say, Mike, where you'd get that submarine?"

1st Vet: "Same place you got your battleship, Al!"

Do you know what this creative source is? It does have a name, you know. Your search to identify what it is begins now. Here's a hint: it's the part of your mind that produces outcomes. Actually, today's computers are modeled after it. Here's yet another hint: it doesn't make decisions or analyze information—it just responds to the type of information given it. This is your last hint: "Garbage in, garbage out!"

One of the most difficult admissions for some people to make is that they have a fault, a conflict, an issue, or a problem that seems to dominate their thoughts on a daily basis. Unfortunately, more energy is expended thinking about the effects of the problem rather than on solving it, of making an end-run around the issue, taking the easy path through avoidance.

It has been said, "It is man's nature to follow the path of least resistance when faced with what may seem like an insurmountable problem."

Consequently, for convenience sake, we have a tendency to take one of two paths of least resistance: (1) going into denial, which is a form of resistance to changing the way and the content of what we think. This means that as far as human behavior goes, resistance is often used as a metaphor for minimizing personal effort, involvement and/or avoiding confrontation altogether or (2) attempting to take shortcuts in overcoming barriers.

Neither of these two paths of least resistance works. With denial, the problem always remains. And taking shortcuts eventually adds new barriers to one that already exists.

It's called the human condition. We tend to do that which is easier, often to the neglect of that which is best. The brain's natural impulse is to take the easy route almost all the time until you think and act otherwise.

Eventually, hopefully, it will become necessary for the individual to do some soul-searching when the decision is made to move forward with their life. In learning to deal realistically and objectively with mental barriers that arise from the past, and even those of more recent times, several compelling out-of-the-box or unconventional considerations emerge:

1. Consider the Zen riddle: "If we know the sound of two hands clapping, *what is the sound of one hand clapping*?" The answer is within each of us. If we can resolve where this riddle fits into this journey we are on called life (notice there was no mention of the word solve), then we are well on our way to learning how to deal with the negative barriers created from past and present experiences.

2. Consider the question: "Is there any truth to the idea that *what we think about intensely all the time expands*"? If so, what is our personal truth?

3. Consider an answer to the idea that *"within every adversity is found the seed of an equivalent benefit."* What, if anything, prevents most people from realizing a benefit?

4. Consider the question: *"Although we are redirecting our mental energies at eliminating attitudinal barriers, what effort have we made to develop a job search plan that provides a sense of empowerment to set and accomplish realistic employment goals?"*

5. Consider the issue of personal perspective: *"Is the glass half full or half empty?"* Your journey to enlightenment is just beginning or continuing, but it never ends so long as you are willing to search for an answer.

2

SHORTCUTS

"What Goes Around Comes Around."

After completing two tours in Afghanistan, Adam was returning home with his Marine Corps Reserve unit. "Miraculously," he thought, "we're going home in one piece." His unit was one of the fortunate few that did not bear those obvious physical scars of war.

The unit was very tight-knit, and everything they did was by the numbers—kicking in doors, going house to house through villages searching for enemy insurgents. It was a matter of survival and training—it was constant, it was rigorous, and it was a group effort. No team member assumed anything; they were all in sync with one another. They recognized the fact there were no shortcuts. Shortcuts can kill you just as quickly as an enemy bullet or a cleverly camouflaged IED (Improvised Explosive Device).

Thankfully, it was over. All Adam longed for on the return flight home was to kick back for a while, party, and eventually find a job. "After all," he thought, "I earned it."

About three months into the good times, the money was running out and he was getting a little uneasy—like searching for insurgents house to house. Most of his buddies had either gone back to school or were getting jobs. Before being discharged, Adam had taken a three-day workshop called the Transitional Assistance Program (TAP). One class had to do with conducting a job search. He now recalled the instructor saying that looking for a job was a full-time job in and of itself. Adam wasn't paying too much attention, though, as his thoughts were elsewhere.

Although attendance at the TAP workshop was mandatory, he skipped the last two days. Thus began Adam's self-initiation into the world of taking shortcuts. His operative mode became more relaxed and out of sync with his survival instincts that kept him alive in the field of battle. He was beginning to lose his edge as the malaise set in. His search for a job was halfhearted at best.

Most of his search efforts consisted of sitting in front of a computer and responding to job announcements on a number of different websites. Adam used the "shotgun" approach, responding to just about every job possibility he thought he could do, not what his training and experience indicated he could do.

Subsequently, his submission of twenty-five applications and resumes a week resulted in four employer responses and one interview in a three-month period of time. Usually the employers who did answer back indicated that he was not qualified for the job he had applied for. They would keep his application on file for the next six months. Should an opportunity he was qualified for become available, he would be notified.

The one application that did result in an interview was for a warehouse job handling returned merchandise. Adam thought that since he needed a job ASAP, any old job would do. He would take it if offered, and then move on when something better came along. Seemingly oblivious to the importance of focusing on his strengths and abilities, Adam's operative idea here was simply to be offered a job.

In the initial scheduling of the interview with Beam Distribution International, Adam was requested to appear thirty minutes early for his 10:00 appointment. Upon his arrival, he was requested to contact the HR manager's secretary, Ms. Joleen Pagent, for additional instructions.

The night before his interview, Adam partied with a few of his friends. When he awoke the next morning, he found himself having to do the "3-S Tango" in ten minutes flat. He wasn't exactly running late, but time was not his friend. Adam was within five miles of his interview destination in the city's heavily trafficked business section when he decided to save some time.

Adam was halfway down the block, going the wrong way on a one-way grid, when the pulsating blue strobe light suddenly appeared in his rearview mirror. The significance of that blue light was immediately and abundantly made clear by the high-pitched sound of the siren that accompanied it.

"Hey," the cop said as Adam rolled down his window. "Where do you think you're goin' at 65 and the wrong way on a one-way street, my young friend?"

Before Adam could answer, the cop behind the tinted sunglasses spoke again. "Okay, sonny, jus gimmie your driver's license, registration, and proof of insurance!"

Adam handed the cop his papers. "Look, man, could you cut me a little slack?" he asked. "I don't want to be late for a job interview. It's the first job possibility I've had since I got out of the Marines three months ago."

The sunglasses covered the top half of the officer's face. They sat high on the bridge of his huge nose. The cop spoke again. "Listen, Marine, the way you were mov'n up this street is called reckless driving. That means you showed a wanton and willful disregard for the rights 'n safety of others. It's a traffic crime, and you could be arrested and taken to jail, requiring you to post bail or a bond to get out."

The cop continued to write in his citation book as he spoke. "So listen up, Marine. What you are telling me is that you were takin' a shortcut to save some time, right?"

"Yes, sir, that's about right," Adam said. The cop sounded just like his old Gunny, his platoon's kick-ass father figure—not a person you would want to tangle with. So, he cautioned himself to keep his mouth shut unless the cop asked a question.

The cop finished writing and handed Adam the ticket. He said, "This ain't no geedunk I'm hand'n you, pal. But, I'm giv'n ya a break. You're gett'n a ticket for go'n the wrong way on a one-way grid. That's it. I should take you in and teach you a lesson, but there were no other cars or pedestrians on the street that you might put in danger. I was in your shoes once when I got out of the Corps years ago. So, you have a safe day, okay?"

As the cop turned to walk away, Adam said, "Thanks, man. I owe you one."

In the side view mirror, Adam watched as the cop walked toward his cruiser, and as he started to roll up his window he heard, "Semper Fi, pal. Semper Fi!"

Adam entered the HR manager's office at ten minutes before the hour—not the half hour as requested. He hoped they wouldn't notice as he walked up to the secretary's desk. The name plate on the desk read *Joleen Pagent*.

Ms. Pagent stood up, and as they shook hands, she said, "You must be Adam Addison. We expected you twenty minutes ago, but we are happy you are here. We're a little behind schedule so you'll have to complete this application as quickly as you can. Please sit at the table next to the window on your left, and be sure to read all the instructions."

"I don't understand," Adam said with a puzzled look on his face. "I already filled out an application online, along with sending a resume. Why do I have to do another app?"

Ms. Pagent's response wasn't what Adam anticipated, "Mr. Addison, if you expect to get an interview this morning, you need to satisfactorily complete the screening process. The application form I just gave you is part of that process. Be sure to read the instructions in each of sections of the application."

There was no Semper Fi this time, not from this lady.

Reluctantly and somewhat tersely, Adam said, "Thanks. I don't understand, but I'll do it." Still irritated, he walked over to the table by the window, sat down, and immediately began to fill out the application.

The first set of instructions asked the applicant to completely fill in the address portion, both the mailing address and the home address.

Adam didn't bother to read the instructions. He merely completed his mailing address, and then filled in the home address with S/A (Same As).

The pen Ms. Pagent gave him stopped working. As he reached into his shirt pocket for his personal pen, he pulled out the traffic citation he had received minutes earlier. The amount of the fine was listed as $150.00. He hadn't bothered to read the citation when it was first issued to him.

"What the hell, son of a—" He cut himself short.

Maybe they had an IED planted in the interview room. The day so far was a bust. He looked over at Ms. Pagent's desk.

She looked up from her computer and watched as he waded up the citation into a tiny ball. He threw it with such force into the nearby wastebasket that it bounced back out onto the floor.

As he bent over to retrieve the missal, he noticed Ms. Pagent eyeing him. She had placed her hand over her mouth, and her face had a peculiar blush to it.

Embarrassed, Adam tried to quickly grab it up but his hand hit the little ball and it rolled away from him. He chased that little ball around the floor and finally captured it, stood up, walked over the wastebasket, inserted his hand all the way to the bottom, and gently laid the citation to rest. He looked over at Ms. Pagent. She still had her hand over her mouth, and her face was now bright red.

Adam returned to the form in front of him and continued to fill out the application, not paying too much attention to the instructions at the top of each section.

In the section labeled **Employment History:** *Please provide, in chronological order, starting with the most recent experience, inclusive of employment, volunteer positions and military assignments within the past seven to ten years,* Adam quickly printed across the entire section "See attached resume."

When he reached the **Education and Training:** *Please specify the degree type or training related directly to the position for which you are applying,* Adam merely attempted a shortcut by listing the title of his degree and the training. The Explanation Notes boxes were filled with "N/A" in capital letters.

Finally, as he approached the completion of the application, there was a set of instruction titled **READ CAREFULLY:** *Information provided that is determined to be false and/or omitted are grounds for being excluded as an applicant or termination at a later date for cause.*

FINAL INSTRUCTIONS: *Please sign, print and date the application at the designated places in acknowledgement of the terms and conditions of employment.*

Adam signed the application where indicated, but neglected to print his name as instructed. He returned the application to Ms. Pagent.

Ms. Pagent took Adam's application. She opened the door to a room behind her office and entered. A few minutes later she stepped out of the room and closed the door behind her.

"Mr. Beam will speak with you in just a few minutes," she told Adam. "Please have a seat."

As he sat waiting to be called in for the interview, Adam figured it should last about twenty to thirty minutes max. Some fifteen minutes had passed when Mr. Beam opened his office door and asked Adam to come in. It only took ten minutes.

Once Adam was seated, Mr. Beam spoke. "Adam, I just went over your application and attached resume and I was impressed with your military experience and former logistics employment, training, and skills. They very closely match what we are looking for in the person we hire to assist our clients."

Mr. Beam looked down at the papers lying in front of him. Shaking his head disapprovingly, he said, "But, I have some concerns with the way you completed this application."

"You have to understand," he continued, "that although we are a small company, we deal with worldwide professional and scientific medical practitioners and facilities. They require our attention to detail in filling their orders. There can be no mistakes made in the products we deliver. There is only one way we do business because people's health and lives depend on our thoroughness, as does the reputation of the individuals who use our products. Unfortunately, your application indicates a tendency to take shortcuts. We hire for attitude and train for and expect competency. Adam, I don't think at this time we want to take the risk of hiring you. So, we are going to pass. Thank you for your time and interest."

Adam sat in silence for a moment. Then he looked directly at Mr. Beam, and stated in a submissive tone, "Mr. Beam, sir, please accept my apologies. I realize now my mistake, and I really do think I can be a productive member of your team. I'm used to working in a team environment where shortcuts could get you killed."

Mr. Beam reflected on what Adam had said. Then he replied, "I'll tell what I will do, Adam. In about a month we will be hiring for another position similar to the one you just applied for. If you aren't employed, and are still interested in coming to work for us, I'll give your new application serious consideration."

Adam thanked Mr. Beam for the interview opportunity. He glanced at Ms. Pagent as he left the interview room. She had his balled-up traffic citation open on the top of her desk. She looked up, smiled, and handed it to him as he passed her desk. "I really am very interested in working here. I'll be back," he said, and opened the door.

Halfway out the door Adam stopped and turned around. Ms. Pagent was still watching him, the blush of amusement still on her face.

"Joleen," he said, "would you have coffee with me sometime and tell me more about Mr. Beam and his company?" There it was ... another beachhead to overcome, another Semper Fi moment. Once a Marine, always a Marine.

VOYAGER BASICS

In an often complex and competitive job market, attempting to take shortcuts can deprive an applicant of the opportunity to experience a productive journey and the ability to project the attitude necessary to successfully achieve meaningful employment.

To further address the destructive and deceptive nature of shortcuts we paraphrase and borrow from the words and works of Dan Waldschmidt, a popular business strategist, professional speaker, and blogger.

His insights suggest a realistic similarity of success as it applies to life pursuits, the world of business operations and the process of job search in today's employment environment as indicated in the following observations:

**Job search, like success ... is a mindset,
not just a point in time.**

It seems as though everything we've been told about job search success generally revolves around a single point in time.

A person completes a three-hour or three-day workshop on job search, then gets an interview, or a job offer. It's all about that celebratory feeling we get from an accomplishment.

Key events in our lives such as getting a DD-214 (with an honorable discharge designation), graduation from college (with a degree), or completion of a training program (with certification), make us feel successful—they are all mementos to indicate achievement. The fact is that without such recognizable results, it is sometimes difficult to gauge success.

This is why it's necessary to understand and accept that success is less about an emotional feeling or symbols and more of a philosophical pursuit that requires disciplined thinking.

Job search, like success, is a way of life ...

It's critical to productive outcomes to seek, promote, and maintain a success-oriented mindset rather than seeking the outward signs of success.

The so-called successes achieved by way of shortcuts generally result in the inability to maintain forward progress over the long haul when it becomes necessary. You can either spend time trying to give the outward appearance of success, or you focus upon doing the difficult things required to realize your dreams, but you really can't do both.

Focusing one's energies and ideas on a dream, and turning that dream into a reality, is difficult enough. It's a stress-loaded, rolling-in-the-mud, the blood, the guts, and the beer kind of struggle. It requires a special kind of mental toughness and endurance to survive and come out on top.

So, while we struggle to bring our dreams and aspirations to fruition, it sometimes seems as though the world at large is putting barriers in our way, tempting us to consider taking shortcuts. And why not? Everybody else is doing it, right?

The answer does not always come easily. We have to work at it. That's because real life is difficult, and shortcuts eventually become more of a hindrance than a help. More time is spent in trying to undo the damage caused by a shortcut, and starting over again, than is spent in doing things right from the start. The following four thoughts about taking shortcuts need to be considered on your journey through life in general, and job search specifically:

1. Initiating a shortcut is admitting failure from the beginning.

Such a consideration can be mentally damaging—if we really believed that realizing the goals we set for ourselves were possible, we'd be less inclined to take shortcuts. Admittedly, we all have similar second-guessing thoughts, doubts and fears—"Can I do this? Am I capable of making this happen? Do I have the intestinal fortitude to move forward into unknown territory?"

If our response to these kinds of questions is taking a shortcut rather than accepting the challenge of what lies ahead, aren't we really saying to ourselves, and eventually to others, that we are self-identifying as an unaccomplished individual?

And yes, entering into that territory requires the posturing and arrogant behavior that says, "I know what I'm doing." All the while the internalized self-acknowledging message is, "It probably won't work, and I'll be lucky if it does."

If we do find ourselves the victim of our delusional shortcut outcomes, getting back on track only requires simple "out-of-the-box" steps like:

- Getting up several hours earlier to start the day.
- Getting in touch with friends and acquaintances and asking for help.
- Avoiding events, activities, and people that tend to distract us from focusing on things that really matter.

2. Taking a shortcut is an inappropriate reaction to handling fear.

When we come up against an overwhelming barrier to achieving a goal, we can either run from it or we can face it (otherwise known as the "Flight or Fight Syndrome"). Sometimes, when we want to do something worthwhile with our lives, it seems as though the whole world begins throwing obstacles in our way. It can get downright depressing, which in turn can create the fear that we will never reach our goal. The temptation to make an end-run around that feeling of fear is an attempt at taking the easy way out. It's called a shortcut.

Just know that it is okay to be afraid. But taking a shortcut is a "flight" reaction, rather than that of "fighting" and championing our own cause. So, if we catch ourselves running away from personal success we should have no expectation of getting closer to achieving personal dreams.

Ralph Waldo Emerson said it best: *"Do that which you fear the most, and death of fear is certain."* Or, to paraphrase: "Do that which you fear the most, and you will no longer fear it."

3. Shortcuts short-circuit the enduring energy required to overcome barriers on the path to achieving goals.

Bowing to the mistaken belief that we can fully realize our ultimate dreams without establishing a vested interest in the outcome through passion, commitment, hard work, and time is an exercise in stupidity. In other words, the expectation that we can get more out of life by doing less is an invalid assumption, and characteristic of a faulty shortcut mentality.

Continuing the struggle in the face of overwhelming odds, and achieving the goal, provides the individual with renewed energy and insight in preparation for the next struggle to come along. Taking shortcuts does nothing to prepare the warrior for surviving the next engagement.

4. Following what appears to be an expedient route on the journey to success is no guarantee that we will reach our destination.

More often than not, it is impossible to determine when we will be successful in attaining the goals we have set for ourselves. Therefore, it is also impossible to initiate a shortcut to a destination that doesn't exist.

So, the question arises for the millions of individuals who suddenly get what they have been wishing and working for, and then find out that they no longer want it: "WHY?"

Part of the answer lies in the fact that the achievement of a goal is more of a "mindset." It is an internalized ongoing development that, when properly nurtured, evolves, and adapts to the environment in which it exists.

Sometimes we realize the original goal is not what we thought it would be after we achieve it. What then? Well, an open mind adapts and continues to move forward seeking new goals. This is not a one-time event. It is ongoing and a ceaseless learning process called *change*.

Yes, eventually we do reach worthwhile end results. And when we do, the focus should not be on what has been achieved but on the journey taken to get there. What did we learn from the journey? Does it provide a model for setting and achieving future goals?

But those who agonize over a failure, or become impatient with the time, focus, and energy required to achieve results, often fall victim to the temptation of taking shortcuts. Once initiated, the learning process becomes stilted.

Frequently, many of us fail to visualize a big enough goal. We tend to compartmentalize and hide the dream in a small, protective cocoon-like environment, out of sight of those who might criticize.

The Universe, similar to our mindset, has an ability to mysteriously materialize dreams far beyond what can be imagined, when shortcuts are excluded.

The Universal Laws of Success dictate that achievement of end goals is built upon incremental steps, not giant quantum leaps. There is no wisdom gained in taking shortcuts and bypassing the struggle. The step-by-step things one needs to do to achieve results always involves a learning process.

Struggles are the best learning experience on this journey we call life. They shape and mold us into better beings.

Remember, we cheapen the experience of life if we try to skip part of that journey.

3

PREPARING FOR THE FUTURE BY ACCEPTING CHANGE

"Change, the One Universal Constant"

Growing up, Dan had been reminded repeatedly by both his old man and grandfather, "There ain't no free lunches in this world. Ya gotta work for everything you get!"

His uncle Mike, a Vietnam vet, added to the family value system: "While you're sleeping, the world is changing around you. You wake up and nothin' is the same. It happens overnight. Sometimes, life is like a train pull'n out of the station, you're late, and now you are runnin' like hell to catch up and get on board. No one told you they changed the schedule."

Now, two years after returning from Iraq, Dan confided to a friend, "I just turned twenty-seven and I feel old. Everything just seems flat in my life. I'm becoming just like my folks told me. I feel out of step with the world, especially in trying to get a better job. The one I got is okay. It's paying my bills but it's also draining my energy. There's no future, no prospects for advancement or a different kind of work that allows me to move forward with my life. Sometimes I feel like one of those little pet hamsters in a cage on their treadmill, running to catch up with myself, goin' nowhere fast."

"Listen, Dan," his friend said, "you might want to consider contacting a Veteran Representative at the American Job Center. They are really good at helping vets make career changes. I know because they helped me."

A few weeks later, following his friend's advice, Dan contacted an AJC Veteran's Representative named Allen. During their initial discussion, Allen asked, "Can you give me an idea of what you think you would chose as an employment goal?"

Dan said, "I'm not exactly sure. All I know is that I want a job that will pay me a better wage and offer a chance to advance."

"Well, everybody wants better pay and a chance to get promoted. So, Dan, how do you think that can happen?"

There was a dumfounded look on Dan's face, and his answer matched the look. "I don't know, man. I just think there is something better out there for me."

"Well, do you have any idea what that something might be?" Allen asked.

Dan, in exasperation, took a deep breath, folded his arms tightly across his chest, then let the air out through pursed lips.

Allen recognized the irritation, an all-too-common trait among a lot of veterans he'd had as clients. It was mostly out of frustration with having to make changes in their lives, from a very structured, team-preservation, and life-threatening survival mode to a free-reigned, very competitive civilian world where the individual is responsible for making decisions that determine the future.

Dan sarcastically quipped, "I was hoping you had the answer, that you would find me a job I would be happy with!"

"Look, my friend, it's not my job to find you a job," Allen said. "I'm here to assist you with making changes that will help you get where you think you want to be. It's all about equipping you with some tools for determining what it is you want to do with the rest of your life. I'm here to help you help yourself, to help you develop a sense of direction, purpose and the right kind of thinking that leads to successful employment outcomes."

"I'm not sure what you mean," Dan replied.

"I guess what I'm really saying is that the goal here is for you to become self-sufficient and independent. That you acquire the tools for job search and employment success without having to depend on others to find solutions to employment issues you might face now and in the future."

Allen continued, "Dan, I want you to ask yourself this: if I had a chance to choose the kind of work I thought I would enjoy doing, I would want to do … WHAT?"

Dan thought a minute, and said, "In the Air Force, I was a 3POX1, Security Police Officer. It was just a job. And, it wasn't like the job I have now as a security guard. I'm just a glorified gatekeeper and I don't see much future in it. I thought about becoming a cop, but I don't see myself carrying a gun and a badge. I did enough of that in the Air Force. To tell you the truth, I wasn't happy or unhappy. It was just a job. My old man used to tell me, 'Just do what you know how to do, and that'll get you by.' So that's what I know how to do and yet I'm not sure what I want to do. So the answer to your question is, I really don't know. I don't know if I can change. Truth is I don't know if I want to change. All I know is that I want something better. I don't just want to get by."

"But, isn't that exactly what you are doing now, just getting by?"

"Yeah, that's what I just said. So, how do I start moving forward with my life?"

"Dan, let me suggest you begin by taking an Occupational Interest Inventory. This will determine where your interests lie, and the career choices you might consider that would provide better pay and advancement."

"Okay, let me give it a try. I'll do just about anything to get away from what I'm doing now."

Allen scheduled Dan to take the exam on the following Tuesday.

The following Tuesday came and went. Dan was a no-call, no-show. Allen attempted to follow up with emails, but got no response. When he called, he got the message: "Tell me who you are, and I'll get back to you sooner or later."

Allen had several other vets who were more receptive to his counseling and recommendations, and so he moved on, giving no further thought to Dan and his apparent reluctance to take on the challenge of change.

Several months after he last saw Dan, Allen was at his desk writing a report when the phone rang. "Talk about coincidence," Allen said when he picked up and heard Dan's voice. "I was just thinking about you."

"Hey, man, I'm sorry about not getting back with you. It was plain stupid. Guess I just didn't want to listen," Dan remarked apologetically.

Allen quickly picked up on the hesitant tone in Dan's voice and instinctively came back with, "Okay, Dan, here's what I think should happen. If you can get here tomorrow morning at ten o'clock, I am willing to sit down with you and explore career options and job possibilities. When you come in, please bring a copy of your DD-214 and your resume."

Dan attempted to end their conversation by saying, "All right, I'll be there and I'll bring my paperwork, but I'm not sure how this will work out. I got fired yesterday from the job I had, and I'm really down right now."

Not wanting to get sucked into his drama, Allen said, "Yeah, Dan, we all get fired at some time in our lives for one reason or another, but it's not the end of the world, it's a beginning. Right now, all you need to do is just show up tomorrow morning at ten o'clock and we'll see how we can make your future brighter. Will you be here?"

There was a pause and finally Dan said, "Yeah, I'll be there!"

The next morning at exactly 10:00 a.m., Dan appeared at Allen's office. They shook hands and sat facing each other. Allen asked, "Dan, just between you and me, why were you fired?"

"It was really for nothin'," Dan said. "The security company at the warehouse where I worked had changed the way they tracked personnel, materials, and vehicles that entered and left the premises. They didn't tell anyone they were going to make the change until the last minute, and they didn't provide adequate training. I wasn't too happy about the change and I let my supervisor know about it. So, he took me aside and explained what needed to be done and how to do it."

"Did you do what your supervisor suggested?" Allen asked.

"Well, sort of. After a few days of trying to make the new system work, I wasn't having much luck. Somehow, it just wasn't working for me. I don't know, maybe I had a mental block or something. Anyhow, I told my supervisor the new system was too complicated and the old way was better. I told him as long as I got my reports in on time and they were accurate, I didn't see the need to make the change."

Allen interrupted Dan. "And that's when he fired you, right?"

"Right!" Dan answered.

"So, what do you think would happen if you were still in uniform and you acted that way when given a direct order by a superior?" Allen inquired.

Dan, now hunched over with his elbows on his knees, sat back up straight in his chair, shrugged his shoulders and smugly replied, "Well, in that situation I wouldn't have much choice. I couldn't just pack up my gear and walk away from it if I didn't like it, especially in a combat zone. If it was a direct order and I refused to do it, I'd probably get court-marshaled, restricted to quarters, bad conduct discharge. They could do any number of things to me."

"So, tell me, Dan, what's the difference between the military and the situation you just went through with your civilian employer?"

"Well, for one thing," Dan replied, "as a civilian, I wouldn't get sent to jail, or get something on my record that would give me a bad reputation. I could just go out and find another job. No big deal!"

"Yeah, Dan, you are probably right about the jail thing. No civilian employer is going to lock you up because you have a bad attitude or for refusing to make changes the company wants to make," Allen replied. "But as far as your reputation, where your employment record is concerned, that's a whole different story."

"What's the big deal? It's only a job."

"But, it is a big deal, because whatever you do, don't, or won't do, has a way of following you from one job to the next. I'm curious, Dan. As a soldier you were trained to follow orders, and you understood that everything changes on a day-to-day basis. It was a matter of survival for both you and the team you worked with. Why, since your separation from the military, does there appear to be a rejection of following directions, of making changes in the way you are asked to by others?"

"I guess there's a big part of me that wants to be in charge of my own life without having to be told what to do or what to think all the time. That's why I got out of the military," Dan said.

But then he admitted, "Since my separation from the military, I've felt a loss of direction in my life. I can't explain it, but I'm having a problem making changes and finding out what I should do. Sometimes I feel like I still have one foot in the Air Force and the other one in the civilian world."

Over the next few weeks, Dan and Allen had several meetings, and Dan appeared to be more accepting of not only making changes in his life, but more importantly, of making life decisions that mattered. It was clear to Allen that Dan, after completing a few career and job-interest assessments, had shown leadership capabilities, was a socially structured individual, and demonstrated strong entrepreneurial-business interests.

Eventually, Dan found a part-time job to provide supplemental income, and decided to pursue a degree in Business Management. In one of their last meetings, Allen offered some additional insight regarding the change process.

"We all have our little world," Allen said. "It requires us from time to time to make changes in the way we do or look at things. It can either be dictated by someone or something, or it is self-initiated out of a personal need. The first example is what we can call our Box of

Life. Everything in the box is pretty smooth—life is good. There are no real challenges. Then, someone or some event comes along requiring us to make a change and do something different. In most instances you aren't really asked if you want to make a change. The immediate reaction most people have is to resist. The question is, Dan, why do you think people resist change?"

"I don't have the slightest idea," Dan admitted. "Well, maybe it has something to do with … like my old man used to say, if things are working, don't screw around with it. Changing things just creates problems! I don't really know what to believe anymore."

Allen said, "Why we resist change is a question that many vets don't have an answer to when they separate from the military, including me when I first got out. But, after a few years of weighing my military experience, comparing it to working with veterans in the civilian world, I think I may have come up with a reasonable explanation."

"What's that?" Dan asked, searching Allen's face intently for the answer.

Allen continued, "The problem is that often when we are forced to make a change, initiated by someone other than ourselves, it's a last-minute thing, and generally it catches us off guard. We get the feeling that we've been blindsided, with little time to prepare, or with little information or training as to what is expected. The only exception would be people who deal with change in an emergency, life-threatening, or survival situation, on an almost daily basis, like cops, soldiers, doctors, EMTs, firefighters, and a few others. But, in those demanding and quick-change instances, their acceptance and readiness is primarily based upon continuous proactive training scenarios. They are designed to promote a conditioned response, most of the time, with a predictable and intended outcome."

Dan interrupted, "So, you're saying that it's different for those who haven't been trained and/or had any warning?"

"Yeah, people typically resist change out of fear because they have no way of predicting the outcome. It can get pretty scary and emotions run high and hot. They say and do stupid things, all in an attempt to resist what they perceive as dictatorial direction, without input from those impacted the most from the change. This kind of behavior is generally seen in the workplace and social groups like families and government organizations and departments.

"With dictated change there is a general feeling of a loss of control over one's work or social environment.

"There is no way of knowing if what has been proposed will be a success or a failure. This is counter to the facilitator's intent of selling the wonderfulness of the change before dealing with any fear that is internally disruptive and resistant. Often, superiors and promoters of change come up against resistance because they fail to observe five key factors involved in the process that determine acceptance or non-acceptance."

Allen went on to explain to Dan the five key factors in this way:

One – Change, to be effective and accepted, must be a well-planned and nurtured event. There should be short and long-term goals built into the plan. It's what is now known as the Strategic Planning Process common to more contemporary organizations like government, corporations, and nonprofit operations.

Two – The process requires input from those whom the change is intended to affect the most.

Three – It's important for change facilitators to understand and deal first with underlying fears before attempting to implement planned outcomes.

Four – Both the facilitator and the recipient of change need to accept that change is identified as an evolutionary rather than a revolutionary process. Nothing happens overnight; it shouldn't be a last minute decision.

Five – Critical to the longevity of change is the ongoing development, implementation and monitoring of clearly written and easy-to-understand policy and procedure, referencing operational and instructional guidelines.

"Dan," Allen explained, "the only reason I mention this is because you indicated a desire to go after a degree in business management.

As a business leader, manager or owner, part of what you will be doing is initiating change. So, everything you do from now on will involve some measure of change. This includes your career development and job search."

"Speaking of job search," Dan asked, "how does all this help me find a job and finish school?"

"Well, Dan, what's that little world or Box of Life called? The one I mentioned earlier that we find ourselves living in where everything is smooth and life is good, and we appear to be content, and in control of our environment. It's the place where we get to decide about change in our lives. What is this place called?"

Dan thought a minute, then said, "Isn't that what we call our comfort zone?"

"You got it," Allen continued. "Within this Box of Life we call our comfort zone, and within LIFE in general, you will find the term if. This is the second kind of change I mentioned earlier. It's the self-initiated example."

He took a piece of paper and wrote the word LIFE. "In a nutshell," Allen said, "our LIFE is filled with ifs. If I had done this, if only such-and-such hadn't happened, if I had only been rich, if, if, if …

"'If' represents personal goals, things we think we want to achieve. We take the risk and we set out on our own. In many instances, once we get in sight of the thing we thought we wanted, it doesn't happen. Or, it doesn't meet our expectations the way we thought it would. This kind of change also results in fear. The fear of being a failure sets in and we resist any further risk-taking."

Then Allen asked, "When that happens, there is a desire to do what?"

As the two men's gaze connected, Dan's response to the question was a blank stare. "I don't know, man. You got me!" Then it hit him as his eyes flashed into high beam. "Yeah, you mean like the person wants to go back to their comfort zone where everything was nice and fuzzy warm, and life was good."

"Dan, you are amazing. You are really getting into it," Allen said. "It's like being in the womb where you have no worries and life is good but once you come out, change is in motion. There is no going back.

"You have to understand that fear will always be there so your only choice is to continue to move forward. To continue to take risks. You need to get into your thinking zone each time you try to make a change in your life."

Allen went on to explain that if things don't turn out as expected, a person should ask these questions:

• What happened?

• Why did it happen?

• What did I learn from it?

• Where do I go from here?

• How do I make a new goal happen?

"More importantly," Allen said, "learn to ask for help. This is what change, like job search, is all about."

At the end of their meeting, Allen said to Dan, "Actually, if you think about it, whether change is dictated or self-initiated, the way you handle it is all pretty much the same. The surprising result is that the more you do it, the easier it gets. The more often you are willing to take risks, the less you fear it, and the more often the results turn in your favor."

As they stood and shook hands, Allen mentioned to Dan, "You know, back in 1964 there was a hippy singer and songwriter. His name was Bob Dylan and he recorded the song 'The Times They Are a-Changin.' One line said, **"You better start swimmin' or you'll sink like a stone."** I think it should be the mantra for all us vets who want to survive in that combative and competitive arena called the job market. Well, pal, good luck to you, and stay in touch."

Two years later Allen received a note from Dan.

Allen,

Please accept my thanks for your help and support. As a business management major, I've been involved in several change strategies courses. You were right, I've discovered no matter what you do in life it will require some sort of change. I'm three-quarters of the way through my degree program and planning my internship with a national organization. When I received their notice of acceptance into their program they said the reason I was selected was the way I presented myself as being adaptable to the future needs of their company.

Dan

Nine months later Allen received a second note from Dan.

Allen,

I just graduated from college. The company I did my internship with just offered me a job. They placed me into a training program to become a Change Facilitator. WOW!

Many thanks,
Dan

VOYAGER BASICS

The reason it's important to understand basic elements of the change process, and its application to the job search process, is that this understanding allows the veteran to become his or her own facilitator of change—a realistic approach to the development of self-sufficiency and sustainability. Thus, the process of change is congruent with the process of job search, as illustrated in the following views:

PERSONALIZED VIEW

The Greek philosopher Heraclitus is quoted as saying, *"The only constant in the Universe is change."*

Similarly, a more contemporary application of Heraclitus' quote is attributed to Isaac Asimov, an American professor of biochemistry at Boston University. He is known as one of this county's most prolific writers of science fiction and popular science books. He is most famous for the quote that singularly explains the basis of how our world functions. He said, *"It is change, continuing change, inevitable change that is the dominant factor in society today."*

For most of us, accepting change is not always easy. We often go through phases in our lives, and that takes time. Elizabeth Kübler-Ross's model, more commonly known as the "Five Stages of Grief," was first introduced in her 1969 book, *On Death and Dying*. She set the stage for the hospice movement in this country. A review of her model helps us to understand and cope with the process of change. The basic stages Elizabeth Kübler-Ross identified were:

- Denial – ("This isn't happening to me!")
- Anger – ("Why is this happening to me?")
- Bargaining – ("I promise I'll be a better person if …")
- Depression – ("I don't care anymore.")
- Acceptance – ("I'm ready for whatever comes.")

The Elizabeth Kübler-Ross Model can be applied to the process one might experience when going through the loss of a job. You are suddenly faced with the traumatic and unanticipated task of conducting a new job search. This processing of events is what many veterans already have experienced, or are currently experiencing. Although the initial cause isn't death, but is separation from a long-held job, the emotional involvement is similar to the following responses:

Denial – ("I didn't do anything wrong. Why was I let go?")

Anger – ("I'm mad as hell. I did all the work while everyone else sat around drinking coffee and goofing off!")

Bargaining – ("Maybe they'll take me back if I offer to work for less or take a different shift.")

Depression – ("I've been with the company for over ten years. I'm too old to start over again. No one will want to hire me. Now what am I going to do?")

Acceptance – ("Guess I will just have to face facts and look for another job. The thing I have to figure out now is where to start. It's been a long time since I've been in the job-hunt mode.")

REDUCING CHANGE RESISTANCE

Whether an individual is a facilitator or recipient of change, the following factors are indicative of why acceptance or resistance may or may not occur:

- **When the status quo is perceived to be satisfactory.**

Resistance will be less if participants clearly understand the basic problem and reason for change, and the possible negative outcome for maintaining things as they are. Presenting real or hypothetical scenarios about what will happen if things are allowed to continue as normal is more likely to result in acceptance.

- **When the purpose of change is not clearly understood.**

Generally, a great deal of resistance can be eliminated or reduced if those impacted by change are allowed to ask questions and are given feedback. There is always a need to know the "why" behind the "what" and the "how." Quite often when adequate information is not available, or withheld, intended participants will become subject to their own invention about what is happening, resulting in imaginary problems.

- **When people become engaged in short-term, narrowly focused thinking.**

Many individuals tend to resist change because they won't or can't put on hold their desire for personal gratification or aren't able to visualize beyond personal views or beliefs.

- **When the person proposing change is not trusted or valued.**

Participants are less likely to resist change when it is supported or endorsed by key figures in an organization, and who already have credibility and earned respect from intended recipients of change. Personality conflicts between facilitator and recipient tend to increase the likelihood of resistance. The guiding principle to increasing acceptance of change is that of treating participants with dignity, respect, and integrity.

- **When the recipients of change are not involved in the planning process.**

Resistance is less likely to occur when recipients have a vested interest in the outcome, and when they have the feeling they have somehow made a contribution to the cause. Recipients should be allowed to offer suggestions from their own knowledge and experience, and facilitators should show respect for the recipients' opinions and feelings prior the implementation of any change.

- **When the impact upon recipient control, confidence, and courage is not considered.**

More often than not, change can and does become a threat to self-esteem. It's important to consider that resistance to change, and the fear generated (e.g. the inability to predict the outcome) can be reduced by assisting recipients to realize the things they can control. Change acceptance requires each stage of the process to be reduced to small manageable steps. Such consideration incrementally produces the courage and confidence of the recipient, providing a feeling of manageable control regarding other aspects of the process as they emerge.

- **When there is a failure to deal with a recipient's possible personal loss of control.**

Resistance begins to increase when participants are not provided with the appropriate training and education upon which informed decisions are made.

Offering information and implementing change slowly and on a trial basis is the most likely way to reassure the anxious recipient that success is not only possible but highly probable. It tends to reduce any sense of loss of control by providing an opportunity to get more facts about change.

- **When there are no provisions for handing the fear of loss of ego, status, power, or resources.**

Quite often the implementation of change, without first considering its impact or emotional bruising on the ego of the recipient, leads to resistance. Those recipients who thought they were finally "in the know" may have to step back and admit they may have misjudged the process or their own assumptions about change.

- **When there is a failure to avoid excessive pressure to implement change, when planning is haphazard, insufficient, or nonexistent.**

Change to be effective and fair needs to be objectively planned and well-timed. If change is implemented unfairly and comes as a surprise, resistance is sure to follow. Participants need time to evaluate and adjust before change occurs.

When change comes within a short period of time from previously implemented change—particularly, change that was difficult to execute ("We know there will be some glitches ..." or "The system isn't perfect ..." or "We'll figure it out as we go ...")—all of this blatantly ignores the pressure put upon individuals who must deal with the change. Highly entrenched resistance is difficult to overcome.

- **When change implementation is rigid or inflexible.**

To keep resistance to a minimum, the process of implementing change must be open to revision and reconsideration, especially when participant response indicates that system modification appears to be warranted.

4

THE VALUE OF LEARNING TO NETWORK

"A Strategy for Self-promotion"

Since her discharge from the Navy, Devina Rose Wright found herself very much unsettled. In her transition from military to civilian life, she had pursued employment in several sectors of the job market. This she had done mainly through employment agencies referred to her by friends. The agencies weren't particularly helpful in providing the kind of career employment she had hoped to find. Her jobs ended up short-term because, as one of her previous employers put it, "You just don't seem to be too enthused about working here," and, "You seem to have a problem connecting with people."

Because of her military training and experience as a paralegal in the JAG Corps, she had been told there was a big demand in the civilian sector for individuals with skills in the legal field. While legal work continued to dominate her thoughts, her employment focus continued to be somewhat uncertain.

Devina Rose attended several job fairs, but there weren't many employers from the legal field at these events. As she sauntered through the crowds of job seekers, she noted several corporations that were looking to fill secretarial and administrative assistant positions. She gave those positions some thought, but every time she began to approach an employer's hiring booth, the fear of personal engagement overtook her. Each time, Devina Rose stepped back and walked away. She couldn't explain it.

Still, Devina Rose continued to doggedly attend job fairs, hoping that whatever was holding her back would break loose and allow her to face the gut-wrenching fear of walking up to a stranger and beginning a conversation.

It was during her last job fair walk-through that providence, the Universe, good fortune, or whatever one would call it, tapped Devina Rose on the shoulder, allowing her to catch the break she had been seeking. The tri-fold reader board on the table of the booth wasn't the standard employer branding. It read, "Job Search, Life Skills Coach & Guru – Network Yourself to A Successful Career and Employment!" Dr. Georg Gojii, Ph.D. Oxford University, Evolutionary Anthropology UK, Johns Hopkins University, Behavioral Sciences, USA."

She stood there reading the message on the board in front of her for the third and fourth time. The question in her mind was, "Who in the world comes right out and calls himself a Guru?" She looked down to the little man with the glistening white hair and full beard seated at the table before her. He immediately looked up at her and sensed a reflection of awe in her expression. Their eyes now focused on one another. Devina Rose continued to stare, noticing the little red dot on his forehead centered slightly above and between his bushy white eyebrows. The red was accentuated by the dark brown of his skin.

"Oh, the little red dot. I see you are wondering about it. It is called a Bindi," the man explained.

Divina Rose continued staring, and wondered, "Does he read minds too?"

Rising from his chair, he brought his hands together in the prayerful salutation, his eyes never leaving Devina Rose. He bent forward slightly at the waist, then stood tall, all five feet four inches of him.

Now with raised eyebrows, he smiled and asked, "I see the puzzlement on your face. I'm George Gojii. My name is pronounced 'Go Gee.' It's a little different than it is spelled, but you can call me George, if you wish. And yes, I am a real Guru. I am a Hindu and in our Hindi culture and language, Guru means teacher or trainer. But, my dear lady, I am hip, tuned-in, turned-on, and I can converse in the American vernacular when it is necessary."

Her response to his speech was silence, although her mouth was partially open, as if to speak.

"May I have your name please?" he asked ever so politely.

Devina Rose struggled in her attempt to initiate a response to this stranger's greeting. Finally it came in a series of excited short statements spewed out all in one breath. "Hi, I'm Devina Rose Wright. It's a pleasure to meet you, sir. I'm not sure if you can help me. I'm not sure what you do. I'm having problems doing a job search. Sometimes I have a problem talking to people and I don't know why. My friends say it's because I need to do more networking, but that hasn't work for me so far!"

There was that penetrating silence again as she thought, "My God, did I just say all that?"

In an attempt to cover up her embarrassment, she extended her arm to shake hands. He took her hand in both of his and bowed again, as was his custom, and pumped her arm up and down twice, gently but firmly. The warmth of his hands and his voice electrified her. She had a sense she knew him, but didn't know him. Despite the weirdness of the situation, she decided to let their meeting play itself out.

"Dee-Veena Rose. What a nice and unusual name. It suits you," he remarked in a very smooth, mostly cultured English accent.

"Mr. Gogii, sir, it's not Dee-Veena. It's Devina, as in Devine," she said, surprising herself with her own boldness.

A sense of calmness began to settle over Devina Rose. For the first time in a long time, she felt at ease talking with a total stranger. There was something about this little man who, with precise pronunciation of his words, made her feel connected to him in a way she couldn't identify.

"A Divine Rose. A name to remember," he said. "Yes, I am very much aware that we should talk further, and I would be most pleased to discuss the possibilities that exist for you."

Before she could respond, Mr. Gogii handed Devina Rose his business card and forthrightly stated, "I would be pleased if you would call my office to make an appointment when you feel ready to discuss your job search." He sensed that it wouldn't be too long before she called. But, his calculation was a little off.

Upon leaving his booth, she noticed that Mr. Gogii's business card had only his name, titles, and the same message he had posted on the reader board, along with his phone number.

Several weeks passed before Devina Rose made the call. When he answered the phone, she heard, "Hello, this is George Gogii. May happiness bless your day. Is that you, Devina Rose?"

"Wow!" Devina Rose thought. "This is really getting weird. How in the world did he know it was me?"

They exchanged a few more pleasantries. Mr. Gogii gave Devina Rose his address, and a time was set to meet a few days later.

Mr. Gogii's office was located on the fourth floor of a six-story business complex. The office suite was made up of several rooms, including a kitchenette break room and two small restrooms. The main room, a very large functional space, was furnished like someone's living room. In the center, two comfortable-looking armchairs sat facing each other on a large multicolored, thickly woven rug. In one corner was an expensive-looking, dark-colored wooden computer module with built-in shelves and drawers. On one end of the desk sat a large multicolored Tiffany lamp. The rest of the room consisted of blank walls, painted in an ancient-looking subdued orange and lemon-yellow trim, with dark-stained wooden folding chairs lined up around them.

As Devina Rose entered the office, Mr. Gogii stood in the middle of the room and greeted her. "I am very happy you decided come," he said. "Please have a seat."

They sat in the armchairs in the center of the room facing each other. Then he began by saying, "I can observe that you appear to be a little nervous, and I would like for us not to be too formal, so will you please just call me George?"

"Okay, that works for me. And you can call me Dee," she replied.

Mr. Gogii continued, "I know you said your job search wasn't going too well, particularly the networking part of it. But before we take a look at that issue, perhaps you could tell me a little bit about yourself?"

Devina Rose hesitated for a few seconds as she entered into a deep place filled with childhood thoughts—some good, some painful. As the words came, she was still remembering, "My mother died giving birth to me, and my dad was left with two other kids besides me to bring up. I was a late baby, and my two brothers were several years older than me. My grandmother took care of us during the day while Daddy worked in the cotton fields. He was one of two other black sharecroppers in Blytheville, Arkansas. That's where they used to hold the National Cotton Picking Contest. I tried pickin' cotton a few times but my little hands couldn't take it."

Mr. Gogii interrupted. "Blythe–Ville … where is it located?"

Devina Rose laughed and said, "Yeah, I know how the name's spelled, but unless you're from the South, words spelled and spoken are two different things. The way you say it is 'Bly Vull,' like you got a big wad of Bull of The Woods chewin' tobacco rolled up on the inside cheek of your mouth. Anyhow, it's between Tennessee and Missouri. It's about seventy-five miles north of Memphis, Tennessee, right on the Big Muddy."

Mr. Gogii asked, "Big Muddy. Isn't that a pie made with ice cream, peanut butter, and chocolate?"

Now giggling, Devina Rose said, "No, no, George, you're thinking about a mud pie. Big Muddy is just another name for the Mississippi River!"

"Well, although I have been in your country for a few years, it is most likely that I still have many things to learn about it," Mr. Gogii quipped. "It is my deepest wish to someday eat a mud pie."

Devina Rose continued, "Anyhow, my daddy always preached he wanted something better for his kids. And since I always had my face in a book, and spent a lot of my summers sneaking in and watching trials in the courthouse, he told me I should be thinking about maybe becoming a lawyer. Right after I turned eighteen, Daddy got sick and passed on. By that time my brothers were living by themselves. That just left me to take care of myself. Granny had moved in with some cousins, and so I decided to see the world I kept reading about in all those books they had in the library."

"So what did you decide to do with your life?" he asked.

"I joined the Navy," Devina Rose replied. "I got real lucky and had, I guess you could call it, a natural gift for legal things, and my test scores were pretty high. They sent me to the Naval Justice School. When I graduated from that training, I had earned about ten semester hours of college credits. I followed that up by getting an Associate's Degree in Paralegal Studies, just in case I decided to go civilian. But I didn't get out after four years. I reenlisted. So, by the end of my fifth year in the Navy, I had made an E-4 Legalman/Yeoman rating. Working in the JAG Corps was great, and I really enjoyed doing legal research and assisting JAG officers in doing preliminary investigations, depositions, and court case preparation.

"And—" Devina Rose abruptly stopped talking. Her silence hung in the air like ground-hugging fog. She had spaced out. She was looking at her new mentor, but she wasn't seeing him.

After minute or so, Mr. Gogii, in a quiet neutral voice, put the conversational vehicle back into drive and asked, "Dee, what was the vision you just experienced that made you stop talking?"

"A 'what-is-happening?' thought just hit me," she replied. "It's about the fact that I came to you because I couldn't understand why I was having a problem starting a conversation when I'm doing a job search.

I know you are supposed to help people with job search and networking. Wouldn't the networking part involve starting a conversation?"

Devina Rose ended her little expository excursion and commented, "By the way, I'm not even sure what networking is. I just noticed I'm not having a problem talking to you, and I don't understand that either."

Mr. Gogii smiled at her, at the blast of words being spewed out by this potential student. He said, "My dear Devina Rose, I have observed that the interrupter, as I shall call him, the little demon that is getting in your way isn't there all the time. He comes and goes. This little fellow lives in a cave, deep inside you. Some people call this place the subconscious mind. He only comes out when he is called. That call is some event or experience you had in the not-too-distant past. It seems that of late he has been getting much more difficult for you to control. So please tell me, if you will, did anything happen to you while you were in the Navy that was unusual?"

For the first time since she separated from the military, Devina Rose let her words run free. "I had been assigned to work with a JAG officer for several months investigating the theft of electronics equipment for the Navy's Reserve Fleet in San Diego. They discovered that someone, most likely enlisted personnel, had been coming aboard these vessels just before they were to be towed to the salvage yard for dismantling. These were aging World War Two, Korean Conflict, and some Vietnam War vessels whose hulls were corroding and disbursing carcinogenic chemicals into the water. This required the Navy to schedule them for destruction to remove their toxic potential.

"Once aboard, the suspects remove classified electronic equipment. According to their source, JAG determined the equipment was being sold to foreign organizations for distribution on a world market."

"What is JAG?" Mr. Gogii asked.

"JAG stands for Judge Advocate General. It's the legal services department for all branches of the military," she said. "The JAG officer and I had information that two suspects were part of a salvage crew that was aboard an old mine sweeper, preparing to tow it to the Navy yard for dismantling. My job was to get a statement from one of the sailors while the JAG officer interviewed the other sailor.

"Once aboard, we quickly located our suspects. The plan was to avoid going belowdecks and to stay topside for our own security, as there was another officer aboard in charge of the crew who had identified the suspects to my JAG. We also brought with us two Naval Security personnel, should we need help taking the suspects into custody.

"Along with my security detail, I contacted the suspect and identified myself. We moved to the aft deck of the vessel and I began my interview.

"After a few minutes I could see the man was really getting agitated, and I had this feeling that he would panic and say or do something stupid. So, I turned slightly to my left to see where my security detail was. He was distracted. I saw him looking down at a Navy motor launch that had pulled up alongside about midships. In another moment I felt myself being lifted up into the air, and I heard the suspect say loud and clear, 'Ain't no one gonna put me the brig!'

"I went over the side and hit the water. It was about a fifteen to twenty-foot drop because the ship was riding low in the water. If the ship had been riding higher, chances are we wouldn't be having this conversation. When I hit the water, it felt like I landed on concrete and it knocked the breath out of me. Everything suddenly went dark. It was real faint, but I thought I heard someone yelling, 'Man overboard!' The next thing I remember is waking up in sick bay.

"We caught everyone involved. The sailor that talked to my JAG officer confessed to everything. He got nine years in the brig. The guy that threw me overboard is doing twenty to life at hard labor in Leavenworth for attempted murder."

"So," Mr. Gogii inquired, "what happened to you? Did you return to … what did you call it … the JAG?"

"The chief surgeon told me that, except for a couple of cracked ribs, bruises, and a slight concussion from hitting the water so hard, I would be okay after a week in the hospital," Devina Rose replied.

Mr. Gogii interrupted her, "I'm not so sure you were all right, were you?"

"Well, I'm still thinking that one through. All I do know is I started to have problems sleeping, and I would sometimes wake up in a cold sweat. I couldn't concentrate at work. But most of all, I started having a problem with investigative and research interviews, and it was particularly bad with people I didn't know."

Mr. Gogii once again interrupted and posed several questions. "Devina Rose, do you still feel you were all right? Is it possible that getting thrown overboard, especially by a stranger, caused you to have problems relating to people and focusing on your job?"

Again, there was that temporary but obvious barrier of silence between them before she finally spoke. "It could be … maybe … I really don't know. Why am I so confused about this?"

Mr. Gogii sensed the beginning of an aha moment, and pursued it. "Tell me something. After the doctor released you to go back on duty, and you started having problems, what happened then?"

"Eventually," Devina Rose replied, "I was sent back for a physiological examination, and the Navy decided I was no longer fit for duty, so I was medically discharged. Up till now, I've been working through employment agencies, mostly taking on no-brainer, minimum public contact, back-office computer and records filing jobs."

Following their initial meeting, Mr. Gogii and Devina Rose met weekly to work through her PTSD issues a step at a time. When he felt she was ready to make face-to-face contacts, he introduced her to the concept of networking.

He asked her, "Can you define what you think networking is, and what it has to do with a job search?"

"Well," she quickly said, "it's all about communicating with others who might be able to influence employers to consider or refer you as a qualified candidate for hire. The job market is the place where your skills, abilities, and training match your job or career goals."

Mr. Gogii nodded his head. "That's a good answer, but it's a lot more than that. All the jobs advertised on TV, in the newspapers, the

Internet, posted on bulletin boards in supermarkets, or offered in professional and career-oriented periodicals, and other media sources—all these jobs only amount to twenty percent (20%) of the jobs that are available. The other eighty percent (80%) of the jobs that provide better pay, better benefits, and opportunities for personal and professional growth and advancement are never or very rarely advertised. This is called the 'Hidden Job Market.' The only way a person doing a job search can access this market is through networking."

"All right, I guess I understand what networking is supposed to accomplish," Devina Rose said, "but how am I supposed to do it?"

Mr. Gogii responded to Devina Rose's request for clarification by providing the following information:

- Networking is something personal. It's establishing a system of relationships that enables the individual to create results based upon the development and maintenance of appropriate contacts and resources. It is the art of questioning and making commitments and establishing personal rapport.

- Networking contacts are people who know you and can refer you to others.

- Networking contacts are connector-type people you know through various associations and activities that are willing to promote you.

- Networking contacts are individuals within an organization who make hiring decisions, create jobs, receive resumes, and facilitate interviews.

- Networks are essentially a combination of personal, professional, occupational, community, and by-happenstance contacts. (An example of the latter is the stranger sitting next to you on an airplane with whom you strike up a conversation).

During their final weeks together, Mr. Gogii instructed Devina Rose in the art of developing and using a face-to-face self-introduction to a stranger. This was also part of his therapy to help her master the fear of initiating a conversation with someone she didn't know.

"Devina Rose," he said, "imagine you are entering an elevator of a twenty-story building that contains prestigious law firms. Your destination is the seventeenth floor to make contact with a civilian law firm that represents JAG defendants. On the elevator with you is a well-groomed executive. He is carrying a large manila file folder, and you can read the title on the folder, Dawson, Dawson & Ligget, JAG Attorneys at Law. You have forty-five to sixty seconds before reaching your destination.

"Dee, do you see yourself on the elevator?"

"Okay, I got it. I'm on the elevator."

"Your assignment is to develop a self-introductory branding statement of who you are, and to determine who they are, what skills and abilities you have to offer, and what you are seeking. Your comments are directed at engaging the executive standing across from you as the elevator begins to rise."

Mr. Gogii explained that this is what is commonly referred to in the job search world as an *elevator speech*. It consists of four basic components:

- **Connecting and Exhibiting Motivation** – What am I all about in the job I perform?

"As a specialist with over ___ years of experience in ___, I'm driven by the fact that I really enjoy what I do and the challenges presented. No day is ever the same!"

- **Skills, Knowledge and Abilities** – What identifiable experience and values can I offer an employer?

"During the last ___ years, I've performed/conducted ___." (Itemize a few of the services or type of work you have been involved in and the kind of results achieved, and why such accomplishment is rewarding. Additionally, indicate a particular skill or ability of yours that has vastly improved because of your work.)

- **Personal Focus of Job Search** – What is my career or employment objective?

"I'm currently in search of ___ opportunity in the ___ profession (occupation, industry, field, arena, etc.)"

- **Inquiry of Opportunity** – How can the person being contacted provide an opportunity?

"Do you know of any opportunities in ___?" or "I would really appreciate your suggestions regarding how I might make a connection with someone who has an opening in the ___ field."

Mr. Gogii instructed, "Please review the four components of an elevator speech, and develop one of your own for our next meeting. The components do not have to be in any specific order, but your dialogue should be a logical flow of information. Just remember, you are still on the elevator with a stranger. This is where your elevator speech begins and ends."

The following week Devina Rose met with Mr. Gogii and presented him with her elevator speech.

"George," she said, "I think part of my elevator speech would be to make eye contact with the stranger, smile, step forward, and extend my arm for a handshake, and then begin. What do you think?"

"Oh, that is excellent," Mr. Gogii agreed. "To be quite candid, I apologize because I forgot to mention that before. Dee, you learn quickly, and I know you will do well in the future."

Then Devina Rose began her elevator speech for Mr. Gogii. "Hi, I'm Devina Rose Wright. And you are? It's so nice to meet you, Mr. Jones. I'm doing some research on possible paralegal opportunities with firms that represent military clients. I'm on my way up to the firm Dawson, Dawson, and Ligget. It's my understanding they handle such clients. I recently separated from the military in that field. It's a pretty exciting field, and no day is ever the same. I've been through the Naval Justice School. I have six years of experience as a Legalman and have an AS Degree in Paralegal Studies. I specialize in legal research, investigative reports, documentation, and trial prep. Do you know of any other law firms that would be able to use someone with my background, training, and skills? I would appreciate any direction or recommendation you would care to provide."

Mr. Gogii smiled and nodded his head in approval, "Yes, yes, yes, that was wonderful! I said before you are a quick study and are very good at expressing yourself, once you get into the rhythm. I do not see you having further problems speaking to strangers or engaging someone in conversation. I think you have done remarkably well during the weeks we have been working together."

As he ended their session that day, he remarked, "I have been working with a group of other veterans with various issues regarding the networking process and would like to invite you to attend our last session together. It is intended to be a graduation exercise, as it would be for you. Will you come?"

"You can bet on it. I'll be there."

There were, according to her count, eleven students of Mr. Gogii's that appeared for the final networking exercise. Devina Rose made it an even dozen. He made a few introductory remarks to the group about how far they had come in understanding the concept of networking.

"This is your opportunity to demonstrate to each other, and to yourself, what you have learned. For your first serious personal network connection, you will be participating in 'The Connecting Exercise,'" he said.

Mr. Gogii removed a large ball of thick white string from his briefcase, and handed it to the student seated immediately to his right—they were all seated in a circle.

"Please pass the string along to the person seated to your right while still holding on to a portion of the string. Will the last person who receives the ball of string please hold onto the ball while gripping your portion of the string?"

When the string had been distributed and every student held a piece of it, Mr. Gogii turned to the last person to receive the string and remaining ball. "Robert, will you please stand and present your elevator speech?"

When Robert had finished giving his speech, the next person stood and gave her speech. They continued around the circle until the last student had had a chance to speak. Then Mr. Gogii said, "This exercise was designed for all of you. It demonstrates that whether by mind energy or physical presence we are all, as beings, and as the string symbolizes, connected to each other in this universe.

"Second, and this is very important, all of you have just successfully established your first personal network of supporters. I have published a list of all the students who are here today, with a copy for each of you. Use the list to stay in touch with one another. Remember to ask for help and support and share your successes with each other. Please notice that I have placed my contact information as the last member on this list. Stay in touch with me and let me know how your life is progressing."

At the end of the meeting, as each student stood to leave, Mr. Gogii gave a slight bow of reverence and respect, shook each person's hand, and said, "Thank you. You will do well." A number of the veterans in the group responded with, "HOOAH," as they exited his office. Mr. Gogii smiled and said, "You are very welcome."

Devina Rose walked to Mr. Gogii's kitchenette and removed a large Styrofoam food container from his refrigerator. She returned to Mr. Gogii and handed it to him. "George," she said, "this mud pie is for you. It tastes a lot different than Big Muddy!"

A few weeks later, Devina Rose read an article in the local Chamber of Commerce newsletter about the local bar association holding a workshop on providing legal services to veterans. She made preparations to be there by making copies of her resume, and by designing and printing up what she called a *professional branding card.*

DEVINA ROSE WRIGHT
(617) 922-2727 / drwright.paralegal@gmail.com
Gifted & experienced paralegal, specializing in Legal Research,
Investigative Reports, Documentation, Trial Prep, seeks opportunity
with veteran-oriented & client-committed law firm.
NJS Graduate - JAG Corps Legalman experience - Certified Paralegal

It was a miniaturized version of her elevator speech on business card stock.

She appeared at the workshop and talked to the bar association's registrar seated at a table near the door, registering and passing out name tags.

Devina Rose explained, "I would really appreciate a chance to contact some of the attorneys in attendance. I recently separated from the military, and I'm attempting to make serious connections with attorneys representing veterans. I'm an NJS graduate, have several years of JAG Corps experience, and I'm a certified paralegal."

The registrar, whose first name was Sherry, said, "Sure, honey, you go right ahead. By the way, as they sign in I'll point out which attorneys you should talk to, and you can give them one of your cards."

At morning break some of the attorneys who had her card spoke to her briefly and accepted her resume. By the time she got home there were four messages on her phone requesting contact. Out of the four calls, two resulted in interviews and one in a job offer, which she accepted. Now she felt connected, and unafraid.

VOYAGER BASICS

Yes, we do live in a changing world of technological wonderment. However, there is too much reliance upon technology for the sake of expedience when conducting a job search. This is especially true when it comes to the networking part of the process.

The social media craze tends to undermine the individual's need to touch skin and to see and speak with others face-to-face as we establish and maintain our interpersonal and professional relationships.

It's no one's fault. This is the world that most modern-day veterans grew up in. Those of us in the "boomer" category grew up meeting people in person or speaking with them on the telephone. In these personal ways, we established relationships and trust.

Yet, as we have all been led to believe, it's necessary to adapt and overcome our resistance to advancing technologies. As a matter of survival, we need to become more social media savvy just to maintain a competitive edge in the game.

In an effort to be competitive, veterans need to ask themselves, "Is face-to-face networking really that beneficial to the job search process?"

The answer, obviously, is yes. Based upon research conducted by the National Association of Colleges and Employers (NACE), 70–80% of jobs are not posted on job sites or other media and can only be accessed through the process of networking. People know people, and it's the traditional word-of-mouth factor that continues to assist those in the hunt with finding jobs and career opportunities.

Often younger veterans, those in Generation Y, return home from deployment with advanced technical skills acquired in the military. These are important skills, and yet these young vets need to learn to take advantage of engaging employers and initiating contacts on a face-to-face basis.

Virtual connecting needs to become more of a bridge to facilitating offline relationships, rather than a convenient means of replacing them. A good rule of thumb would be less texting and tech-talking and more face-to-face involvement.

For the veteran, such mindfulness is critical to making the adjustment from a tightly structured military group effort to re-engagement into an open, competitive, civilian, and often "one-on-one" environment.

Some of the advantages and benefits of face-to-face networking include:

- **Developing Interpersonal Contact Skills**

These are most often referred to as people or communications skills. This involves listening and having an interactive conversation, mastering the ability to relate to someone personally. It is almost impossible to get better at this with a smartphone.

- **Perfecting the Art of Light Conversation**

Learning to engage in small talk about things you like or enjoy—can establish a commonality with others. The ability to "chit-chat" provides the opportunity for others to gain a better insight into the real you.

- **Establishing the Intuitive Connection**

The intuitive connection is the unspoken language. It's the difference between personal versus a virtual connection. It can only be affected through eye contact, the projection of humor, neurolinguistics (body language), and self-authentication. It's the creation of real-time live energy as a result of being around people. How else is it possible to get a vibe, a sense of someone's spirit or personality? The marvel of Skype is no match for the down-to-earth handshake and the warmth of a "glad to meet you" smile.

- **Experiencing the Power of a First Impression**

There is no substitute for making an enlivened and lasting impression through face-to-face contact—because of the way someone made you feel, but more importantly, how you made them feel.

So, a veteran might ask, "Is there a different set of rules for older and younger veterans with regard to the networking process?"

The answer is probably not. The continued assertion that social media provides a completely new method for interacting with potential employers is a little out of step with the basic (boot camp) cadence of how effective relationships are established and maintained in the real world.

If you are a veteran engaged in a job search, then you need to realize that the most important activity, above all others, is research. You have to do research, which means looking into, considering the possibilities, asking questions, searching out, etc.

In the business world it's called "due diligence"—checking out the credentials of others, looking at the books of a business you are considering buying into or partnering with, assessing your ROI (Return On Investment). It's all business and, it's all R-E-S-E-A-R-C-H.

If you consider social media to be the ultimate tool for your job search efforts, you might want to do a little research first. Read articles and blog posts about people using social media in their job search. Or, consider and evaluate Twitter or whatever other technical networking tool the media says is the greatest thing since sliced bread.

The fact is, social media doesn't play as crucial a role in obtaining employment as is popularly believed. Most of the "hype" out there is just that—overindulged myth making.

According to researchers writing about the impact of social media on job search, the numbers just don't match. Statistically, social media contacts only result in a very small percentage of hiring done by employers, roughly 3.5%.

Most employer/recruiter/job seeker connections are made through referrals, job boards, company and government websites, and outside recruiters, marketing professionals.

This shouldn't be interpreted to mean that social media cannot or does not play a role in getting someone a job or that it's not becoming more accepted as a valid form of job search, because it is. But as experts in the field of job search and career development indicate, job hunting through social media is not as big a phenomenon as projected by the media. But, it can and should be used as an evolving and natural addition to other job search tools utilized by contemporary employment seekers.

Here's the bottom line: it's more about leveraging online social sites with old-school job-hunting techniques. No job search should focus exclusively on social media.

For example, establish and maintain a few LinkedIn relationships with people in your professional field. Then, following a period of trust building, set up an in-person get-together over coffee, beer or a meal and go from there. Once the meeting appears to be flowing smoothly, ask for referrals.

The secret to social media networking is to mix and incorporate it with off-line strategies. A person can't do a job search exclusively online and expect to achieve their employment goals. Networking is a face-to-face, person-to-person function. The people you meet with in person should represent a wide range folks from different fields who can help you achieve your goals.

So, what kind of people do you want in your network? Let's consider the people who can be most helpful in guiding you on your path to employment:

- **The Advisor**

This is an individual who has reached a level of success you aspire to achieve. This person provides an opportunity for you to learn from their successes and their mistakes. Pay attention to their words of wisdom from their life experiences. Such a relationship often offers unique perspectives, especially if they have known you for a while and have watched you evolve as a person.

- **The Benefactor**

This is someone who has periodically entered your life at different times. They may have helped with making critical life decisions, personal transformations, or offered objective insights with no strings attached.

- **The Insider**

An insider is someone in your career or occupational field who can provide an expert level of information or access to it. You can depend on them to keep you informed of what is occurring now, and the next big thing anticipated to occur in the field. Ask them to be a sounding board on new ideas you have for moving forward with your job search.

- **The Guru**

This person is generally outside of your chosen career or occupational field, but has the latest job search information. The guru can help you to be innovative and creative in developing and utilizing unconventional job search methods.

• The Connector

This individual provides access to people, resources, and information. As soon as the connector come across something related to your specific job search goals, they send an email or dial you up on the phone to tell you about it. Connectors are great at uncovering unique methods of making connections and locating resources or opportunities most people tend to overlook or ignore.

• The Innovator

Including this person in your network offers you someone with whom to share out-of-the-box ideas. Innovators are exceptional at brainstorming methods of making things happen in nonconventional ways.

• The Realist

This person is a co-planner with a gift for providing periodic reality checks. They can help you focus on your employment goals. They tell you when your expectations exceed your capabilities without destroying personal ambitions and dreams. They are there to challenge you to make things happen.

• The Collaborator

Here is an individual whose road to success is similar to your quest. This person is a collaborator and a planner, similar to the realist, but they can plant seeds of accomplishment on the path to reaching your goals.

Sometimes only one contact with this person can significantly impact the way you think and the outcome of your life. Be sure to include this person in your network, for they help you see the possibilities.

• The Partner

This is someone who is in a place and on a journey similar to yours, who is willing to share resources, opportunities, and information, and who encourages you to do the same. This relationship is mutually beneficial, as you both work toward the same goal.

• The Veteran Player Promoter

This person is a real player and contributor in the game of networking. They are willing to encourage you on your journey with the hopes that you in turn will encourage others in the future. The veteran player understands the concept of contributing to the success and well being of others by "paying it forward."

The veteran player's mantra: "As a brother or sister, not in arms, but as collaborating seekers of truth, communal advancement and personal transformation, you freely give to fellow veterans, young and old alike, a helping hand whenever the opportunity presents itself."

Their reward for such generosity is the feeling of satisfaction one achieves through the mere act of giving—one of the most powerful ROIS in existence. Paramount to the success of their network is the Universal Principle of learning to give before you receive—their network is a reflection of this principle. If, out of all the network participants listed, you were given the choice of selecting only one to be involved in your network, it would be this individual.

5

THE APPLICATION CHALLENGE

"It's All About Paying Attention to Directions."

It was Monday, usually a day with a hectic pace at the career center where Matt interviewed and helped veterans register for job search assistance, especially vets with barriers to employment. But an hour and a half had gone by since the last vet left his office.

The time was crawling now, like molasses oozing uphill in winter. He knew the phone could ring any second and the reception desk out front would tell him a veteran wanted to speak to a Vet Rep. Just as he thought of that possibility, the phone rang.

"How did I do that?" he questioned himself. Was it just a coincidence?

Matt quickly picked up the phone on the second ring and listened to the brief message. Then he hung up and made his way to the front lobby.

The receptionist gave that "It's a joke, right?" kind of smile and nodded her head toward the woman standing at the front counter. She appeared to be around thirty-five. It was apparent that she had spent considerable time in the sun, perhaps too much. It made her look overly healthy, but not unattractive. The windburn tan of her face, her demeanor, and the way she resolutely walked up to him–with an uncommon graceful rhythm, as though in cadence with the universe, seemed almost predatory, like feline stalking.

Her jeans were styled with a permanent crease in the pants legs. She wore an oversized yellow sweatshirt with red lettering that read, "Marines Believe Pain Is Just Weakness Leaving the Body!" Tightly wedged onto her head was a military camouflaged soft hat with the brim lowered over her eyebrows, shading but not covering her eyes. The hat covered glistening, dark brown hair tightly rolled into a bun at the back of her head.

Matt picked up his pace and walked toward her. Their eyes met, making an initial introduction. In sync, they smiled at each other. They reached out and touched skin. For Matt it was an impressive handshake. "My God," he thought, "my whole arm aches!"

He imagined a well-defined six-pack on a five-by-five sinewy and well-muscled android just beneath that yellow-and-red sweatshirt.

Matt could barely get the words out—the pain now radiated up his arm to his tongue. "Hi, I'm Matt. You're a vet, right?" When she nodded, he said, "Thank you for your service to our country."

She continued smiling, attempting to mask her bone-crushing charade. "Thank you," she said. "I'm Jackie June-bug Jenkins, but you can call me JJ. It's a pleasure to meet you, sir."

They walked back to his office, sat down, and began with some light get-acquainted talk.

In answer to Matt's questions, JJ began to tell him her story. "I joined the Marines after completing an ASN two-year degree, with the initial goal of becoming a registered nurse. I was about fourteen months into my BSN training when I realized the Marine Corps doesn't have a medical field of operation.

"I found out that when a person enters the service as a Marine, they train as a Marine, and when training is completed as a BSN, which covers all fields of the nursing profession, they come out as a Navy Ensign. When a person applies for admittance to the program, it's through the Medical Enlisted Commission. I only later discovered that the Marine Corps is a department or branch of the Navy, and upon graduation, Marines are switched over to the Navy. They then provide medical services to both Naval and Marine personnel.

"When I first entered the Corps, I had to complete boot camp. I was sent to Parris Island, South Carolina. Although the Marines do have boot camps in San Diego, California, at Camp Lejeune, which was where I would have preferred to go, the Marines only train women at Parris Island. I was in with no way out. So, I told myself I would deal with it."

"So, how long were you in the Navy?" Matt asked

"Well, to tell you the truth, I never finished my BSN degree. And looking back at it all, now that I'm out of the military, quitting was a dumb thing to do. When I got out I was still a Marine.

"I was just beginning my second year of training, and the day-to-day grind of studying was getting to me. So when I heard about openings for female Marine Drill Instructors at Parris Island, I had no second thoughts about applying for the program.

"One night I had my face in this book about medical procedures, and the words began running together. I don't know why or how it happened but a thought struck me ... 'too much thinking and not enough doing.'

"Right then, I remembered boot camp and the way all of us in my squad were doing things together, and the respect I had for the DI who made it all happen. It was something I knew I could do. The next day I saw a billet posting, something about volunteering for women DI Training at Parris Island, and that was it. I spent the next three and a half years as a DI."

Matt, not meaning to, fired several questions at her. "Why did you get out? Why didn't you stay in? It seems to me, from what you've been saying, you liked what you were doing. What happened?"

There was a pause in their conversation. It was as though JJ went to another place. Matt saw her eyes begin to fill with tears.

"Well," she said, "we were doing an early morning five-mile run on a fairly wide dirt road. One of the trainees, Angie Marks, was really struggling. She was this real cute petite girl, and I was always pushing her. I had just yelled at her to keep up and get out of the middle of the road. I told her to get behind the rest of the squad, who were jogging along the side of the road, but Angie looked like she was about to do a belly flop in the dirt. Anyhow, a four-by-four ammo carrier came around the curve and took her out. She was gone.

"When re-up time rolled around at the end of 2010, I promised myself I would get out because … well … I felt responsible for the death of one of my recruits, even though the follow-up board of military inquiry cleared me of any wrongdoing. I should have toughed it out with the medical studies.

"For the first few months of trying to get adjusted to civilian life, all I did was think about that little Marine dying in the dirt, and I still do."

Matt suggested, "You know the VA has programs for vets who have experienced traumatic events like yours while serving in the military."

"Yeah, I'm in a treatment program now. I go once a week and I'm trying to work it out. But I need to get a job so I can move forward with my life. So far, I've sent out dozens of resumes and filled out about the same number of applications, and they are not producing anything, especially the applications. A lot of them just don't make sense. They ask for information that's already on the resume I sent in. I've had most of them returned with the word 'Unacceptable' written across the front."

At this point in their conversation, Matt asked JJ, "Do you have any idea what you want to do career-wise? I'm thinking since you had almost three years of nurses training, that would be something you might want to finish."

"Yeah, I did give that some thought. As I said before, I joined the Marines with an Associate of Science in Nursing. That's what made the nursing program I signed up for so attractive at the beginning of my enlistment. I saw it as a solid medical career opportunity.

"So, now you know what happened," she concluded. "I've been applying at medical clinics for positions. I know I can handle it, but nothing is happening. I must be doing something wrong because I've received letters from employers telling me my applications were not acceptable."

"JJ," Matt said, "I think we both know the direction you want to go career-wise, but the big question is, how are you going to get there if you're having an application problem? I think I may have an answer for you. But before we get into that, I have another question for you."

"What's that?" she inquired.

"Where did you learn to shake hands?"

She started laughing almost uncontrollably, caught herself, and swallowed hard. She choked back another giggle as she wiped away the remaining tears in her eyes.

Out of emotional relief, she half whispered, "Yeah, man, I'm truly sorry about the squeeze stunt. It was one of those things I trained myself to do to survive with my macho Marine male counterparts. The whole thing about the Marine Corps is staying fit. I did some running and rock climbing before I joined up. Once I got in, I had to get even fitter to keep up. After I became a DI, I began weight training and working out almost every day."

"Really," Matt remarked, "I kind of suspected something like that. Just by the way you carry yourself, I could tell you were into fitness."

"Every day I did, and still do, body planks, and I can hold one for five to twenty minutes, depending on my energy level. I also do push-ups on my fingertips and chin-ups on a bar one inch thick. You really can develop a grip that way. When I'm at home, I squeeze a tennis ball constantly."

"Impressive," Matt said. "But let's get down to business. Why don't you tell me what you think the problem might be with your applications?"

JJ thought for a few seconds. "I guess I'm not what the employer is looking for. Maybe it's because I'm ex-military. To tell you the truth, I really don't know," she replied.

"Okay, JJ, give me an idea of what kind of applications you have been submitting. Were they just basic two-or-three pagers or in-depth multipage documents? What kind of jobs have you been applying for?"

"Well, in spite of the leadership and drill instructor training I've had, most of the jobs I've applied for have been either as a medical assistant or in medical records."

JJ went on to explain, "Because of my previous civilian and military medical training, most of the applications I've filled out are only two to three pages. The only exception was the one time I filled out a federal job application for medical assistant at the VA Hospital."

"What happened with the VA app?" Matt asked.

"There were numerous attachments I had to submit, and the resume that went along with them was incredibly detailed, resulting in a ten-page application. The strange thing about that application was that I never received any response from the feds."

Matt gave out with a short laugh. "Yeah, I know what you are saying about the federal job applications. They can be pretty intense and detailed. We can examine the federal application process later. But for right now, I think we need to focus on your standard, everyday application. I think if we can achieve some success with a regular application, and get you into a medical job to handle your immediate employment and economic needs, the federal application will be more doable later on."

Matt presented JJ with the following basic blank application form and suggested that she fill it out as though she were applying for a medical assistant position.

EMPLOYMENT APPLICATION

- Please complete this application by typing or hand-printing in black ink. INCOMPLETE or UNSIGNED applications will not be considered.
- We are an equal employment opportunity employer. We do not discriminate on the basis of race, religion, color, sex, age, national origin, marital status, or disability.
- Do you need an accommodation to participate in the application or interview process? __Yes __No

Employer: _____ Job Order # _____

Job Title: _____

PERSONAL INFORMATION

Name: _____

Address: _____ City: _____

State:____ Zip: _____

Phone: (___)_____ Message: (___)_____

Email: _____

Driver's License: _____ Operator: __ CDL Type: ____

Endorsements: _____

Veteran: __Yes __ No Branch:_____

From:___/___/___ To:___/___/___

Have you ever been convicted of a crime: _____Yes _____ No

EDUCATION / TRAINING

High School Diploma / GED: __Yes __No

Post-Secondary Degree: _____

Name of institution beyond high school: _____

Training or academic dates of attendance: From Mo.____/____ To

Mo.____/____

Degree: _____ Major: _____

Minor:_____

Additional training or occupational certification: _____

_____

WORK EXPERIENCE (List most recent work experience first, include volunteer & military experience)

Company Name: _____

Immediate Supervisor: _____

Address: _____

Dates: _____/_____To: _____/_____
Reason for Leaving: _____
Employer's Phone: ____/____/____ Employer's Email: _____
Your Job Title:_____ Job Description: (Duties, Skills,
Equipment Used)

_____

_____

_____

_____

_____

_____

WORK EXPERIENCE (Continued)
Company Name: _____
Immediate Supervisor: _____
Address: _____
Dates: _____/_____To: _____/_____
Reason for Leaving: _____
Employer's Phone:____/____/____ Employer's Email:_____
Your Job Title: _____Job Description: (Duties, Skills,
Equipment Used)

_____

_____

_____

_____

_____

_____

Company Name:_____
Immediate Supervisor:_____
Address:_____
Dates:_____/_____ To:_____/_____
Reason for Leaving:_____
Employer's Phone:____/____/____ Employer's Email:_____
Your Job Title:_____ Job Description: (Duties, Skills,
Equipment Used)

_____

_____

_____

_____

_____

_____

ADDITIONAL QUALIFYING INFORMATION (Certifications, Licenses, Training, Equipment, etc.)

_____

_____

_____

_____

_____

_____

REFERENCES (Provide only those individuals who know of your work ethic, training, performance)

Name:_____ Address:_____ Phone:_____

Name:_____ Address:_____ Phone:_____

Name:_____ Address:_____ Phone:_____

Note: Information provided in this application, and any subsequent information provided, is subject to verification. Falsification or misrepresentations are grounds for disqualification or termination at a later time. Therefore, I certify that all information provided is true, correct and complete to the best of my knowledge, and contains no willful omissions, falsifications or misrepresentations.

Signature of Applicant:_____ Date:_____

Matt explained that he often used this application form with his clients who seemed to be experiencing problems with employer rejections similar to JJ's. A few days later JJ returned with her completed application:

EMPLOYMENT APPLICATION

- Please complete this application by typing or hand-printing in black ink. INCOMPLETE or UNSIGNED applications will not be considered.
- We are an equal employment opportunity employer. We do not discriminate on the basis of race, religion, color, sex, age, national origin, marital status, or disability.
- Do you need an accommodation to participate in the application or interview process? __Yes __No

Employer: **Central City Medical Center**   Job Order # **N/A**
                                                Job Title: **C.M.A.**

PERSONAL INFORMATION
Name: **Jackie J. Jenkins**
Address: **1422 Oak Ave**   City: **Detroit** State: **MI**   Zip: **48201**
Phone: **(313) 187-7723** Message: (___)_____ Email: **jjj21@yahoo.com**
Driver's License: **MI 112217398** Operator: __ CDL Type: _____
Endorsements: _____
Veteran: **X** Yes__ No Branch: **USMC** From: **06 / 13/ 00** To: **06/ 12/ 06**
Have you ever been convicted of a crime? _____ Yes ___No

EDUCATION / TRAINING
High School Diploma / GED: **X** Yes __No
Post-Secondary Degree: **Assoc. Sci. Nurs.**
Name of institution beyond high school: **Central City Voc-Tech Institute Detroit, MI**
Training or academic dates of attendance: From Mo. **09/ 04** To Mo. **06 / 06**
Degree: **ASN**   Major: **Nursing Admin.**   Minor: **Patient Care & Clinical Diagnosis**
Additional training or occupational certification: **MI # 4297 ASN**

WORK EXPERIENCE (List most recent work experience first, include volunteer & military experience)
Company Name: **SEE ATTACHED RESUME**
Immediate Supervisor: _____
Address: _____

Dates: _____/_____ To: _____/_____
Reason for Leaving: _____
Employer's Phone: ____/___/____ Employer's Email: _____
Your Job Title:_____ Job Description: (Duties, Skills,
Equipment Used)

_____

_____

_____

_____

_____

_____

WORK EXPERIENCE (Continued)
Company Name: **SEE ATTACHED RESUME**
Immediate Supervisor: _____
Address: _____
Dates: _____/_____To: _____/_____
Reason for Leaving: _____
Employer's Phone:____/____/____ Employer's Email:_____
Your Job Title: _____Job Description: (Duties, Skills,
Equipment Used)

_____

_____

_____

_____

_____

_____

Company Name: **SEE ATTACHED RESUME**
Immediate Supervisor:_____
Address:_____
Dates:_____/_____ To:_____/_____
Reason for Leaving:_____
Employer's Phone:____/____/____ Employer's Email:_____
Your Job Title:_____ Job Description: (Duties, Skills,
Equipment Used)

_____

_____

_____

_____

_____

_____

ADDITIONAL QUALIFYING INFORMATION (Certifications, Licenses, Training, Equipment, etc.)
SEE ATTACHED RESUME _____

_____

_____

_____

_____

_____

REFERENCES (Provide only those individuals who know of your work ethic, training, performance)

Name: WILL _____ Address:_____ Phone:_____

Name: PROVIDE AT _____ Address:_____ Phone:_____

Name: INTERVIEW _____ Address:_____ Phone:_____

Note: Information provided in this application, and any subsequent information provided, is subject to verification. Falsification or misrepresentations are grounds for disqualification or termination at a later time. Therefore, I certify that all information provided is true, correct and complete to the best of my knowledge, and contains no willful omissions, falsifications or misrepresentations.

Signature of Applicant:_____ Date:_____

After reviewing the basic application JJ had completed, Matt highlighted several obvious errors that were most likely the reason for many of the rejections she was getting from employers:

- Page one – neglected to complete the Yes or No response at the top of the application form.

- Page one – neglected to indicate N/A (Not Applicable) in blank spaces for: Message Phone, Operator CDL & Endorsement sections.
- Page one – neglected to answer the Yes or No crime conviction question in Personal Information section.
- Pages one & two – failure to provide work experience and entering "See Attached Resume."
- Page two – failure to complete additional skills/certification/training section.
- Page two - failure to provide references.
- Page two – failure to sign application acknowledging conditions of employment at bottom of page.

Matt ended their discussion that day by advising JJ, "Most likely employers would consider your lack of response as an inability to follow directions. You are not answering their requests for information. As you know, in the medical profession, paying attention to directions is critical to achieving positive patient outcomes and the maintenance of accurate medical records.

"JJ, you need to remember that it's an employer's market and they get to set the requirements for applicants. Even at the risk of repetitiveness of information, it is always best to provide whatever information an employer is requesting. Not paying attention to requirements is not an option you want to consider."

JJ met with Matt for several more weeks, and gained insight into the art of completing an application. Her attitude began to change as she realized there were only a few options open to her. She could:

- Apply to employers who she believed only required a resume—this approach, however, would limit her exposure to employment opportunities.
- Wait for employers to come begging her to work for them—it is highly unlikely she would ever experience becoming employed following this method, or …

- Seriously consider taking her time and completing all applications according to employer requirements.

Matt suggested, "JJ, you need to consider doing some research on your own regarding the application process. In the meantime, I'd like you to review this Application Completion Process Questions and Answers (Q&A) Summary. It will provide you with basic principles required in the proper completion of employment applications."

Application Completion Process Q&A

Q: Do most employers require an applicant to complete an employment application?

A: *Yes, the majority of today's employers still do ask an applicant to complete an employment application. In fact, a large number of employers require the applicant to complete an application on-site. This is especially true when a screening interview is scheduled to follow the submission of a completed application.*

For the employer, the application serves as a guide during the interview to determine the general qualifications of the applicant. Some application forms contain an "Employer Comments" section that allows the employer or interviewer to jot down additional notes concerning applicants and their specific answers to qualification questions.

Q: Why is it necessary for an applicant to completely fill out the application form when a resume is being submitted?

A: *It's the employer's prerogative to require anything within reason as a condition of application and employment to determine an applicant's qualifications.*

Additionally, most employers, hiring managers, and HR people in general know candidates will tend to embellish and present themselves in the most complimentary light as possible in a resume. This is what a resume is supposed to do—it is, after all, a piece of personal advertisement and branding. It's designed to capture the employer's attention by marketing and promoting the applicant's skills and abilities, hopefully resulting in an interview.

However, employers also realize that a resume seldom points out personal weaknesses of the applicant/candidate that might impair or jeopardize business operations.

Many applications are designed by employers to be skills and experience specific as a method of eliminating unqualified applicants. Generally, the contents of an application, when compared to similar items presented in the applicant's resume, tend to support or invalidate alleged qualifications.

Additionally, such comparison may also bring to light other inconsistencies that might necessitate verification and a careful background check before an offer of employment is made.

Q: What kind of weakness or inconsistency are employers looking for in an application compared to the information contained in a resume?

A: *The primary purpose of an application is to determine if the applicant has enough of the required qualifications to do the job, or has the capability of learning how to do it.*

The work or employment history section of most employment applications generally provide some indication of the skills, abilities, and work experience that function as a qualifier. If not, then education and training can usually establish the capability or probability that the applicant can learn to do the job with some additional training supplied by the employer.

Example: Suppose the applicant, before and while attending a junior college, had experience in the fast food and warehouse industry, but had a college major that focused on the Medical Assistant career field. Does this mean the applicant is not qualified for an entry-level position in a doctor's office, medical clinic, or hospital?

No, it means the employer can still consider the applicant for a medical assisting position, but not one which requires a lot of experience. However, if the applicant has the benefit of an internship/externship in that same medical field while in college, it may qualify as experience for an above entry-level position. This is particularly true when the internship/externship turns into an offer of full-time employment by the same employer when that training period has been successfully completed.

A secondary function of an application is to assist the employer in determining the applicant's stability by reviewing past employment history, although it may not have been in a career-related field. This is why dates of employment receive a critical review—continuity and stability of employment need to be established.

Keep in mind that employers as a whole are still reluctant to consider or hire people who appear to be "job-hopping." Putting time, effort, and financial resources into the training of a new employee just to have that person quit after a short period of time on the job is not conducive to being considered for future employment. This is why it's so important for an individual who, after being on the job for only a week or two, when offered what appears to be a better-paying job by a different employer, should seriously consider staying on-board for a while—to establish a stable work history. This is particularly critical for the person just beginning their career.

The employer will also use an application to determine if the applicant demonstrates a team-player attitude. The probability that an applicant will get along with others, responsibly carry an assigned work load, and yet be willing to help others progress is an inherent concern with most employers.

Attitudes reflected on paper are continually being measured throughout the application, screening, interview, reference, and background check process. It is the completed application that becomes the indicator as to what kind of person the applicant is.

Q: Does an applicant need to provide references in an employment application?

A: *Yes, but only if the application requests them. Otherwise, it is suggested to disregard furnishing them. However, in today's competitive job market, and with the scrutiny most employers give employment applications, the request for references is most always included. Remember,* *some employers may require more than the traditional three (3) refer-ences—this is generally the accepted standard for most employment ap-plications, but be prepared for a maximum of up to five (5) references.*

Q: Although many employers indicate there will be a back-ground check or investigation, do they really conduct one?

A: *Whether or not there is an indication by an employer that a back-ground check will be made, an applicant will be much further ahead in the job search game by always assuming one will be conducted. The in-tensity and thoroughness of a background check or investigation usually depends upon the employer and the nature of the job being applied for.*

Example: When applying for government work, the applicant can always expect verification of references, schools, previous employers, credit agencies, military records, and previous neighborhoods lived in. The more confidential the work being performed in government and/ or in the interests of national security, since 911, the more intense and thorough background checks becomes.

In the private sector of employment, it is becoming more common for employers to complete a very thorough background check.

This is especially true of employers when the job involves the hand-ing of proprietary or confidential information such as manufacturing or production processes, copyrights, secret formulas, and development patents associated with high tech industry and U.S. Government con-tract work. Associated with in-depth background checks are the signing of NDAs (Non-Disclosure Agreements).

Where background checks are concerned, an applicant would be well advised to seriously consider the negative consequences of embellish-ment (exaggerating or stretching the truth beyond what seems reason-able and acceptable) in an application just to create the illusion of being more qualified.

The best and only approach to providing requested information in an application is to be honest, especially JIAs (Justice Involved Applicants) —previously incarcerated veterans and/or felony convictions.

Q: How should an applicant answer a question that appears unfair or illegal, or that creates discomfort by involving too much self-disclosure (the revealing of personal history that has no apparent relationship to the general qualification for performing the job)?

A: *Some authorities suggest that the proper way to respond to such questions is to leave the space blank. Unfortunately, this response does not take into consideration that many employers, when reviewing an application, generally reject any application with a blank space. It is assumed that the applicant is attempting to hide something, and so the employer will reject the application. Also note that large corporations and government agencies with online applications are using tracking and skills verification and matching systems, and blank spaces tend to lend themselves to automatic rejection.*

Again, the best way to stay ahead in the job search process is to fill in every space on the application, unless otherwise instructed. So, if the answer does not apply, simply insert "N/A" (Not Applicable).

When the answer to a question is the same as a previously asked question, consideration should be given to placing "S/A – (#)" (Same As, and the included number of the previous question where the answer was the same). However, the simplest and most practical response would be to provide the same or similar response as before, even at the risk of being repetitive.

If the response to a question or requested information causes an applicant concern as to its legitimacy or fairness, or the applicant is unsure, or the answer would require more space than is provided, then the following two options apply:

• Use an additional sheet of paper to address the question, or

• Insert "Will discuss at interview" in the space.

Remember, when considering blank spaces employers seldom ask about them at interviews. Applicants who leave blank spaces (unless otherwise directed in the application form) seldom get selected for an interview to explain why a space was left blank.

Q: How can an applicant be prepared to complete an application at the employer's place of business?

A: *If an applicant goes to an employer's place of business to apply for a job or to be interviewed and is requested to complete an application before any hiring-related decision is made, it will prove beneficial if the applicant comes prepared.*

Even when an applicant has submitted a cover letter and resume and is coming to an employer for an interview, all too often upon arrival the applicant is asked to complete yet another application before the interview can take place.

Although the applicant has brought a copy of their resume with them to an interview, any attempt to use the resume to assist in completing the unanticipated employment application will prove inadequate, frustrating, and time consuming.

These three factors can be unnerving to the point that any eventual interview will result in poor performance. The applicant will appear unprepared and the employer will be unimpressed.

The best preparation involves the construction and use of an Application Prep Sheet. This completed document should be carried with the applicant to any job search event. It provides an applicant with essential and additional information beyond what has been included in a previously submitted cover letter and resume. In a manner of speaking, it becomes their "cheat sheet."

Keep in mind that a cover letter and resume are only summaries or personal branding messages regarding who you are and what you can do for the employer. The information presented in those documents does not include complete detailed background information normally captured and contained in an Application Prep Sheet.

Note: Regardless of the circumstances, an applicant should always be prepared to handle, efficiently and accurately, an unanticipated request by an employer to complete an on-site employment application.

APPLICATION PREP SHEET

1. Full name: _____

2. Correct mailing address and correct street address if different:
_____/_____/_____/_____
(Street address)   (City)   (State)   (Zip)
_____/_____/_____/_____
(P.O. Box number)   (City)   (State)   (Zip)

3. Email address/Website address:_____

4. Telephone: _____ - _____ - _____   Message: _____ - _____ - _____
   Cell Phone:_____ - _____ - _____   Pager: _____ - _____ - _____

5. Driver's License number:_____
   Classification/Rating:_____(Include recent DMV print out)

6. Military Service – Date of enlistment: ____/____/____
   Date of discharge: ____/____/____
   Branch of service:_____ Military Serial Number:_____
   (Make available discharge documents/DD-214)

7. Skills and Abilities:

Note: The list of skills can be varied and go beyond those included in a resume. They are based upon what has been acquired up to the time of the current application. These skills and abilities are based upon personal on-the-job work experiences and include: volunteer activities; college internships; educational work-study programs; military service; vocational and technical studies; and professional training programs and those that were self-taught.

The objective is to move from multiword phrases used to describe what it is the applicant does or did, to one-to-four word descriptors or images. Example: From: "entered shipping and receiving information from warehouse into computer records system." To: "shipping/receiving data entry."

Under column "A" just brainstorm with acquired skills and abilities as the applicant sees them or might describe to another person. Under column "B" rephrase those skills and abilities into one-to-four word descriptors/images.

Similarly, veterans need to exchange military job descriptions to civilian descriptors.

Column "A" Phrases   Column "B" Descriptors/Images

_____   _____

_____   _____

_____   _____

_____   _____

_____   _____

_____   _____

_____   _____

_____   _____

_____   _____

_____   _____

Note: This method of going from phrases to descriptors and images will be useful with providing essential and specific information when completing the [Employment History] job descriptions section of the application. Additionally, this brain storming/Application Prep Sheet can be used when planning a resume and cover letter. As new skills and abilities are learned the Skills and Abilities section outline in the next section [Employment/Work History] should be updated.

8. Employment/Work History:
Start with most recent employer, moving back in chronological order (by dates, in sequence) to the earliest employment situation for the last seven years. If the skills, experience, and/or expertise now possessed were obtained beyond the last seven years, and are applicable to a current prospective employment situation, be sure to include them.

Note: The following Employment/Work History format represents only one employer; therefore, several copies of the format should be made to meet the desired number of previous work histories. Employment/work histories are handled similarly to Skills and Abilities in Item #7 (including on-the-job work experience, volunteer activities, internships, work-study, and military service).

Employer/Organization:_____

From: _____/_____ to _____/_____
      (Month) (Year)   (Month) (Year)

Total time worked: _____/_____
             (Months) (Years)

City: _____ State:_____ Zip: _____

Phone: _____/_____/_____ Fax: _____/_____/_____

Email: _____

Job Functions/Tasks Performed:

_____

_____

_____

_____

Skill Required/Acquired:

_____

_____

_____

_____

Assess Major Accomplishments (awards, achievements, employer recognition, commendations, new inventions/procedures/systems developed, etc.)

_____

_____

_____

Supervisory/Managerial Responsibilities:

_____

_____

_____

Additional Training/Professional Development/Education acquired working for this employer:

_____

_____

_____

Reason for leaving this job/position:

_____

_____

_____

9. Education/Training/Certification/Licensure:

College Name	Major	Degree	City	State	From:	To:
_____ /	_____ /	_____ /	_____ /	_____ /	_____ /	_____
_____ /	_____ /	_____ /	_____ /	_____ /	_____ /	_____
_____ /	_____ /	_____ /	_____ /	_____ /	_____ /	_____

High School	Graduate?	City	State	From:	To:
_____ /	__ Yes __No /	_____ /	_____ /	_____ /	_____

G.E.D. (Organization/Agency)	City	State	Date of award/Certificate
_____ /	_____ /	_____ /	_____

Junior High School	City	State	From:	To:
_____ /	_____ /	_____ /	_____ /	_____

Professional/Specialized Training/Certification / Licensure : _____

_____

_____

_____

_____

10. References:

Name	Title	City	State	Phone
_____ /	_____ /	_____ /	_____ /	_____
_____ /	_____ /	_____ /	_____ /	_____
_____ /	_____ /	_____ /	_____ /	_____
_____ /	_____ /	_____ /	_____ /	_____
_____ /	_____ /	_____ /	_____ /	_____

APPLICATION PREP SHEET ESSENTIALS

The use of an Application Prep Sheet during the job search process, although it may initially involve time to assemble, will prove beneficial to those applicants serious about being prepared. As outlined, the document contains the following essential background information:

1. Full name (include middle name).

2. Correct street address and mailing address, if different.

3. Email address (and/or website address if applicable).

4. Telephone number, message phone, cell phone, (pager number if applicable).

5. Driver's License information, including DL number and DL classification and endorsements according to state DMV. (Include a recent DMV printout of driving record.)

6. Military service information. (If in National Guard or Reserves, provide printout of the applicant's military status. If active duty, provide copy of discharge document—DD-214.)

7. Provide complete list of all skills and abilities. The list should exceed that which is generally provided in a cover letter, resume, or portfolio by including your personal work record, volunteer positions, internships, and military service. Also suggested are work-related experiences; education; vocational, technical, and professional training; and skills self-taught.

8. Provide complete work history since high school. Although employers currently request employment histories covering seven (7) to ten (10) years, it is best to be prepared for those employers who sometimes ask for work experience exceeding ten (10) years.

Work or job histories are usually provided in chronological order, in reverse, with the most recent employment listed first, including:

- Name of business or organization, including all volunteer positions, internships, and military service (indicating the beginning month and year to ending month and year).
- Correct mailing address of business or organization, city, state, zip code, and phone number with area code.
- Name of immediate supervisor or superior.
- Name of department or division assigned.
- Name of job or designated title of responsibility. (Veterans should refrain from using military slang or descriptions, listing equivalent designations in civilian terms.)
- Brief description of major tasks or jobs performed. (Again, avoid the use of military descriptors.)
- List accommodation, awards, letters of recommendation, endorsements, references, and letters of referral.
- Indicate reason for leaving each employment situation listed.

9. Complete academic education, training, and certification (and any academics and training received in/through military service), including the following:
   - List of educational institutions, beginning chronologically with the most recent.
   - Include dates of attendance (beginning month and year to ending month and year).
   - Provide city and state.
   - Include high school and junior high school attendance and graduation. Provide GED (General Education Development), if applicable, and name of institution or agency where it was obtained.
   - List all professional certifications and licenses obtained.
   - Identify all special training courses and programs completed. (Avoid listing participation in coursework not completed).

10. Provide five (5) references. (Generally three (3) are required for most applications but some employers may ask for more).
    - Provide name and title of reference.

- Indicate profession, trade, or special skill.
- Complete mailing address, telephone number (home and work if known) and email address.

JJ read through the Q&A summary Matt gave her and completed the Application Prep Sheet, taking care to review it and making sure everything had been completed. After two weeks of research, JJ was confident she was headed in the right direction. She sent her resume to a large medical clinic and received a phone call from the employer two days later to come in for an interview.

When she appeared for the interview, the receptionist handed her a three-page application and said, "Please sit at the table in the corner and complete the application. When you're finished, bring it back to the reception desk."

JJ took the application but was tempted to tell the receptionist they already had her resume, and she was there for an interview. But she caught herself. Smiling, she took the paperwork and went to the corner table as instructed.

After sitting down at the table, JJ removed her Application Prep Sheet (her carefully documented cheat sheet) from her briefcase and completed the application in less than twenty minutes.

A few minutes later, she found herself sitting with Mrs. Chase, Central City Medical Center HR Manager. Things went well for JJ that day. During the interview, Mrs. Chase stated, "JJ, it was very impressive how quickly and accurately you completed our application. Usually, most of the candidates we invite for an interview take anywhere from forty-five minutes to an hour to complete the application. We are looking for someone who is qualified, efficient, and accurate. If an offer is made, would you consider becoming a member of this clinic's medical team?"

JJ had no doubt as to what her answer would be.

VOYAGER BASICS

In today's job market it's important to remember that all veterans looking for employment opportunities are not always those who have been recently separated from the military. The truth is, the majority of veterans seeking employment today may have been employed in the civilian sector for several years. And, they may have held more than one or two jobs. A growing number of these veterans are, or are fast approaching, the rank of senior citizen. Still, they are out there "pounding the pavement" just to make ends meet.

Equally important to remember is that being a veteran does not entitle anyone to preferential treatment in the eyes of many employers. Employers will consider all applicants equally. So, to simplify your approach to the application process, all veterans referred to in this guide are applicants, and the rules of applicant status still apply.

On the other hand, at American Job Centers (AJCs) throughout the country, all qualified veterans are given Priority of Service, especially those veterans with significant barriers to employment.

Similarly, in recent years the federal government has created and mandated special programs for veterans experiencing recent deployments and military separations. The emphasis of these programs is directed at employers giving qualified veterans first consideration when making hiring decisions and/or job creation, especially those employers who are federal government contractors.

All too often, applicants inadvertently commit errors on their applications that result in rejection. In almost all of these situations, applicants are never made aware of the reason for rejection. So, the following items should be considered when completing an application for employment. These are the top ten:

1. Mentioning Referrals – Many applications ask if an applicant knows anyone who works for the company or has made a referral.

When mentioning a referral the applicant needs to be careful. In some cases, a referral may be a lazy or mediocre performer or may have fallen out of favor with the employer. In such instances, the employer could assume that the applicant has a similar work ethic or performance issues. The employer may then not give the applicant the consideration they deserve.

2. Arrests, Convictions, and Criminal Records – In every state it is inappropriate, and very often illegal, to ask an applicant if they have ever been arrested. Unfortunately, thousands of people in this country are arrested every year for crimes and offenses they didn't commit but were assumed to be guilty of at the time of arrest. However, our system of jurisprudence (the study, science, and philosophy or rule of law) promotes the concept that an individual is presumed innocent until proven guilty in a court of law. Being arrested is not an indication of wrongdoing.

Therefore, if an applicant is faced with the question of ever having been arrested, some consideration should be given to responding "No" or "N/A" (Not Applicable) even if the answer would have been technically "Yes."

Consider a situation in which a person was detained and released, as opposed to actually being physically incarcerated (put in jail) for a period of time and then released some time later. This would require a "Yes, with an explanation at interview" notation beside it on the application.

Being detained and/or arrested and released (even under the posting of a bond) is not the same as being convicted of a crime. However, in many states an employer is permitted to ask about prior convictions if the employer can demonstrate a rational basis or compelling business reason for doing so.

Example: The employer is an armored car carrier used in the transporting of money for banks, lending institutions, and other businesses handling large sums of currency, and is therefore required to demonstrate the honesty and trustworthiness of its employees to clients.

Hiring ex-offenders (individuals with felony convictions) may create some doubt in the minds of clients and the subsequent loss of business. And felonies aren't the only crimes that may keep a person from being hired. Consider also convictions for misdemeanors such as spousal abuse which is abhorrent to employers needing to maintain public trust.

It should be noted that in most states it's required that personnel hired by an armored car carrier service (including security service agencies) must be licensed, thereby insuring the hiring of individuals without criminal convictions or questionable backgrounds.

If a question appears on an application that does not apply to the applicant, then answering "No" or "N/A" should be considered. Answering a question even when the applicant knows or feels the question is inappropriate is advisable, as leaving blank spaces is to be avoided rather than risk exclusion from consideration.

When an applicant has been convicted of a crime, whether or not time was spent in prison or jail, answering the question "Yes" is a must. Being dishonest and attempting to conceal a conviction would likely result in termination from the job later. So, if the applicant has a "skeleton in the closet," it is appropriate to respond with "Will discuss at interview" or "Please discuss later." It is inadvisable to leave the space blank or to answer "No."

Many employers do realize that it is human to make mistakes, and giving an ex-offender a second chance is something they are willing to do. In many instances, an applicant with a criminal conviction will be allowed to explain what happened and the life lesson learned from it before a final hiring decision is made.

Applicants with an extensive criminal history or a conviction for a sex crime and listed on a state registry as a sex offender can expect considerable resistance and rejection from employers. But even with this kind of record the task is not totally impossible—it's just a little more difficult and requires continuous pursuit of the goal and a "never give up" attitude.

3. Involuntary Termination of Employment (Getting Fired) – Involuntary termination can cause a high level of anxiety if dwelled upon too long. It can interfere with maintaining a positive and healthy view of the application process. Then again, applicants also need to look at that situation to determine if something in their job performance may have contributed to termination to avoid repeating it in the future.

To reduce unnecessary anxiety, it's important to understand and accept the fact that at least once or twice during a lifetime of work, applicants may experience an involuntary termination. This may come about through a variety of reasons or even through no fault of their own.

Involuntary termination is generally defined as being given the option of leaving the job before being fired, as opposed to an immediate termination, which does mean getting fired in about ninety-five percent (95%) of the cases. In today's world of employment, the use of the word "termination" by employers generally covers any exit from employment.

For any applicant who is serious about properly completing an application, it is important to remember not to exclude an involuntary termination, no matter how distasteful the experience might have been. To do so may leave a large gap in an employment history, which may exclude the applicant from consideration during the initial screening process. Even if the applicant makes it to an interview, the gap in employment would be difficult to explain.

Again, it is always advisable to provide a complete work history in an application. An involuntary termination can be addressed in the "reason for leaving" section of the application form.

A response similar to these can be used effectively: "Left under exceptional circumstances and will discuss at interview," or "See separate attached document," or "Please discuss with me at interview."

If the question is raised at the interview, an applicant can explain that some superiors are easier to satisfy and get along with than others, and in this case the supervisor was a difficult person to please. The applicant should explain that they have usually been a top performer and generally get along with everybody.

4. Layoffs / Personnel Cutbacks – Due to economic changes over the past decade, many businesses and public service organizations continue to downsize, enter into mergers, reorganize, or close down. This subsequently leads to personnel cutbacks and layoffs. These situations are a fact of life beyond the control of applicants. It's a probability that many applicants will experience at least once or twice during their lifetime.

Therefore, applicants should be prepared to provide such information on an employment application regardless of how embarrassing or ridiculous it may appear. Without hesitation the applicant needs to consider answering the question "reason for leaving" with a brief notation such as "Company downsizing led to layoff," or "Personnel cutback," and/or, "Business reorganization or merger." Most employers these days are aware of changes in the employment cycle and tend to accept these responses.

5. Gaps and Periods of Unemployment – When an applicant indicates a gap in employment, a reasonable explanation needs to be given.

Today, because of the erratic ups and downs of the economy and the job market, it may take from nine months to a year or longer for some individuals to find a job, particularly veterans making the transition from the military to the civilian sector.

Thus, a job search can and should be used as a legitimate reason for being unemployed. Other legitimate reasons include pursuing an education, career assessment, research, retraining, exploration of self employment, extended vacation, travel, pregnancy/parenthood and/or domestic support, and recovery from a traumatic life event (illness or an accident).

Regardless of the reason for being unemployed, it should be stated clearly in the application (even if it takes a notation included on the application or an addendum attached to the application). The applicant also needs to be prepared to explain it during the interview, should the question be asked.

6. Dealing With the Appearance of Being a "Job Hopper" – When an applicant has an employment background reflecting a history of short-term jobs, it is known as "job hopping."

To avoid the label of Job Hopper, an applicant should be able to offer a legitimate reason for moving from one job to another, which should be noted in each time period reserved in the employment application for "Job Held" or "Employment."

An acceptable response might involve layoff, personal and family considerations (death in the family, loss of a loved one), health problems and accidents (time needed for recovery), relocation, career changes, bored or stuck in a position with no opportunity for advancement—most any legitimate reason that is compelling is acceptable.

7. Educational and Training Embellishments – During the past several decades considerable emphasis has been placed on academics and specialty training in an effort to keep pace with the demand for high-tech and business management career field growth. Some applicants, in an attempt to remain competitive, have gotten caught up in exaggerating or embellishing their academic and/or training accomplishments.

In other instances, applicants have taken liberties with one or two courses or short-term training programs they participated in but never completed, making untrue claims. Similarly, some applicants have worded educational experience in such a way as to create the impression they have a college degree or special certification or licensure, when in fact they do not.

If there is one area of the application/screening process that employers are now paying a great deal of attention to it's the awarding of college degrees and professional training certifications and licenses.

8. References –These days, with most application submissions, employers are inclined to follow up and check all references listed, especially where the job involves the handling of sensitive and/or confidential materials and information or where there is a high-priority security requirement.

In many of these situations, employers are more frequently asking the reference, "Do you know anyone else who might be acquainted with our applicant?" Thus, it would be wise for the applicant to ensure that the person given as a reference is discrete. Also, always ask someone's permission before using them as a reference.

There is nothing more detrimental to an otherwise solid application than for an applicant to list a reference who, as it turns out, doesn't remember the applicant. This is why it is recommended that references only be listed within a ten-year period of time, unless there has been periodic contact with the reference that exceeds this time frame.

When the applicant knows his former boss would not provide a favorable reference, even though the application asks for the name of a supervisor or superior, it would be wise to check off the "Do Not Contact" box. This precaution is especially relevant if you are still employed and are seeking new employment. In situations where there was some sort of conflict with an immediate supervisor, the applicant should consider using that person's superior, another manager who is familiar with the applicant's skills and work ethic, or a fellow peer—but not without their prior approval.

9. Answering the Salary/Wages Expected Question – For many applicants unfamiliar with this part of the application process, it can be a little tricky and daunting. If the applicant specifies a certain dollar amount and it is too high, they may price themselves out of consideration for the job. Generally, if there is uncertainty in the mind of the applicant, it is best to state "Open" or "Negotiable."

If an applicant feels compelled to declare a dollar amount, then select an amount from the middle of the salary or wage scale. The amount chosen should be based upon experience, education, and training. In some instances, job announcements will state what the salary range is. If not, a little research will help in determining what the general salary or wage scale is for a particular position. An excellent resource is the Occupational Outlook Handbook (OOH) published by the U.S.

Department of Labor and available at many American Job Centers. An equally helpful resource is O'Net Online (www.onetonline.org) .

10. Application Review – Although job applications have deadlines for submission, taking the time to review each section of the document for errors, omissions, spelling of names, and correctness of data can pay great dividends.

Inaccurate or incomplete data and failure to follow directions are the number one reasons for application rejection. Once the applicant has completed the application, has reviewed it, and is satisfied with its contents, it is recommended, if possible, that a copy of that application be made for future reference. If the application is completed on-site, it is not unreasonable to ask the secretary or clerical person to please make a copy for your records.

6

THE FEDERAL APPLICATION PROCESS

"Uncle Sam Wants You!"

After she started her new job at the Central City Medical Center, JJ sent Matt a thank you note for teaching her the right way to approach the application process. It was his insight that led to her successful employment. She reminded herself that success had more to do with attitude—the right mindset—than the mechanics involved with completing an application. She admitted to a friend, "What Matt taught me was invaluable and mainly responsible for my moving forward with my life."

Four intensive, passion-filled years working with patients went by quickly. JJ was feeling pretty good about herself and what she had accomplished. Her work had given her a fresh new outlook on life. From the medical center, she moved on to a second job at the Detroit Regional Corrections Center. There, JJ's manager really liked her and encouraged her to enroll at the local university to complete her BSN degree. This encouragement motivated JJ to go for it.

Upon graduation, JJ began looking for higher paying professional career opportunities in the federal employment field. Although JJ was on her way to establishing herself as a professional in the local government sector, she gave strong consideration to the federal arena. She was especially interested in the VA, where she could better apply her skills to serving veterans with whom she strongly identified. However, the biggest deterrent to becoming a federal employee, as she soon discovered, was the federal application process itself.

After several attempts at completing a federal application, she became completely bewildered and challenged by a process she simply could not understand. About to put the whole idea on hold, she thought of Matt. He had, after all, guided her through her civilian application hurdle.

When JJ met with Matt, she explained, "I discovered that the resumes used for civilian and local government jobs are very different from those used by applicants for federal jobs. I had this friend who applied for a nursing job with the VA, and when she let me look at her resume, I couldn't believe the difference."

JJ continued, "My friend told me that the resume was to be designed according to the department in the Federal Government I was applying to. She said that in a general sense, the application process and the resume submitted were almost the same. Actually, it seemed as though the resume was the application, or maybe it was just the reverse."

Matt agreed, saying, "Your friend's observations are fairly accurate. The Federal Government application process is definitely very different from that of the civilian and local government employment sector. As a matter of fact, the federal resume/application is more of a legal document. You need to prove on paper you are qualified, and you need to complete other associated documents, such as a questionnaire focused specifically on your qualifications. This differs from the civilian resume, which usually is simply a summary of qualifications as it relates to a job announcement.

"You need to understand the feds are making changes to their application process in an attempt to parallel the civilian sector. However, they seem slow to provide information allowing applicants to understand the distinction between the two, but they are moving forward."

Matt explained to JJ some of the changes that were made, based upon recent research he had done. They included the following:

Federal Hiring Reforms – In 2010 the President issued an Executive Order resulting in sweeping reforms to the federal hiring process, including five (5) major initiatives:

- The elimination of requirements that applicants respond to essay-style questions (frequently referred to as Knowledge, Skills, and Abilities, often referred to as KSAs) when submitting application materials.

- Allowing individuals to apply for federal employment through the submission of resumes and cover letters and the completion of plain-language application/occupational questionnaires.

- Selecting qualified applicants utilizing category ratings rather than using an outdated and mandatory "Rule of 3" approach traditionally used by managers to select only from the top three highest-scoring applicants.

  Note: Traditionally, applicants were scored with a numerical rating requiring hiring managers to select from only among the top three highest-scoring applicants and could not pass over a veteran to select a non-veteran (e.g. the "Rule of 3").

  The new process, however, provides for the categorizing of applicants, allowing hiring managers to select from top categories, as long as they do not select a non-veteran if there are qualified veterans in the same category.

  Its purpose is to increase the number of qualified applicants overall while preserving Veteran Preference rights. (Currently in use are the following categories: Veteran Preference, Highly Qualified, Qualified, and Not Qualified.)

- Notifying applicants of the status of their application at key points in the process, and

- Requiring the timely notification of applicants regarding their status throughout the selection process, facilitating a reduction in hiring time.

Matt went on, "Here's the bottom line, JJ. Federal agencies are continually changing their application process in order to select only the best qualified candidates."

"I'm still a little confused," JJ confessed. "Why does everything seem so drawn out with the process? Where do I start?"

"Look, JJ, let me tell you the number one principle that vets need to consider when applying for a federal position. Always, always read the job announcement in its entirety first to determine if you can make the fit. You would be surprised at the number of vets who don't and can't figure out why their application never results in a response from the feds."

Matt continued, "Here's the number two most important thing you need to consider: always follow the specific application requirements or instructions exactly and don't deviate in any way. And number three, always submit documents only if they are requested in the 'How to Apply' section of the job announcement.

"There's also a fourth item you need to be aware of and that is testing. Tests are given in only specific instances. It is not an all-inclusive thing."

According to Matt, tests are required only for certain occupations. More than 80% of federal/government jobs are filled through a competitive analysis of the applicant's background, work experience, and education. Mandatory testing is currently required and limited to the following occupations:

- Air Traffic Control Specialist (www.faa.gov/trainingtesting/schools)

- Border Patrol (www.cbp.gov)

- Central Intelligence Agency (www.cia.gov/careers)

- Federal Bureau of Investigation (www.fbi.gov)

- Foreign Service Written Exam (www.careers.state.gov)

- Internal Revenue Service (www.irs.gov)

- Mail Handlers USPS (www.usps.com/employment)

- Secret Service (www.secretservice.gov)

- Transportation Security Agency (www.tsa.gov/join/index.shtm)

- U.S. Customs (www.ice.gov/careers)

As their meeting was coming to a close, Matt provided JJ with a set of instructions designed as a basic navigational tool for the USAjobs.gov website. Matt indicated that these were the general rules for navigating USAjobs.gov when applying for a federal vacancy.

He also mentioned that because the federal application process was constantly evolving to meet federal employment demands, it would benefit her to continually anticipate and look for changes.

www.USAjobs.gov

NAVIGATIONAL TOOLS

The Federal Government works diligently to hire qualified applicants and is currently looking to fill a multitude of vacancies. Although the Federal Application Process will continue to change in the years ahead, the following information provides access to the federal hiring process as it exists today.

Note: USAJOBS is currently recognized as the official jobsite for Federal Government employment. Prospective applicants can search www.USAjobs.gov to locate thousands of available federal jobs.

It is recommended that prospective applicants utilize the job search tools provided here to focus their search on jobs that best match their interests and qualifications.

1. Initiating Your Job Search:
- Go to http://www.USAjobs.gov.
- Enter a key word or job category and location.
- Click the "Search Jobs" to see results.

- Use the "Refine Your Results" categories located on the left side of the search results page to refine your search further.
- Click on the position title to view full job announcement.

2. Create a USAJOBS Account:

- Ensure that you have an active email address. (Your email address needs to correspond to a single person and can only be used one time.)
- Go to http://www.USAjobs.gov.
- Select "Create an Account" located in the upper right-hand corner of the page.
- Complete the biographical data page.
- Create a username and password (create a unique username or use your email address).
- Select three (3) questions and answers to help reset your USAJOBS account if password forgotten or locked out.
- Select "I Agree, Create My Account" following the completion of all sections of the form.

3. Uploading a USAJOBS Resume:

- The USAJOBS website allows an applicant to create and upload resumes, inclusive of a maximum of five (5) different resumes when applying for different federal job opportunities.
- In responding to federal job announcements, it is important to ensure that each resume is searchable, enabling agencies to locate you.
- Go to www.USAJOBS.gov and select "Sign in" located in the upper right-hand corner of the page.
- Log in using your username (email address) and password.
- Select "I Agree, Sign Me In."
- Select "Build New Resume" or "Upload Resume," and follow instructions.

4. Applying For a Job:

- Search and review the "Search Results Pages," and decide which jobs you are interested in applying for.

- Read the entire job opportunity announcement (job posting) carefully to ensure your eligibility to apply.
- Be aware there is a difference between being eligible and being qualified. Just because the individual is able to establish eligibility to apply via status as a veteran, a U.S. Citizen, VEOA (Veterans Employment Opportunity Act), etc., does not mean they are qualified or able to meet KSA, experience, training, or educational requirements.
- Once you have determined that you are both eligible and qualified, follow the instructions under "How to Apply."
- Under "How to Apply" locate any additional forms required and a contact name and phone number for the hiring agency.
- Should any questions arise, use the contact phone number to find an answer to any question you may have about the vacancy.

5. Planning & Preparation:

To carefully prepare your application, you need to plan ahead to take your time, as each agency has their own requirements and application procedures.

- When a position is chosen that you are eligible and qualified to apply for, select "Apply Online" located to the right of the job opportunity announcement. Log into your USAJOBS account, if not already logged in, and select one of your stored resumes, along with any other required forms (e.g., college transcripts, DD-214, etc.) and submit for the vacancy.

6. Application Website Referral:

- Upon submission of your resume and accompanying documents, USAJOBS will reroute you to the Talent Acquisition System (application website) used by the hiring agency to facilitate completion of the remainder of the application process.

- If the Talent Acquisition Systems (application website) requires you to create an account on their site, then do so before attempting to continue further.
- Complete all biographical data pages.
- Complete the Assessment Questionnaire by following the prompts to submit answers, and view/print the answers.

Note: Assessments/Occupational Questionnaires are frequently used to collect information about experience, education, knowledge, and skills (KSAs) to determine your qualifications for the position. Be aware that check-marking a box that indicates you are uniquely qualified, and/or are an expert in your field, will most likely result in being rated as "Highly Qualified," and subject to telephone and/or in-person interviews to determine if in fact you are "Highly Qualified." At which point, a job offer may be forthcoming.

As they were wrapping up their meeting, JJ asked, "So okay, I get the idea about accessing www.USAjobs.gov, but since the resume is much different than what is used in the civilian and local government world, how do I construct a resume that meets federal requirements? What should a federal resume look like?"

"JJ," Matt explained, "you need to spend some time reviewing the USAJOBS website format and required informational material. I would also suggest you review a copy of *The Book of U.S. Government Jobs*, 11th Edition, by Dennis V. Damp. Pay particular attention to chapter 6 for a complete understanding of the federal resume process. This text provides current examples of the type of resume needed to meet the needs of federal employers."

Following her meeting with Matt, Jackie June-bug Jenkins was determined to make the federal application/resume process work for her. Armed with some basic information from her counselor, she began her research. JJ quickly discovered the following facts about Federal Applications, some of which were explained in the Navigating USAJobs.gov provided by Matt:

- All federal applications consist mainly of a detailed federal-styled resume, required documentation, the completion of occupational questionnaires, and knowledge, skills, and abilities (KSA) statements.

- Most federal applications are completed online, with a few fax and/or hand-delivered exceptions.

- Very often highly qualified applicants fail or ignore what is required to properly complete the detailed application that the Federal Government requires. The application isn't complete until all the paperwork is done … and done right.

- Applications/resumes need to be tailored to the vacancy/job description to which the applicant is applying in order to obtain a "Highly Qualified" ranking.

- Applicants need to be prepared to read the entire vacancy announcement and the position description as it is posted.

- In many instances applicants, especially those transitioning from the military to the private sector to the Federal Government, fail to read the entire announcement. Unfortunately their focus is directed at the salary and basic job description and, if they like what they see, they decide to apply.

- Applicants need to keep in mind that federal employers do not give favorable consideration to applicants who "think" they can do the job. To capture the government's attention, specific examples to demonstrate the applicant "can do the job" are required.

After several weeks of research, JJ returned to Matt's office. "I feel ready to seriously begin to apply for federal employment. So, what's next?"

Matt provided her with a sample of the recommended USAJOBS resume format, reminding her to follow the guidelines.

NAME
ADDRESS
PHONE / EMAIL

CAREER OBJECTIVE:

WORK EXPERIENCE:

Employer Name	MM/YYYY to MM/YYYY or present
Employer City/Town, Sate, Zip	$XX,000 per year
United States	Average hours per week: xx
Job Title	Supervisor: Name (Contact: yes/no)
Pay Plan-Series-Grade (if Federal civilian)	

Phone: (Only if contact is yes)

Duties: Brief description of company, duties, and responsibilities.

Accomplishments: List any significant accomplishments made.

EDUCATION:

School Name	Major:
School City/Town, State, Zip	Minor:
United States	GPA (Only list if 3.0 or higher)
Degree/Level Attained	XX Semester /Quarter Hours

[Credits]

Earned (Include if no degree completed)

Honors (If applicable)

Completion Date: MM/YYYY

RELEVANT COURSEWORK, LICENSURE, AND CERTIFICATIONS:

(List only coursework relevant to a school program of study that might correspond with potential job duties of the position you are applying for. For example, if applying for a GS-2210 Network Administrator, be sure to include related courses such as: Introduction to Networking, Networking Basics, etc. Only list licenses obtained from this program (e.g., a nursing license). If you attended an individual program to obtain a license (e.g., a CPA), list that under the heading Additional Information.

JOB-RELATED TRAINING:

List all programs (civilian and military) you took that are job related, including one-day seminars, workshops, and conferences even though they did not result in course credit or count toward a degree or certification.

OTHER RELATED INFORMATION:

REFERENCES: Should include at least one professional. Provide name, title, employer, phone number, and email of each reference. (Always contact a reference before including them in a federal resume/application).

AFFILIATIONS: Should be fairly current and in some capacity job related.

PUBLICATIONS: Include articles, books, and contributing research. Ideally, such work is job related.

ADDITIONAL INFORMATION:

Professional Summary   Professional Licenses
Career Highlights   Professional Training
Awards   Affiliations
Military experience

Once JJ had the general federal resume format, she located an announcement that she felt fit her qualifications. She began to assemble her personal background information similar to the model produced by her research, and she meticulously constructed the following document:

Jackie J. Jenkins
1422 Oak Drive
Detroit, MI 48201
(313) 187-7723 / jjj@yahoo.com

OBJECTIVE: Certified Registered Nurse: John D. Dingle VA Medical Center, Detroit, Michigan
Announcement Number: CRN/VA10-2850A

CAREER FOCUS: Qualified BSN, ASN with diversified nursing and volunteer experience seeks career opportunity serving veterans.

WORK EXPERIENCE:

Detroit Regional Corrections Center	01/2013 – Present
1521 Manchester Blvd. Detroit, MI	$35,000.00 Annual
USA	37.5 Hours/week
Job Title: Internship /Registered Nurse	Supervisor: (May Fields, NP)

Duties: Served as RN at hospital located within maximum-security correctional facility housing approximately 4,700 inmates. Assigned to the mental health crisis unit and played a key role on the interdisciplinary team of psychiatrists, RNs, social workers, and corrections officers. Actively participated in the development and implementation of individual treatment plans for patients exhibiting a broad range of health issues. Ensured that doctor's orders were effectively carried out, including testing, medical procedures, consultations, and restraint orders.

Key Accomplishments:

- Assisted in developing and defining unit policies and procedures regarding suicide watch, safety measures, discharge planning, and documentation.
- First responder to numerous volatile situations and violent outbreaks, earning the respect of physicians and coworkers for restoring order through demonstrating calmness in stressful situations with staff and patients.

- Completed training in team-building management and assaultive behaviors and the administration of psychotropic medications.
- Successfully completed internship/practicum and based upon performance offered full-time employment.

Central City Medical Center	12/2011 – 01/2013
# 42 Chester Nimitz Parkway Detroit MI	$28,000.00 Annual
USA	40 Hours/week
Job Title: Cert. Med. Assist.	Supervisor:
	Jacob Page, PRN

Duties: Performed front office duties and patient clinical examinations under the supervision of medical center RN. Assignments included cardiac, oncology, and medical surgical departments. Tasks included medication administration, dressing changes, IVs, and other associated nursing disciplines. Clerical duties involved admissions, discharges and transfers, preparation of chart notes, confidentiality of medical records, appointment, scheduling, and billing and coding.

Key Accomplishments:
- Volunteered for assignments as a medical team member to engage in cross-training in front office and patient clinical functions.
- Treated an average of 12 patients daily (at a 100 percent above average student case load), gaining experience in procedures such as cryotherapy and trigger-point injections.
- Established a reputation for service delivery excellence. Supervisory performance evaluations reflect comments such as, "JJ has excellent interpersonal skills and readily creates a cooperative rapport with patients—her clinical skills are impressive and would be a welcome addition to any nursing team."

U.S. Marine Corps (Dept. of the Navy)	10/2006 – 10/2010
MCRD Parris Island, SC	$26,000.00 Annual
USA	60 Hours/Week
Job title: Drill Instructor/Navy Student Nurse	Supervisor:
	M GY/Sgt.

Duties: Provided basic instruction and military indoctrination to civilian recruits new to the military service, regarding the customs and practices of military life, and instruction in the proper execution of military drill, instilling discipline and willingness to immediately obey all lawful orders given by superiors, and instruction in basic armed and unarmed combat training.

Key Accomplishments:

• Successfully changed military career goal from Marine/Navy Nursing program to Training Instructor (Drill Instructor of female recruits) attaining the rank of Corporal, after earning a 99 percent score on the Armed Forces Vocational Battery Test at the time of admittance to instructor training and graduating with top honors.

• Completed first year of nursing school with GPA of 3.7.

EDUCATION & TRAINING:

01/2013 - **Western Michigan University-Bronson School of Nursing, Kansas City, MI**

• Bachelor of Science in Nursing (BSN), GPA 3.6 (Dean's List)

• Course highlights: family and community nursing, healthcare delivery models, professional Nursing Synthesis Theory, Nursing Health Assessment, Clinical and Chemical Therapeutics, Biophysical Pathology, Human Anatomy and Physiology, Statistics, Nursing Research, Psychiatric Nursing Practices.

06/2004 – **Gardner-Webb University-Hunt School of Nursing, Boiling Springs, NC**

• 1st year military nursing student with ASN Degree pursuing BSN Degree.

• Course highlights: Community and Public Health, Health Assessments Protocols, Informatics, Medical Leadership and Management, Nursing Research and Evidence-Based Practices, Pathophysiology, Professional Roles and Values, Trans-cultural Nursing.

09/1999 – **Central City Voc.-Tech. Institute Nursing Program, Detroit, MI**
- Associates of Science Nursing Degree (ASN), GPA 4.0 (Deans List)
- Course Highlights: Human Anatomy & Physiology, Medical Terminology, Chemistry for Nursing Professionals, Pharmacology, Treatment of Psychological Disorders, Patient Histories, Clinical Evaluations, Charting, Medical Records, HIPPA & Confidentiality of Information, Contemporary Medical Ethics, Public Health Issues & Treatment.

SPECIAL SKILL SETS:
Case Management; Critical Care Nursing; JCAHO Standards & Compliance; Medication Administration; Patient & Family Education; Patient Advocacy; Patient Assessments; Psychiatric Nursing; Quality & Continuity of Care; Medical Records/Confidentiality Protocols.

AFFILIATIONS& CERTIFICATIONS:
- Michigan RN Certification (#6787).
- Michigan ASN Certification (#4297).
- Michigan State Nurses Association Member (06/99 – Present).
- Psychiatric Unit, Central City Medical Center Volunteer (06/13 – Present).

Upon completion of her federal resume, JJ submitted her application. A few weeks later, she received a Highly Qualified notification followed by a brief phone interview. Finally, an in-person interview landed JJ a new federal career position as a BSN at a nearby veteran's hospital.

VOYAGER BASICS

Although there is still considerable debate regarding the pros and cons of the federal application process for veterans seeking employment with the Federal Government, the fact remains that the Federal Government does offer some of the best jobs, salary, and benefits in the U.S. And, it has a number of veteran-oriented hiring programs based upon utilizing job search recommendations that tend to increase the odds of qualifying for federal employment, as follows:

- To determine which federal jobs match as closely as possible the individual veteran's background, experience, training, and education, a search of the Office of Personnel Management Classification Standards (OPM) is recommended.

- Veterans should consider networking via LinkedIn and other similar accounts (e.g., VA4vets, etc.). These sites offer veterans an opportunity to provide a summary of their experience, certifications, skills and abilities, and associated specific qualifiers. Too, these sites allow veterans to conduct informational inquiries of persons already employed in a career or occupational field of interest.

- Consider including in your resume information from performance evaluations (military fitness reports) that reflect an outstanding work ethic to a potential superior, promoting you as a "Best Qualified" candidate.

- Familiarization of federal employment opportunities by veterans frequently searching www.usajobs.gov, and applying for jobs listed on USAJOBS.

- Subscribing to weekly federal government jobs updates for the state within which a veteran resides by going to www.federalgovernmentjobs.us.

- Analyze each job description for key words before constructing and/or submitting a federal job resume, and include those words in each resume.

- Be aware that when you are applying for a federal job, the resume becomes, with few exceptions, your federal application—usually involving from three (3) to five (5) pages in length.

- Samples of federal resumes can be obtained through Google.

- The primary goal when submitting a federal application (resume) is to obtain a "Highly Qualified" rating. Veterans can check the status of their application through www.applicationmanager.gov. Be sure to have or create a USAJOBS username and password before attempting to determine the status of a federal application.

Note: While federal employment offers opportunities specific to veterans, some consideration must also be given to the fact that not every veteran's career goals fits into a government-oriented environment. It may require the veteran to explore broader opportunities in the civilian/ private sector of employment. Venturing into the nongovernmental sector of employment will require job-search methods very much different from the government arena.

7

THE REALITY OF RESUMES AND COVER LETTERS

The Voyage of Rockland "Rocky" Cahill

As he sat in the VFW hall waiting for the guest speaker to be introduced, Rocky reminded himself it had been a while since he had attended one of these meetings. Being surrounded by fellow vets gave him a sense of camaraderie he hadn't experienced in a long time. But it wasn't the real reason for his attendance this night.

The post commander began his introduction. "Our guest speaker tonight is the local Veteran Representative at the American Job Center. He is going to provide information on conducting a job search. For those of you who are looking for a job or want to improve future job prospects, or have vet buddies who you think need some job search help, pay attention to what this guy has to say. Please put your hands together and welcome our guest speaker Rudy Lamar."

The first few words out of the speaker's mouth unexpectedly grabbed Rocky's attention, as it did the majority of veterans in attendance. "When we are discussing job search for veterans, we need to understand the term 'there are no free lunches' as it applies to today's job market. Most of us are familiar with that term, after having served in previous campaigns like Vietnam, the Gulf War (Kuwait & Iraq), Bosnia, Kosovo, Afghanistan, and the current war on terrorism. We know there is no such thing as getting something for nothing. Armed conflict is serious business and some, as we know, have paid the ultimate price. For those of us who are still around, it's a matter of fine tuning and successfully employing those skills for survival. Some would add to that, luck.

"So," Rudy continued, "when it comes to job search we need to get serious because it too is a matter of survival. But as you will soon realize, luck has nothing to do with it. As a matter of fact, in today's business world where we seek employment opportunities, you will come to experience the reality of 'no free lunches'—there is always a price to pay. There's another old saying: It takes money or capital investment to make money. Your capital, when it comes to looking for a job, involves the investment of time, development of abilities, application of experience, and creatively experimenting with what works and determining things that don't work in finding your place in today's job market.

"The world of employment, in many respects, is similar to the field of combat. A successful mission is dependent upon how well one develops and uses their planning skills. Just as in a combat zone battle plans are designed and followed, so too is the development and implementation of a business plan necessary when seeking employment. It's called job search. It's a lot like going into business for yourself."

Rudy continued for the next thirty minutes or so explaining and comparing the various aspects of a business model to the job search process. At the conclusion of his presentation, he stated, "As a Veteran Representative working with fellow vets on a daily basis, I've discovered that what I do is less about providing a handout—you know, just giving out free advice—and more about providing a hand up and a hands-on approach to personal achievement. I do that by showing vets how to design, develop, and use their own job search skills.

"For me, working with veterans is all about developing life tools and preserving one's dignity as a means of encouraging, establishing, and maintaining a respectable level of self-sufficiency and sustainability."

After the presentation Rocky introduced himself to Rudy. "Hey, Rudy, I'm really in need of some help here. Here's my problem. I've been unable to find steady employment. I'm fairly skilled at the things I can do in the construction, maintenance, and carpentry trades. I'm wondering if you'd be willing to work with someone like me?"

They made an appointment for the following week.

During their initial meeting, Rocky explained, "For the past several years I've been more or less self-employed as a carpenter and building-maintenance specialist. One of the reasons I went into business for myself was because I spent a few years in the state pen. I was a felon, and no one would hire me."

"So, what were you in the joint for?" Rudy asked.

"Well, when I got back from Nam, I went through what a lot of guys who survived that war went through. I did a little drinking, smoked some pot, and took prescription drugs. I was using Oxycodone. I took some shrapnel in the back and right knee and the VA prescribed it to deal with chronic pain. So, I had a ready supply of painkillers.

"Anyhow, I was out buzz-driving one night and blew a stop sign. The guy in the other car I hit died a few days later, and I was convicted of vehicular manslaughter. I did my time. Yeah, in many respects, I'm still doing time, and I guess I'll always be doing time!"

"I'm not sure what you mean, Rocky," Rudy replied.

"Well, it was like this. I tried looking for a job when I got out of the pen, but no one wanted to take a chance on me. I'm an ex-con. That's the long and the short of it.

"I did all right on my own, built this tool trailer on wheels, and towed it behind my pickup truck."

Rocky borrowed a pen and a sheet of blank paper from Rudy and began to draw. He said, "A friend of mine painted a large bright green shamrock on each side of the trailer, and under it, in Kelly green block letters, the words 'CUSTOM CARPENTRY & BUILDING MAINTENANCE by CAHILL.'"

"Okay, Rocky," Rudy replied. "I get the self-employment thing. Seems you are doing all right for yourself, so my question is, why do you want a job? Why do you want to work for someone else?"

"I'm not doing that well anymore. Over the years I've been edged out of business by large companies who can afford to low-bid on carpentry and building maintenance projects I apply for. I'm getting older and need steady employment just to survive. I have a 70% disability rating based upon injuries sustained while in Nam. My knee is getting worse and I'm in constant pain. The VA hospital said eventually I might need knee replacement, and my back is still giving me a problem too. Besides, I'm almost sixty years old. Right now I'd be happy finding a job doing medium to light maintenance repair work. I'm also qualified to do basic electrical and HVAC work."

Rudy interrupted Rocky, "Well, if you are looking for a job, you're going to need a resume and a cover letter in order to compete with everyone else who is seeking employment in your field. It's really competitive out there, Rocky, but I believe you can do it."

Rocky handed Rudy a copy of an old resume he had put together several years ago. "It's sort of a letter resume document I used in the past to bid on carpentry and maintenance projects and contracts with potential clients," he explained.

Rudy studied the resume for a few minutes, then placed it in a manila folder along with a copy of Rocky's DD-214. "Well, Rocky, that kind of resume was probably okay back in the day, but what you need is something that establishes and markets you as a skilled professional."

Rudy paused for a few seconds, then asked, "Tell me, Rocky, what's the purpose of a resume?"

Rocky didn't give his answer a second thought. "To get a job, that's pretty clear."

"You're right, Rocky. In the overall scheme of things that's the ultimate goal. By the way, just about every time I ask that question of the vets I work with, that's the stock answer I get. But there is a basic, underlying reason for writing and submitting a resume to an employer. Do you know what that is?"

"Yeah, man, it's to sort of outline for the employer what you are capable of doing for him. It lets the employer know you got what it takes to get the job done, and the skills and experience he is looking for, right?" Rocky replied, sounding a little irritated.

Sensing some agitation in Rocky's voice, Rudy leaned forward in his chair. In a hushed tone, he said, "Hey, pal, you are almost there. You're getting closer to the answer, but you need to understand where you are going with a resume for it to be effective with an employer."

He slowly leaned back in his chair and went on, "So, Rocky, after you submit a resume to an employer, what has to happen for you to get a job offer? What is the process called where you sit down face-to-face with an employer and you discuss who you are and what you can do?"

Rocky's eyebrows flew up as understanding suddenly illuminated his face. "Yeah, I got it! It's the interview, right?"

Rudy nodded. "Let's face it, Rocky, nothing is going to happen until you get an interview. As long as I've been working with vets, I have never heard of any one of them being offered a job based solely on their resume. Just like when you are developing a business contract with one of your clients, there is always a face-to-face event. So, the real purpose of a resume is what?"

In sync now, they both laughingly and simultaneously cried, "It's to get an interview!"

"Look, Rocky," Rudy explained, "Too many vets get all pumped up and in a hurry to apply for a job they believe will start their career or offer better pay. They always seem to be a big hurry when it comes to getting their resume out."

"Well, yeah, I would be too if I saw a job that I wanted," Rocky replied.

"But, Rocky, too many times I've seen where they have merely copied someone else's resume. Not much thought is given to its effectiveness in getting the employer's attention, or whether it's relevant to the position being applied for. In some instances, I've worked with vets who have unnecessarily spent good money having someone else write their resume for them. These resume writers don't even know who the person is they are writing about and don't have a vested interest in the outcome, except for the fees they charge.

"When I assist someone it's to help them build a basic job-search foundation. Once that is established they begin to move toward becoming self-sufficient and achieving sustainability. I want my vets to no longer be dependent upon another person's idea of a resume. Once that foundation is set you, can experiment with different versions of the basic format to meet the qualification requirements of each and every employment opportunity that comes your way."

Rudy added, "We need to get you pointed in the right direction. I have nothing but respect for carpenters and those in building and construction trades. They are pretty smart and independent people. So, I know you know all about things like planning your work and then working your plan. What's that old carpenter's saying? 'You measure twice and cut once.' It's all basic thinking and ideas. Here's another way to look at it. When you build a house, what generally, in the simplest of terms possible, do you do to get the project, the basic structure, moving along?"

Rocky, now seemingly more engaged with Rudy but still a little resistant, said, "In the simplest of terms you start with building a foundation and a sill to anchor the walls to, then up go the walls, followed by the roof, then you do the finish work inside. That's basically it."

"So," Rudy interjected, "think about it this way. A job search is just like building a house. What do you build first when constructing a house, the roof or the foundation, and why?"

"It's the foundation because it establishes a solid supporting mechanism upon which the rest of the building is based. The roof comes last. If you don't have a strong base or foundation, everything else attached to it will eventually fall apart."

"Rocky, you got it, enough said," Rudy replied. "Now, let's move on to the job search process. Since you've been in business for yourself most of your life, I don't think you will have any problem accepting the use of a business model approach to your job search. Your cover letter becomes your marketing tool where you target the employer as if he were a potential client. Your resume becomes your brand. It's used like an advertisement to create interest with the employer, similar to attracting the attention of a prospective customer—like the message on the side of your tool trailer. And the interview is the opportunity to sell a product or service. In this case the product is you along with your skills, abilities, and experience."

Rudy handed Rocky a guide of basic resume concepts and commentary about resumes and their relationship to the job search process. "Rocky, I would like you to go over this information before our meeting next week."

Rocky took the list, promising himself he would review it when he got home, which he did.

BASIC CONSIDERATIONS TO EFFECTIVE RESUME-BUILDING

- A resume is designed to attract the attention of an employer by creating enough interest to want to meet an applicant face-to-face.

- A resume is a document that reflects an applicant's accomplishments, specific qualifications, and overall potential—much the same as any other promotional advertisement about a product or service.

- A resume must represent the applicant's organizational and communications skills. The applicant shows his ability to pay attention to detail because the resume itself is neat and clean, and all spelling, grammar, and punctuation are correct.

- A resume needs to be concise and compelling at the same time, avoiding run-on wordy sentences. Employers on the whole are very busy and sometimes reluctant to spend too much time reading or trying to interpret a resume. The text and layout must capture an employer's attention within the first five to seven seconds after it is picked up and read.

- A resume is most effective and appealing to an employer if it efficiently utilizes action verbs such as "managed," "developed," and "orchestrated," and getting away from using terms like "was responsible for." The applicant should avoid declarative phrases such as, "I developed," "I facilitated," or "I performed." The "I" word has little value to an employer and should be excluded.

- A resume is easy on the eye, using normal margins of approximately 1.0 inch on the top and bottom and 1.25 inches on the right and left sides, with evenly applied "white space" between headings and paragraphs.

- It is recommended that a resume's layout include subtopic headings centered above each major division (topic area) of the document to avoid the distraction of forcing the reader to read from side to side to introduce new material. The practice of "centering" promotes the quick targeting of qualifying information the employer needs to see.

- An effective resume presents an appearance that is clean, clear, and sharp. This is best accomplished with white stock paper and black ink/print, using standard text fonts. The use of colored paper and ink makes photocopies appear dark and sometimes blurred and difficult to read.

- A resume needs to be an honest representation of accomplishments and qualifications, avoiding exaggerations, embellishments, and false statements. More often than not, inappropriate claims are usually detected during a background check, and when they are, it generally results in the applicant's disqualification.

Sometimes an applicant manages to get hired as a result of inaccurate statements made on a resume or during an interview. But weeks, months, and even years later these inaccuracies may be discovered, resulting in immediate termination of employment for cause.

- Every resume submitted should contain an objective or brand statement (focus of employment) in a clear, concise, and sincere manner. Statements similar to "Seeking a position that offers a rewarding and satisfying career" should be avoided. Such statements are more about applicant self-interest and little about meeting the employer's needs.

- An attention-getting resume presents a clear and concise description of the applicant's skills and abilities, and lets the employer know immediately the applicant's qualifications for a particular position. If a resume fails to do this, it is a waste of time—for both the employer and the applicant.

- A focused resume reflects the applicant's experience relative to and supportive of previously listed skills and abilities. Experience also reflects job-oriented accomplishments and a positive attitude toward work performance.

- A strong resume presents an applicant's education and training directly related to skills and abilities and stated experience, and/or the potential for meeting current and possible future needs of the employer.

- A resume ends when all critical information related to the position being applied for has been provided. The use of superfluous (unnecessary) information or details such as "height," "weight," "gender," "health," "marital status," and "hobbies" is a waste of time and space. Many applicants new to the job search process, and those reentering the employment arena after an extended absence, are of the mistaken belief that it will look better to fill in any leftover white space at the bottom of the page.

Note: This approach to using leftover space is similar to the compulsive behavior of individuals involved in a conversation who run out of things to say and feel uncomfortable with an extended silence, and so attempt to fill the void with idle chatter and prattle. Most astute employers and HR managers are quick to notice this and will tend to view the applicant as a novice and possibly unsuited for the job.

- Generally, a resume should use as many pages as is necessary to properly inform the employer of an applicant's qualifications, depending upon the nature of the position and qualifications the employer is looking for. However, it is important to remember that, in the overall scheme of things, all resumes are merely summaries, not long biographical presentations. Most contemporary resumes are between one and a half to two pages in length, unless otherwise specified by the employer.

Note: With many of today's applicants, especially veterans who have been away from the private sector or mainstream job search arena for extended periods of time, there will be differing beliefs about how many pages a resume should contain:

- There are those who subscribe to a one-page document containing only a bare minimum of information relative to the character of the job being applied for, usually presented in a manner likely to highlight only key skills and experience and accomplishments.

- All too often the use of a one-page resume tends to sacrifice essential and critical information an employer may need in order to make an informed interview decision. In many instances, applicants reduce the font size (the standard is #11 to #12) in an attempt to fit everything on one page. Such a tactic makes a resume difficult to read and sacrifices needed white space to attract and hold the employer's attention.

- In many instances, the importance of white space and its aesthetic appeal is ignored, especially when attempting to produce a one-page document. Used properly, white space becomes your friend.

It allows the reader to quickly scan key points while deciding whether he wants to read the resume more closely. White space is pleasing to the eye and avoids a cluttered look. Remember, most employers determine in approximately five to seven seconds whether a resume is worth reading thoroughly, so make yours attractive.

Question: What is the proper length (number of pages) for a resume in today's job market? The answer is this: preferably one page, if it can adequately summarize the last seven to ten years and demonstrate the applicant's critical skills and abilities relevant to the job announcement. The resume should never be more than one and a half to two pages.

Other factors that vet applicants may want to consider are:

• Military personnel with college degrees and officer ranks should lean toward a one-page resume, summarizing their leadership experience, professional skills, and potential to a civilian employer.

• Military personnel without degrees, and those in the enlisted ranks without high in-demand technical skills, may need to consider obtaining employment in non-professional fields while they acquire additional technical skills or academic credentials. Non-professional and non-high-tech applicants may want to consider more than one page in order to highlight contributions and accomplishments that depict work ethic and the ability to learn quickly.

• In today's competitive job market it is not uncommon to find some employers accepting only five (5) to seven (7) years employment history for highly qualified applicants in critical high-demand career fields where extreme shortages exist.

Yet, in many private companies and government agencies, extended and formal applications require applicants to provide a minimum of ten (10) and sometimes more years of employment history. This is based upon the belief that anything less will make it difficult to substantiate employability and stability of the applicant. While the importance of a resume cannot be denied as a general indicator of the applicant's potential to the employer's business needs, its impact regarding the hiring decision is less than it has been in the past. Greater emphasis is now placed upon the sophistication of today's interview process. Again, the applicant needs to keep in mind what the true purpose of a resume is—"to get an interview."

- Resumes during the latter half of the 19th century and all of the 20th century catered to America's industrialization, including the move from an agrarian to a mechanized economy. The design of those resumes and the way they were used are no longer applicable in the current high-tech and service-oriented 21st century. Major trends in employment tend to keep pace with the rapid and constantly changing technologies, communications, and services that directly impact today's job market.

- A resume may or may not include a short statement about references. It is often enough simply to include the line: "References Furnished, Upon Interview," rather than listing the names of references. (Note: It is better to say "Upon Interview" rather than "Upon Request" as a cue to the employer that your desire is for your resume to lead ultimately to an interview.) If there is any doubt in the mind of an applicant about the usefulness of mentioning references, then an applicant is better off not mentioning the subject at all.

- A referral to "References" in a resume, when utilized, should be presented on a single sheet of paper, as an addendum, with the applicant's header information centered at the top of the page, the same as indicated in the resume. Below the header put the word REFERENCES in all caps, bold-face type, and underscored. Then give the name of each reference. For example:

<u>**REFERENCES**</u>

JACK SMITH
Electrician
1250 Maple Street
Memphis, TN 38118
901-515-2288 / jack.smithe@yahoo.com

The next time they met, Rocky indicated he read the material Rudy had given him and expressed a better understanding of the relationship of the resume to the job search process.

During the discussion that followed, Rudy presented Rocky with a basic model for constructing an effective, simple and foundational resume:

NAME
(In BOLD, in CAPS)
Street Address / P.O. Box
City, State, Zip
Phone Number and/or Cell Phone / Email address

_____

_____

The above "Center Lines" are designed to subtly and subconsciously direct the reader's eyes down the middle of the page to each of the subheadings presented.

Note: the double line is achieved by doing the following:

- Begin by centering the curser in the middle of the page.
- Hit the Enter key, dropping down one space.
- Activate the **Bold** and <u>Underline</u> definitions. (Remember to deactivate to facilitate normal text.)
- Hold down the Shift key while activating the Hyphen key just below the F9 Key on the keyboard.
- Let the first line travel its full length across the page.

- If the first line goes to a second line merely back space until the blinking curser is back to the end of the first line.
- Hit Enter, dropping down one space.
- Repeat the process of holding down the Shift key while activating the Hyphen key if a second is desired.
- Hit enter dropping down one space again, centering the curser in the middle of the page, and begin with the first subtitle "**OBJECTIVE**" (in caps).

OBJECTIVE

(Other titles to consider: **CAREER FOCUS** or **EMPLOYMENT FOCUS**)

The **OBJECTIVE** statement should be designed to project a creative and upbeat message (like an advertising "hook") or word image (like a "brand" statement) about the applicant's skills and achievements and how they will directly benefit the employer. This statement should be no more than two short sentences, and preferably one sentence limited to a maximum of twenty-one (21) words. It's an old copywriter's tool to eliminate unnecessary words.

Example: "Experienced, innovative business development and community service professional seeks opportunity to take your sales and clients to the next level."

SKILLS and ABILITIES

(Other titles to consider: SUMMARY of TALENT and SKILLS or just plain SUMMARY.)

"SKILLS and ABILITIES" is a section of your resume designed to match up your skills and abilities with the employer's requirements. What you include here is critical to capturing and maintaining the employer's attention and interest. It provides an immediate answer to the typical question on the mind of most employers, "Why should I interview or consider hiring you?"

This section prevents the employer from having to second-guess what it is the applicant has to offer—it is said up front. Highlighted categories associated with the OBJECTIVE (see statement above) are supported by short advertisement-like descriptors of acquired skills and abilities.

Example: "Business Acumen: marketing; sales projections/promotions; workshop trainer; surveys; client development; customer relations; project/records management. **Community Service**: grant writing; nonprofit operations; volunteer venues; gifting program implementation. **Technical** or **Computer Competency**: IT Certified (data base program management; CRM; Oracle; QuickBooks; MS Office; Word; Excel; Access; Power Point)."

Again, this section provides the employer with a "no guesswork" look at what the applicant can do, and the applicant's potential for accomplishing performance-related new tasks in the future. Skills and abilities are generally connected to and supported by actual work-related experience, education, training, and on-the-job accomplishments and other life-related experiences.

EXPERIENCE

In this area of the resume the applicant needs to support the acquisition, development, and use of stated **SKILLS and ABILITIES.** Reflected are the experiences and the current ability to perform in a work-intensive environment, including on-the-job accomplishments, using descriptive phrases and/or words that are action oriented. *Note: Most employers are not interested in "I was responsible for" comments. An employer needs to know what was achieved, what goals were set, and how they were reached.*

Such positive-outcome descriptions of work performed may coincide later with possible behavioral-focused questions that have now become commonplace in today's interview process.

Example: "Tell us about a time when you were given a project to complete within a limited time frame. How did you handle it and what was the outcome?"

Generally, employers recommend that all work experience, internships, volunteer projects, and employment history be presented chronologically, and dated from the most recent/current to the earliest job, usually within the last ten years. Dates need only reflect Month/Year to Month/Year.

If the applicant is currently employed, list Month/Year to "Current Employment." In some instances an applicant will have worked for only one employer for more than ten years—this is especially true for individuals who have retired from the military. In such cases it is recommended that the applicant list different assignments and their attendant duties as separate jobs, using the appropriate location and date format.

Yet, in some instances the veteran may have had many different jobs of varying length which, when listed, could be confusing to an employer, and would exceed the recommended one-and-a-half to two-page limit. In such instances it is better to consolidate assignments (job titles) under one subheading, within a specific date range.

In order to relate job experience to employer qualifications, military veterans should use words or descriptions common or familiar to the job or occupation being applied for. Avoid using military jargon at all costs. Many veteran job-search websites have word translation functions useful to maintaining civilian descriptors of similar work performed in the military. (See military.com, e.g. MOS Translator, or go to Google and enter MOS translator).

Key job functions and results achieved should be bullet-point accentuated. Attempt to stay within the 21-word guideline used in the "Objective"/"Brand" statement.

Example: The following format is recommended.

Name of Job, Title of Specialty   **Dates: Mo. /Yr. to Mo./Yr.**
Name of Business or Organization
City, State
• Job performed and results/outcome achieved.

Example:

- Designed and delivered sales training, resulting in the increase of monthly sales by 30% within six months of program implementation.

NOTE: Individuals constructing a resume need to be aware that more often than not most applicants using resume bullet points make the mistake of using the same words and phrases—most generally "I was responsible for" or, "My duties involved ..." Quite honestly, hiring managers grow weary of them because such phrases tend to lose their meaning and fail to show creativity, results and/or accomplishments. What is required are more action-oriented verbs that energize past and current outcomes and forecast future accomplishments with the new employer. Note the following examples:

You Provided Project Leadership.

If you managed an assigned project or initiative from start to its completion consider:

Coordinated. Executed. Orchestrated. Organized. Headed. Controlled. Operated. Programmed. Oversaw. Produced.

You Brainstormed and Activated A Project.

If you actually created or introduced a project concept into your organization, consider:

Charted. Envisioned. Administered. Devised. Designed. Established. Formalized. Spearheaded. Engineered. Constructed. Incorporated. Pioneered.

You Saved the Organization Money or Time.

Hiring decision-makers give top marks to applicants who demonstrate operational efficiency or cost effectiveness, thereby indicating the potential for bottom line increases. In this case, consider the following:

Reconciled. Reduced. Decreased. Yielded. Conserved. Multiplied. Gained. Diagnosed. Realigned. Consolidated. Restructured. Conserved.

You Improved a System or Changed a Process.

Your creative concepts led to discarding a worn-out logistics process via the introduction of a viable IT system. Allude to the changes resulting from your ideas. Consider injecting energy into accomplishments with the following words:

Converted. Influenced. Clarified. Integrated. Remodeled. Restructured. Simplified. Streamlined. Transformed. Overhauled. Merged. Modified.

You Led a Team.

Showcase your management skills by avoiding the use of "Led a team…" or "Managed employees…" descriptors. Instead, use inspirational terms such as:

Cultivated. Enabled. Facilitated. Fostered. Inspired. Shaped. Unified. Supervised. Encouraged. Trained. Guided. Mentored.

You Maintained Reliable Customer/Client Support.

What did you do to establish productive relationships with customers, clients, and/or vendors?

Advised. Arbitrated. Advocated. Coached. Consulted. Fielded. Informed. Resolved. Partnered. Forged. Acquired. Established.

You Conducted Research Leading to a New Company Program.

Did you initiate inquiry into how to improve business, company programs, or services?

Evaluated. Measured. Explored. Identified. Assessed. Forecasted. Investigated. Qualified. Analyzed. Audited. Tested. Examined.

You Were Involved in Writing or Company Communications.

You conducted company writing, training, and speaking engagements. Explain just how effective and results oriented you were with the following descriptors:

Briefed. Defined. Promoted. Publicized. Co-authored. Counseled. Documented. Illustrated. Composed. Edited. Convinced.

You Handled Compliance Regulations.

If you managed operational protocols or supervised enforcement of your company's business principles, use descriptors such as:
Delegated. Ensured. Authorized. Monitored. Verified. Maintained. Screened. Reviewed. Inspected. Verified. Investigated. Inquired.

You Accomplished Something Unique.
Reached. Achieved. Exceeded. Succeeded. Attained. Outperformed. Surpassed. Earned. Obtained. Completed. Demonstrated. Maintained.

EDUCATION and TRAINING

When presenting formal education information, list the major field of study or program first, the degree upon graduation followed by the dates of attendance, all on one line. Degrees are presented with the highest awarded first, followed in descending order by lower degrees, certifications, diplomas, and related awards.

It is not necessary to include a high school diploma or GED if there has been attendance at college—high school diplomas or GEDs are a given since it is not possible to be admitted to a college or university without one or the other. A high school diploma or GED should be listed when no college has been attended. The following example or format is recommended:

Business Administration (MBA)　　　　**09/2015 – 06/2017**
Name of College or University
City, State

Computer Science (BS)　　　　**09/2009 – 06/2013**
Name of College or University
City, State

Business Accounting (AS)　　　　**09/2007 – 06/2008**
Name of College
City, State

Basic / Intermediate Bookkeeping　　　　**01/2004 – 05/2006**
(Certified)

Military Branch and/or Installation
City, State or City, Country

High School Graduate   **09/2000 – 06/2003**
Name of High School
City, State

Using "References Furnished Upon Interview"

As previously mentioned, the primary purpose of a resume is to create enough interest in the applicant that the employer will want to meet with them to assess their qualifications and to determine their potential for making future contributions to the business or organization. This is called an interview.

Using the **References Furnished Upon Interview** message at the end of the resume is intended to subtly plant the "interview seed" in the mind of the employer, and serves to reinforce the applicant's desire for an interview. The request for an interview statement is optional. If an applicant feels uncomfortable with the statement, then do not use it. On the other hand, when it is used, be prepared to furnish the references mentioned. Generally, three references are standard, but be prepared to offer more should the employer request them.

References should never be included in a resume unless requested by an employer. References when furnished should be confirmed before they are used, and are submitted on a separate page using the following format:

Example:

Name of Applicant
Mailing Address
City, State, Zip Code
Phone / Email Address

REFERENCES
Name and Title of Reference
City, State
Phone number / Email Address

References should be taken to the interview whether or not the employer has requested them. They are presented to the employer or interviewer at the conclusion of the interview. WHY?

They are presented because you advertised that they would be "furnished upon interview" in your resume. Remember, a promise or guarantee made concerning your product or service is all part of being in business for yourself and tends to lend credibility to what you have accomplished and who you are.

Note: Any remaining space at the conclusion of a resume should not be interpreted as the time to supply additional personal information such as height, weight, marital status, and hobbies unless specifically requested by the employer. Generally, such information is no longer considered appropriate. It is better to leave any remaining space blank.

RESUME FORMAT PRACTICE

Note: The practice of writing the content of the various subtitles requires following the Model for Construction of An Effective Resume. Hand copy each format using additional sheets of paper to expand your practice and options. Remember, resume perfection can only be achieved by following the three basic rules of resume construction—practice, practice, practice! The same goes for cover letters too.

PERSONAL DATA / HEADING INFORMATION

NAME

(In caps & bold – use 14 or 16 point font – Times New Roman or Calibri)

Address

City, State, Zip

Phone / Email

OBJECTIVE

(Practice writing attention-grabbing declarative statements of not more than 21 words. Be creative about addressing your brand relative to the employer's needs.)

SKILLS and ABILITIES

(When projecting or summarizing specific skills and abilities, use one main highlighted descriptor [one or two words, in **Bold**] followed by supportive descriptors.)

Example: Business Acumen: sales; marketing; advertising; office operations; customer/vendor relations. Computer Literacy: MS Office; Access; Excel; Power Point; Peachtree; Outlook; Word.

NOTE: Skills and Abilities support, and are related to, the contents of the statement under the **OBJECTIVE** subtitle. Things accomplished in previous positions are noted under the **EXPERIENCE** subtitle using bullet points to accentuate accomplishments or positive outcomes.
Example:

- Researched, designed and implemented a three-stage plan for developing a diverse customer base resulting in a 50% increase in customer growth.

EXPERIENCE

Name of Job Title or Occupational Specialty Dates:00/00-00/00
(In **Bold** and Underlined)   **(Bold)**
Name of Business or Organization
City, State, Zip

Note: Recently discharged military personnel should avoid using MOS titles and instead research and use equivalent civilian job descriptors/occupational titles. Such "Skills Translator" information can be located at www.military.com at the Job Search link, or the U.S Department of Labor's online Occupational Outlook Handbook and/or O'Net. List out two or three employers when practicing this format.

EDUCATION and TRAINING

Note: The advantage of listing the academic discipline (field of study) or occupational subject first, as opposed to the traditional practice of listing the institution first, is in establishing a relationship between formalized instruction and work performed and objectives accomplished in the **EXPERIENCE** section of the resume—demonstrating the ability to put theory (things learned) into practice.

Major Field of Study or Degree Program   **Dates: 00/00 – 00/00**
(In **Bold** and underlined)   **(Bold)**
Name of College/University/Training Facility
City, State

REFERENCES FURNISHED UPON INTERVIEW
(Optional)

The following week Rocky and Rudy met again and discussed the actual hands-on development of Rocky's resume. Rocky appeared a little hesitant, but with some additional coaching and convincing from Rudy he agreed to put together a resume according to Rudy's instructions.

As they parted company, Rudy said, "Hey, Rocky, take your time, there's no big hurry. Let's say we meet up in two weeks. If you get stuck or have any questions, just give me a call."

Well over three weeks went by before Rudy received a call from Rocky, who sounded a little weird—his words and the thoughts he was attempting to convey seemed a little disconnected. There was a lot of heavy breathing as well as long pauses and some slurring of his speech.

Finally, Rudy said, "Okay, Rocky, bring your new resume with you, and I'll see you at ten o'clock tomorrow morning."

After he ended the call, Rudy calculated that actually it had been over a month since he and Rocky had had contact. "Wonder what's going on with him?" Rudy mused.

The following day they sat down, and Rocky laid a copy of his resume on Rudy's desk. "Here's what I came up with. I pretty much followed your instructions and the model you gave me for a basic resume. What do you think of it?" Rocky asked.

Rudy moved his chair closer to his desk, bent over and read the following:

ROCKLAND J. CAHILL
4675 Sunnyside Ave
Oakland, CA 94601
Rockj1944@earthnet.com / 510-899-2004

EMPLOYMENT OBJECTIVE

Master carpenter with construction project management, building maintenance, and business acumen seeks opportunity to exceed expectations for quality work and satisfied clients.

SKILLS and ABILITIES

Professional Carpentry: framing; insulation/drywall; tile/trim work; windows/doors installation; cabinets/appliance installation; patio-deck construction; roofing/siding; handicap accessibility design/applications; motor home remodeling. **Project Management:** demolition; subcontractor hiring; personnel supervision; resource management; cost-overrun/benefit analysis; construction progress audits. **Building Maintenance:** HVAC; electrical; plumbing; remodeling; general carpentry; floors & windows. **Business Acumen:** sales; marketing; advertising; client & vendor development; customer & contractor relations, budgeting; A/R & A/P; payroll. **Computer Literacy**: Windows XP; 7 & 10; Word; Outlook; Power Point; Access; Excel; QuickBooks; Fresh Books; Wave. **Work Ethic:** willing to do whatever it takes to get the job done.

EXPERIENCE

Cahill's Custom Carpentry /   07/04 – Present
Building Maintenance
Self-Employed
Oakland, CA

- Successfully conducted home remodeling and commercial projects according to customer specifications resulting in 100% satisfaction, client referrals, and repeat business.

- Managed subcontractors in the repair and maintenance of historical buildings and homes, establishing reputation for detailed and meticulous work among customers and peers.
- Maintained exceptional array of tools, hardware, and building materials, providing access to nontraditional building and maintenance contracts exceeding $200,000.00.
- Established the ability to respond to emergency repairs on short notice.

Cahill & Associates   04/96 – 12/03
Contract Builder
San Mateo, CA

- As company owner and Master Carpenter established reputation for quality workmanship, competent employees, and honest business operations.
- Orchestrated contractual agreements for the completion of 20 custom home projects, with budgets ranging from @150,000.00 to $300,000.00 with no cost over-runs – with all projects completed on or before established deadlines.
- Managed all company business operations inclusive of contract negotiations, vendor relations, subcontractor/employee hiring, A/P, A/R functions and material/resource management.

EDUCATION and TRAINING

Electro-Mechanical Engineering   09/92 – 06/95
& Drafting (AS Degree)
Herald Institute of Technology
Santa Clara, CA

U.S. Navy (Seabees)   02/86 – 05/91
Construction Battalion Center (NCBC)
Gulfport, MS

References & Business Recommendations Furnished Upon Interview

As Rudy read through the resume, he was somewhat surprised by how well Rocky had grasped the simplicity of constructing a basic resume. He looked up at Rocky. "Hey, Rocky, you did an outstanding job. Now we have to get into developing a cover letter, and once that is done, you should be close to doing some serious job search."

Rudy went on, "So, Rocky, if I were to ask you to define a cover letter and what its purpose is, you would say what?"

Rocky's face reflected bemusement. His eyes were wide open now, rolling up like an automated garage door toward the top of his head. He was in deep thought ...

"Well," he finally admitted, "you kinda caught me off guard here but, in short, I'd have to say it's a letter to the employer introducing myself and briefly explaining my interest in the job. I'd present some of the major items I have listed in my resume and touch on things he advertised for in the job announcement. It's a way of getting the employer to want to look at my resume to give me an interview, right?"

"Wow, Rocky, you're really getting into this!" Rudy said. "Remember, it's just like going into business for yourself. I know you know that because you've already been there, right?"

"Well, yeah, but it's not exactly the same. I mean, my former letters were mostly about making a bid on a job."

"True enough," Rudy said. "There are similarities and differences. But on the whole, a cover letter is a concise, focused, and well-written communication designed to be an attention-getting marketing tool, targeting the employer. And in your business, Rocky, that would be a prospective client, right?"

"That's right. I never thought of it that way," Rocky admitted.

Rudy continued, "The cover letter is focused on promoting, in a general sense, your skills, abilities, and personal attributes to an employer. It presents your personal acknowledgement of the employer's needs and the probability of those needs being met by you, with a referral to specific qualifications found in your resume.

"Sometimes it's not necessary to send a cover letter. For a number of years it has been thought that every time an applicant submits a resume, a cover letter should accompany it. In many instances, though, the employer asks only for a resume without requesting a cover letter. This is especially true of online applications."

Rudy's rule for cover letters included always sending one under these circumstances:

- When an employer requests one.

- When responding to a job announcement and your research of the employer provides adequate identification and contact information for a follow up. Forget blind job announcements (name of employer withheld (e.g., Progressive Company, Confidential Employer, etc.), as they usually result in the applicant using generic greetings such as "To Whom It May Concern:" and/or "Dear Madam or Sir:".]

- When you consider initiating an unsolicited letter of inquiry regarding the possibility of future employment with an employer you have researched, and whose business or operations reflects a close match of your qualifications. Also, when inquiring about internships/externships. Letters of inquiry and cover letters are similar in content and construction but are intended to differ in outcome.

Note: The practice of using a generic cover letter (one letter fits all) is a waste of the applicant's time and energy, and a cause for employer rejection. Contemporary job search protocol suggests that cover letters and resumes alike be directed toward the subject of a job announcement or posting. In other words, the applicant needs to show how their qualifications relate to the needs of the employer regarding a specific employment opportunity.

As he did before with Rocky's resume, Rudy provided him with the following instructional guide regarding some basic ideas for writing a cover letter:

<u>COVER LETTER COMPOSITION BASICS</u>

As an essential marketing tool a cover letter, to properly showcase candidate qualifications and personal attributes related to the job being applied for, should include the following basic considerations:

- The use of a personal heading is optional. However, if one is used it needs to be consistent with the same heading used in the resume. The advantage of using a heading is that it provides the employer with an immediate reference for any future contact with the applicant. The disadvantage is that it sometimes reduces available writing space for the contents of the cover letter.

- A cover letter should be a personal communication to the employer or decision-maker. If there is no name of reference to whom the letter can be addressed or if the applicant chooses to respond to a blind job posting, then merely begin with the first paragraph of the letter. In such instances avoid using the greeting "To Whom It May Concern" or "Dear Sir or Madam."

  Example: Your current posting for the position (enter job title).

  Note: When the name of the company or organization is known but no referral information is given with which to personalize a cover letter, check the Internet, local library, Chamber of Commerce, Better Business Bureau, local business journal, or informational websites to track down the name of the person to whom your letter should be addressed. A call to the business or organization under consideration could also reveal the proper contact name and title of the employer, decision-maker, or HR representative. If the application process seems a little daunting or just too much work, then consider the fact that this is why it's called job search (research).

- Attempt to develop a writer's voice when generating a cover letter. The flow and use of words and ideas should be a written representation of the applicant's conversational expression. In other words, just be natural and write as you speak. Be careful not to overdo it with slang or use of words and terms you are not familiar with—employers are quick to notice self-aggrandizement. It's a big turnoff, even when you are super qualified for the job.

- Do project yourself in a straightforward manner, but take care to avoid appearing too stiff or formal. A little formality is okay, but guard against trying to sound like something you are not. Use the same action-oriented words to describe your skills, abilities, and experience that you used in your resume—subtly establishing a link between your cover letter and your resume while offering a dynamic expression of who you are.

- Remember a cover letter introduces the employer to your personal business model for achieving career-oriented employment. It should be a marketing tool that entices the employer to look at your resume, while not simply being a carbon copy of your resume. From an employer's perspective it addresses the question, "Why should I consider this person?" Or, "What is in the resume that I need to know to make an interview decision?"

- The tone of a cover letter needs to be positive, exuding confidence in your ability to meet the employer's needs. Avoid referring to anything negative about previous employers, including undesirable assignments or experiences, even if they are true. Perceived negative attitudes toward previous employment will most often make applicants appear to have questionable work ethics. Additionally, persons who have the responsibility for making hiring decisions are very wary of individuals who sound or project a desperate image—"Desperate people do desperate things."

- It is essential to present yourself as being confident. But take care to avoid appearing overconfident—overconfidence can cause an applicant to appear arrogant. It's necessary to say you are qualified, but coming across as though you are demanding consideration or that you are doing the employer a favor by applying, whether intentional or not, is a huge turnoff. Confidence mixed with a little humility can go a long way.

- Attempting to create the impression that you know more about an organization than you really do is to be avoided at all cost. The only way to come across as knowledgeable is to do research of the employer first. It is always a good idea to briefly explain at the beginning of your cover letter why you are attracted to the employer, but there is no need to go beyond that point. Keep it brief.

- Show respect for the employer's time by being efficient with your sentences. Ensure that every line addresses the employer's need or explains your interest in his business or organization.

- Specifically indicate your availability and how the employer can contact you by using the same heading you used in your resume. Indicate that you look forward to his follow up to your resume in the near future.

- Avoid having your cover letter appear as though it is a form letter by using a little variety throughout each paragraph and staying away from repetitious words and phrases. With the exception of computer-generated documents, remember to sign the cover letter.

- Cover letters appear more businesslike and professional when produced on white paper with black ink/print—it is a sign of being organized and focused when the cover letter and the resume are produced in the same manner.

- Always keep a copy of each cover letter sent to an employer for future reference.

- Avoid starting sentences with first-person words like "I" and "my." Give the impression that the letter is not about you so much as it is about the employer's needs.

Example: "Ten years previous experience in marketing ..." compared to "I have ten years of experience in marketing."

- Be sure to proofread both cover letter and resume carefully to check for proper use of grammar, spelling, and punctuation. Avoid becoming too dependent upon computer spell-check programs. Instead, use a dictionary.

Rudy suggested to Rocky, "Be sure to read the Cover Letter Composition Basics a few times before attempting to write the letter. As far as the actual construction of a cover letter goes, you should have no problem getting it set up. I'm taking you through this scenario because a lot of the vets I work with have never written a cover letter, and it's one of the most crucial pieces of the application process. So, just take your time and you'll get it."

Rudy then handed Rocky a copy of a document titled **Cover Letter Construction Format** and reviewed the document with him.

When they shook hands at the end of their meeting, Rudy noticed Rocky's eyes had a glassy appearance. He's also noticed during their conversation that Rocky was yawning constantly, and his attention span fluctuated.

"Hey, Rock, anything wrong?" Rudy asked.

"No, man, it's just the damn meds the VA gave me to kill the pain in my back when I get to hurtin' too much. Sometimes they make me really zonked. I think I better get home and take a nap before I try to get into the cover letter material you gave me. See ya later, Rudy."

Later, sitting in his favorite easy chair, Rocky awakened from a numbing, dreamless sleep. He was groggy from the painkillers and not even sure how he had made the drive home. He spent the rest of the day watching TV, then he had an early supper and went to bed. Taking several deep breaths, he drifted off wondering where his whole day went.

Next morning, the voice in his head screamed "Reveille" as the alarm clock kept cadence with the pain in his head. Rocky got up, did the "triple S" routine, had a little "chow," and was at the desk in his home office by 0700. He laid out the paperwork Rudy had given him and turned on his computer.

He read through the Cover Letter Composition Basics several times as Rudy had instructed, and then carefully read the Cover Letter Construction Format:

COVER LETTER CONSTRUCTION FORMAT

The following Cover Letter Construction Format and instructional four paragraph commentary, paragraph by paragraph, is designed to produce an effective marketing message, targeting a specific employer, compatible with your resume, focused on the job for which you are applying:

Date:

Name and Title of Person (Employer/HR Person/ Decision-maker)
Name of Company/Organization
Street address
City, State, Zip Code

Greeting

Dear_____:

This greeting should only be used when the name of the individual is known. The use of "Dear Sir or Madam" is not recommended. Similarly, the greeting of "To Whom It May Concern" is not specific and concerns no one in particular; it should be avoided. When there is no specific person to address, just begin with the opening paragraph.

Example: The Baker Organization's current posting for Director of Public Relations has captured my attention and interest…

First Paragraph

This paragraph should consist of from three to five concisely constructed sentences. It acknowledges the employer's business or organization and the vacancy to be filled. The applicant expresses an interest in the position and a desire to work for the employer. It's also time for an applicant to let a little creativity shine through. This paragraph may vary somewhat when the cover letter is an unsolicited inquiry by an applicant pursuing an internship possibility or future employment.

Example: The Baker Organization's reputation as a leader in the field of marketing and advertising, evidenced by its recent Better

Business Award for Midsized Business Innovator of The Year, has definitely captured my attention. Of personal interest is your current opening for Director of Public Relations. It presents an incredible opportunity to make contributions to the clients you serve and to learn from the best. This is a position that previous experience and training have led me to pursue. "The only client worth having is a returning and satisfied one."

Second Paragraph

When constructing this paragraph, the applicant uses two to four concise statements/sentences briefly outlining basic experience, skills, abilities, and personal characteristics that fit the employer's business or organization. This is the place to strategically highlight some of the applicant's background that is relevant to the employer's requirements. Here, the applicant declares a personal conviction that he or she has the necessary qualifications to fit the position and can be an asset to the company. It is recommended that several short bullet-point declarative statements be used.

Example: Previous education, training, experience, and commitment to successful client development and building of customer relations over the past ten years, involved the following accomplishments:

- Graduate Degree in Business Communications, including a successful nine-month internship with a top public relations firm, leading to offer of full-time employment.

- Director of Communications and co-author of texts and articles on the establishment and maintenance of customer relations and service programs.

- Completion of two-year Project Management assignment in customer relations.

- Contributing public relations consultant in private practice.

Third Paragraph

In this paragraph the applicant directs the employer's attention to the enclosed/attached resume which, according to the business model approach to job search, becomes the "Advertising Hook." A cover letter should be designed to foster continued interest in reviewing the applicant's resume, and only two short sentences are required.

Example: As the attached resume demonstrates, I come equipped with the sincere desire, commitment, training, experience, and expertise necessary to take The Baker Organization to the highest level possible in business communications, as your next Director of Public Relations.

Fourth Paragraph

The final paragraph should consist of one or two short statements confirming the applicant's ability to meet the employer's need and expressing interest in an interview. It sets the stage for follow-up contact between employer and applicant, and presents an opportunity for continued dialogue until an interview decision is made.

Example: An opportunity to interview with you and/or members of your staff, to determine the match between The Baker Organization's Director of Public Relations requirements and my qualifications, would be very much appreciated.

Closure

The cover letter simply ends with one or two words: "Sincerely," or "Sincerely yours."

Between the statement of closure and the applicant's typed name, leave sufficient room for the applicant's signature, usually one space.

Example: "Sincerely yours," or, "Respectfully yours,"
Applicant's Signature
Applicant's Name Typed
Note: If an email cover letter is used, then merely enter your name.

Rocky spent the rest of that morning practicing each of the cover letter sections—writing and rewriting sentences and paragraphs.

It was 3:00 p.m. when he finished his cover letter in response to the Maddox Realty Investment Corporation posting for a Property Maintenance Manager. He read it over several times just to make sure it related to the resume he had constructed earlier. It was time for his meds—the pain, he convinced himself, was becoming a distraction. Satisfied with his work, he left the cover letter laying on his desk.

The next morning began with questionable clarity, but it was a new day. Rocky reviewed the cover letter he had left on his desk the previous afternoon. "That still looks pretty good," he mused. He read it again, and again, and was satisfied.

ROCKLAND J. CAHILL

4675 Sunnyside Ave.

Oakland, CA 94601

Rockj1944@earthnet.com / 510-899-2004

January 20, 2015

Maddox Realty Investment Corporation
1856 New Start Drive
Oakland, CA 94607
Attn: Alice Rawllings, HR Manager

Dear Ms. Rawllings:

Your current posting for Property Maintenance Manager with the Maddox Realty Investment Corporation is an attractive opportunity just made for the quality of work I perform. If you are seeking someone who meets all aspects of your requirements and is dedicated and committed to complying with stringent building codes and producing work that results in client satisfaction, then look no further.

With over twenty-five years of experience in contract building maintenance and a reputation for quality workmanship and repeated client referrals, I excel when it comes to:

• Professional Carpentry: both interior and exterior work.

• Project Management: personnel supervision, cost-containment, and material resources.

- Building Maintenance: remodeling, electrical, plumbing, HVAC repairs and installation.

- Business Acumen: bookkeeping, vendor relations, budgeting, AP/AR disciplines.

As the attached resume outlines, I have the skills, abilities, experience, and credibility as a professional to enhance the quality of work your properties demand and require.

An opportunity to meet with you and your business associates, to discuss the match between your Property Maintenance Manager requirements and my qualifications, would be very much appreciated.

Respectfully yours,

Rockland J. Cahill

A few days later, Rocky asked Rudy to review his cover letter, got his blessing, and began to submit his cover letter and resume to employers in the light carpentry and building maintenance fields.

Much to his surprise Rocky began to get responses to his applications. Rudy wasn't surprised. As he related to Rocky in a follow-up meeting, "If you remember what I said in the beginning: it's a step-by-step process. Job search never really stops, even after you're hired."

"Why is that?" Rocky asked.

"Because once you've established the grove, you never stop looking —nothing breeds success like success."

Then Rudy asked the inevitable, crucial question, "Hey, Rock, have you had any interviews?"

"Yeah, as a matter of fact I have. I don't have a problem talking to people, like I had in the beginning with writing things like a cover letter and resume. It seems I was born with, as they say, 'a gift for gab.' I'm just waiting for them to get finished doing my background investigation."

"Well, while you are waiting for those employers to finish your background checks, are you doing any job search?"

"Not exactly. I thought I would take a little break until I get word back from these guys."

"Okay, Rocky, here's the deal. You always keep searching, even after you've had an interview, and even while an employer is doing a background check."

"Why?" Rocky blurted out. "Why is that?"

"Because all those things that appear positive are never set in cement—there are no guarantees. You never know what might interfere with an employer's hiring decision until there is an offer of employment on the table. And even then, you haven't been on the job yet."

Ruby finished their session by saying, "You always keep looking, as a backup. You can always turn down a job, but you can't always turn one up when you need it. It's called hedging your bet."

After a few weeks of submitting cover letters and resumes, Rocky ran into Albert, a friend he hadn't seen in a few years. Albert worked for one of the management companies Rocky had initially applied to.

Over coffee, and after some preliminary conversation, Rocky finally mentioned his application to Al Property Management, and the fact that during the interview the HR Director indicated that he was what the management company was looking for.

Rocky said, "They even had me fill out a simple two-page application and some payroll papers after I was interviewed. I really thought they were going to hire me. They said they would give me a call in a few days. It has been a couple of weeks now and no one has let me know where I stand with this company."

"Look, Rocky," Albert said, "you didn't hear this from me, but I heard through the grapevine that A1 Property Management was getting ready to hire you. Your resume and cover letter and interview indicated that you were what they were looking for. Then your background check returned and there was something about a conviction for vehicular manslaughter and three years in the state pen. Wow! Rocky, what happened?"

Rocky sat stunned. The silence became a deafening roar in his ears. Then as he spoke, his memory played back the event that indelibly stamped CONVICTED FELON in his mind's eye.

"That was over twenty-seven years ago, right after I was discharged from the Navy. I was in a hurry to get home after work one night, and I was a little 'high.' I blew a stop sign and ran into this old guy and killed him. I was young, made a stupid mistake, and I paid for it. All this time, I've regretted unnecessarily taking the life of another. I guess I'm still paying for it. I have nothing to hide. I even checked the box 'Yes' on the initial application next to the question 'Have you ever been convicted of a crime?'"

Leaving his friend that day, Rocky thought everyone should be entitled to a few mistakes in life. He reminded himself that his felony conviction, and the fact that he did a little time in the joint, had never been a problem with all the other building maintenance and carpentry contracts he had before.

Emotionally drained, he called Rudy. "I talked to my friend who works for the company I applied to, and he said they were getting ready to hire me but when they found out I was a felon, they backed out. I told them on the application I was a felon, so they knew that. So, I can't figure out why they never called me back! Now what do I do?"

"Okay, Rocky, I understand," Rudy assured him. "Let's meet at my office the day after tomorrow. Just don't give up. These things do happen. Job search is not always a smooth road, especially for those with felony convictions. We'll get through it."

When they met to discuss the felony situation, Rocky had a bruised right eye, several scratches on his face, and an ugly bluish-green bump in the middle of his forehead. His left wrist was freshly wrapped in white tape.

Rocky limped his way back to Rudy's office. As gingerly as he could, with every muscle and joint in his body aching, he slowly and cautiously sank into the soft-cushioned chair in front of Rudy's desk.

Not unexpectedly the first words out of Rudy's mouth were, "What the hell happened to you, man? Surely, it wasn't from doing job search?"

With intended sarcasm in his voice, Rocky explained, "Well, it was, sort of. Right after I called and told you what happened with the job I thought I had, but didn't get, my back started to pain up, so I popped a couple of meds. Anyhow, I stopped by a friend's house on the way home from the store and we knocked down a few beers. By the time I left his house the pain was gone. So, when I got to the big curve in my driveway at home, I guess I was going a little too fast and I end up rolling my truck over. It's kind of banged up, like me. My neighbor who owns a tow truck helped me get it back up, and it's still running."

Now imitating his ancestral Irish brogue, he said, "Like dey say in de old country of me fore-faders, shite happens, then you move on to a higher order of tings!"

Their conversation that day was short.

Attempting to control his exasperation, Rudy commented, "Listen, Rocky, there's no getting around the fact you've been convicted of a felony. So the only approach to becoming employed is to be up-front and direct in all applications and interviews. Honesty is the only policy here. The fact that you have been self-employed for the past twenty years has established you as a credible individual and a reputable businessman since your conviction. It will carry considerable weight with most employers."

Remorsefully, Rocky said, "Okay, Rudy, I got it."

They awkwardly shook hands. Rudy put his free hand on Rocky's shoulder, his eyes fixed on the bruised mass before him. "Hey, pal, if there's anything you need or you just want someone to talk to, let me know. In the meantime, watch the damn meds and booze. They can get away from you if you're not careful."

Rocky's response surprised and disturbed Rudy. "Yeah, man, you're right about the meds, but then again, it's a peaceful way to go."

A month later Rudy ran into Rocky at a Veterans Day event. They shook hands, gave each other a man hug, and simultaneously asked, "How's it going, brother?"

Rocky said, "Man, I've responded to mega job announcements and written so many cover letters and resumes that the process has become automatic now."

Rudy explored Rocky's face. It still had a few scars, barely noticeable but enough to remind him how they got there. Quite noticeable, though, was his skin's ashen pallor. He appeared to move a lot slower now and was more deliberate in his steps when he walked. Rudy said, "Rocky, I got to be honest here. You don't look so good. What's going on, my friend? You look tired."

"Well," Rocky responded, "I went to my annual physical a few of weeks ago, and they told me my kidneys aren't working like they should, something about my retaining too much water in my system, and my heart giving off some weird beats. The doctor said I would probably need a few more tests in the very near future. For now, they gave me a bunch of meds, including Lasix, in addition to the painkillers I'm already on. Now I'm peeing like a fire hose. It's wearing me out, man. I feel like a race horse all primed to run, but I never get to enter the race. I just keep running to the latrine instead. I've lost ten pounds already!

"On the other hand, the doctor said I'm not active enough, and I need to get some exercise. I told the doctor that I was looking for a job, and if I had the kind of work that I normally do, it would keep me plenty active. If I had a job I know I'd be feeling a lot better. It's a real bummer.

"Some days I feel like taking a handful of Oxies and calling it a day, but then I tell myself I'm not ready to give up the search for a job yet."

As empathetic as he was to this veteran's situation, and yet wanting to avoid getting sucked into someone else's drama, Rudy interrupted. "So tell me, Rocky, how has the job search really been going?"

"As I said before, I'm getting pretty good with basic resumes and cover letters. At least I think I am because I keep getting interviews.

When I finish an interview I always feel like I did well. I answer all their questions, and they keep telling me I'm what they are looking for. I just think it's the background check and the felony thing that is hanging me up. I'm starting to get a little depressed."

They broke up their impromptu meeting that day agreeing to meet the following week. Rudy indicated he would furnish Rocky with a new listing of felon-friendly employers.

They met as previously arranged, and Rudy gave Rocky three pages of employers that hire veterans with felony records. Rocky was instructed to research and apply only to those employers who appeared to match his experience, skills, and abilities.

A few days later, Rocky made a follow-up call to Rudy. "Hey, man, I found eight employers that matched my qualifications, and I submitted resumes and letters of inquiry regarding employment opportunities."

Their phone conversation was brief. Rudy ended the call by saying, "Listen, Rocky, I have a good feeling about what you are doing. I'll give you a call in a few days, and we can discuss what's happening. Just be patient. These things take time, especially when it involves a felony in a vet's background. I've worked with some of these employers before, and as long as you are straight with them, they'll give you every consideration. Just know that if they interview you, their hiring decision will be based strictly upon you being a top qualifier, not because you are an ex-felon who deserves a second chance."

When Rudy did his follow-up call, he sensed a lack of energy in Rocky's voice. He sounded weak, distant, and apprehensive, not decisive, not like the old Rocky.

Rudy didn't waste any time getting to the main question. "So, what happened with the eight employers you contacted?"

Rocky cleared his throat and spoke with a little more resonance in his voice. "I don't know what to think. Out of the eight employers that I sent my resume and letters of inquiry to, three of them invited me to an interview. I've already had two of them email me back saying they thought I was well qualified, but they selected another candidate. I still haven't heard anything from the third employer."

Rudy interrupted Rocky and asked, "What was your general impression, your gut feeling, when you left your last interview?"

"This company was called the Hastings Property Management Group. Out of the three, Hastings really made me feel at home. I was very comfortable with these people. There were four of them sitting in on the interview. One of them was a woman HR person, and the other three were regional big shots and the owner of the company. They were all vets. From what they told me, the company is an international organization. They asked me about my felony conviction and about my experience with property and building maintenance. Toward the end of the interview they agreed everyone needs a second chance. They told me they would get back to me with their decision in a few days."

"What did they say when they called you back?"

"Man, it's been over a week now and still no contact from them. To tell you the truth, Rudy, my gut tells me their decision will be the same as the first two. When I left that interview, I really thought I was going to get a job offer. Now, I'm not so sure. I even tried to call them a couple of times, but all I got was that their mailbox was full."

Rudy sensed the disappointment in Rocky's voice and attempted to move the conversation forward. "Rocky, remember we agreed to continue with job search until you got an offer on the table so, have you done any job search while you are waiting? Just between you and me, I really feel your best chance is with Hastings. I know these guys pretty well. They are more likely to make you an offer than not. But for right now, you need to keep busy."

With some irritation in his voice, Rocky responded, "No, I haven't done any job search this week! I think I'm going to take a break. The holidays are coming up, and I think I'll just kick back for a while."

Then Rocky continued in a more apologetic tone, "Look, man, sorry about snapping at you like that. I appreciate everything you have done to help me out, but I got this darkness hounding me. I'm trying to break free of it, but I can't seem to catch a break. I just want some peace in my life. I'll give you a call in a week or so and let you know how I'm doing."

The last lingering reminder of their conversation that day for Rudy was the dial tone right after Rocky hung up the phone in the middle of their conversation.

A week later Rocky's family planned to make their annual pilgrimage to relatives in Oregon to celebrate Thanksgiving. Rocky declined to go. He said he needed some alone time. They left without him.

When they returned, Rocky was in his easy chair in front of the TV. The TV was tuned in to the History Channel, and a Vietnam War documentary was playing. There he sat, still as a silent moment, a silly smirk on his ashen face. Here was a voyager, a veteran exploring a new and different kind of world now, where job search was no longer in the scheme of things to come. Sitting on a small end table next to his chair was an empty bottle of "Black Jack" and next to it a small empty prescription bottle labeled Oxycodone. In his lap lay unopened mail. One large envelope had the return address of the Hastings Property Management Group.

After the funeral the family gathered around the dark-stained oak dining room table Rocky had made for his wife years before. They started going through all the papers he left behind. His wife opened the large envelope that was on his lap the day they found him. As she began to read, she unconsciously reached up and pulled hard on her hair, stretching the skin so tight that her facial features became distorted. Sobbing lightly, she read the letter aloud.

Dear Mr. Cahill:

Please accept our sincerest apologies for the delay in informing you of our hiring decision. We had an unexpected water line break in our main office, causing severe flooding and requiring us to vacate the building. We had to suspend business operations until repairs were completed.

We are happy to announce that after a review of your qualifications, background, and forthrightness in your interview, you were our top candidate for Manager, Building Maintenance Operations. Therefore, and it is with a great deal of pleasure, that we make this offer of employment. Welcome to the Hastings Family!

Your starting salary will be $70,000.00 per year, along with an outstanding benefits package. If this offer is satisfactory, please contact Helen Morris, Director of Human Resources, (510) 177-2298 by December 1, 2010, to complete all paperwork. Your start date is scheduled for December 15, 2010.

Sincerely yours,

Victoria Manning, HR Assistant

Robert Hastings, Founder, Owner & CEO
Hastings Property Management Group

VOYAGER BASICS

Resumes and cover letters have a reality and life of their own, once put into motion by their creators. When the basics of a winning resume and cover letter have been applied and implemented, no matter how the applicant's life situation develops, they will eventually bear fruit. It's all about making the right connection with the right employer. But it's not easy to predict exactly when, after an interview, a job will be offered.

To be sure, not every resume and cover letter submitted will resonate with an employer. It's just the way the world works. Life is not always fair, and it is continually driven by cycles of successes and failures.

Again, not every attempt to gain employment will be rewarded. The main key to a successful job search is persistence, relevance, and creativity in the development of a winning resume and cover letter. To ensure a greater degree of success, these documents should be designed to fit the employer's need.

When it comes to the resume and cover letter, the idea that "one size fits all" will not work very well in today's diverse, rapidly changing, and competitive job market.

Unfortunately for veterans, the transition from the military to the civilian sector can be difficult. It may be that, during the time they were serving their country, the whole job search scene changed. It's as though one were beginning anew. There are also many veterans who have been employed for a while but who have lost their jobs for a variety of reasons (e.g., business downsizing, business closure, business relocation, the desire to change careers, etc.).

Thus, the use of a simple basic format for resumes and cover letters as presented here provides both the transitioning and seasoned veterans with an effective and adaptive tool to begin or renew their job search.

The development and implementation of cover letters and resumes can be compared to going into business for yourself and should include the following rudimentary considerations:

Cover Letters

- A cover letter becomes the primary marketing tool with which you introduce your product or service to a targeted prospective client (the employer). The letter is used to create interest in your qualifications and invites the employer to review your qualifications in more detail in your resume. This is your marketing strategy.

- Don't downplay the importance of the cover letter—its use is proper business etiquette. Get in the habit of sending a cover letter along with every resume submitted, unless there is sufficient evidence indicating that it is unnecessary.

- Be as concise as possible. Remember that most HR managers and recruiters are extremely busy individuals who don't have time to struggle through a lengthy introduction. This is especially true when initiating an email response.

Email communication requires conciseness because it is often more difficult to read text on-screen than on paper. Conversely, one-liners similar to "Your attention to the attached resume establishes my qualifications for (name of position)" are inadequate and unprofessional. The best strategy is to send a brief email, then include a cover letter and your resume as attachments.

- A convincing cover letter, aside from being the applicant's primary method of self-introduction, also needs to be both professional and personable. The primary goal is to demonstrate that the applicant would be a good fit for the position while projecting a friendly, down-to-earth demeanor. Engendering acceptability through a mix of friendliness and professionalism works best.

- Always attempt to direct your greeting to a person. When responding to a job announcement in which no specific contact person is indicated, make every effort to identify the individual responsible for handling cover letters, resumes, and applications. Calling the employer's business or organization to obtain information is part of the job search process. However, if the job announcement specifies "No Phone Calls Please," then respect that request.

- The primary purpose of a cover letter is to express an applicant's desire and ability to fulfill an employer's needs, so avoid beginning sentences with "I" or "my" (first person references). Again, some research should be done to determine the employer's greatest needs. The most compelling letter will clearly convey your ability to solve or proactively prevent problems—it's all about what you can do for the employer, not what the employer can do for you.

- Being creative with your cover letter will make it stand out. For example, you could include a summary of your success facilitating effective logistics through the efficient handing of materials, resources, and personnel. Or, you may include excerpts of awards in recognition for outstanding performance.

- Regardless of how convincingly a cover letter demonstrates your ability to meet employer expectations, failure to proofread your document for spelling, grammar, and punctuation errors will likely eliminate you as a competitive applicant. Avoid computer spell check and use a dictionary. Yes, it takes a little more time and effort to proofread your cover letter, but the rewards are so much greater. Most importantly, be sure the name of the person to whom the letter is addressed is spelled correctly.

Resumes

Based upon the number books, videos, and lectures presented by experts in the field of job search, it seems as though there's an endless source of ideas and recommendations available for resume-writing. The following concepts are some of the most critical to the development and use of a winning resume:

- Of all the recommendations and instructions an applicant receives regarding the development and use of a resume, it is most important to remember that the primary purpose and function of a resume is to facilitate an interview.

- Adhering to the job search business model, the cover letter needs to function as a marketing device that targets the client/customer (in this case the employer). The resume functions as your brand, telling who you are and what you do, and serving the same function as an advertisement. It presents the product (you), your skills, abilities, experience, training and education, and it matches your qualifications to the needs and goals of the employer. It's designed to create a clear and convincing reason for the employer (HR manager/hiring official) to extend an invitation for an interview.

- Taking time to carefully review the job description for key words and phrases used to describe job functions and responsibilities allows you to use the same descriptors in your resume. Doing so provides you with an opportunity to establish a connective link with ideas and words the employer is familiar with, creating a

195

sense of commonality. So, if the employer is searching for someone with strong communications skills, using terms like "presenter," "trainer," or "speech writer" may hit the mark in gaining their attention.

- Make good use of white space and effective fonts such as Helvetica, Times Roman, and Arial. It is important to make your resume a clean and easy-to-read document by being consistent with the use of headers, bold, and italics. Avoid the use of colored inks and paper—they make document copying dark, unclear, and difficult to read. Black ink and white paper is the standard when attempting to provide a professional look.

- Putting aside the debate of how many pages a resume needs to be, you can be certain to provide an acceptable document if you stick to the guideline of one and a half to two pages. Veterans who have been in the workaday world for a number of years will have held from two to four jobs, and the two-page maximum is a good fit. Veterans experiencing a more recent separation and who have ten or more years of military service may still manage a two-page resume. The trick is to break down your various military assignments and to present them as different jobs, much like the various jobs you would hold in the civilian sector.

- Your resume should include only the last seven to ten years of your work experience, unless otherwise requested by an employer. A veteran who has had civilian employment with one employer for more than ten years, or who has recently retired from the military, should select only those jobs closely related to the position she/he is applying for.

- Be aware that applications for federal jobs may require from five to seven pages, and may use a format much different from that of the standard one- to two-page resume used to apply for private employer jobs.

- A veteran, recently separated with four or less years, might want to consider a one-page resume, including civilian employment and/or volunteer work that relates to the job being applied for.

- When developing your resume, some research needs to be conducted regarding the hiring manager and the organization. A little knowledge about their hiring practices should provide insight into the employer's operation.

  Such research may also reveal the culture of the company—whether it is strictly business as usual or informal. Understanding the company's culture can aid you in developing an immediate rapport during the interview.

- If you are a veteran recently separated from military service, you may tend to use military jargon and terms in describing experience, job descriptions, skills, and responsibilities in your resume.

  To avoid this dilemma, it's recommended that you translate military lingo into terms that an employer can understand and that fit qualifications in the original job announcement. Internet military translator tools are available through Military.com and/or O'NET (onetonline.org).

- Remember a resume is not a rehashing of previous job duties that might relate to the position being applied for, but rather an opportunity to indicate what was accomplished. Highlight the results of the functions you served, quantify those results. For example: "Managed the installation and preventative maintenance of four $6.3 million military base facilities, with a cost savings of over $100,000.00 per annum."

- Consider placing your resume in PDF to ensure that any email you send retains your document's original format.

- If you have done volunteer work, be sure to include those experiences in your resume. It's a way of showing your ability to be diverse and to develop new skills. However, include volunteer work only if these experiences relate to the job being applied for.

- Again, and this bears repeating, be sure to proofread your resume before sending it to an employer. Simple grammatical, punctuation, and spelling errors are a huge turnoff for many employers.

References

- Always confirm your references before submitting their names and contact information to an employer.

- References are presented on a separate page unless otherwise requested by an employer.

Persistence

- Never give up; job offers come when you least expect them.

8

PREPARING FOR AND PARTICIPATING IN THE INTERVIEW

"Practice Makes Perfect."

Vet Rep Michael Ishioto and Nathan Stores, a somewhat belligerent vet, were having an intense discussion about interviews and their outcomes. Michael tried to be patient as he explained, "Look, Nathan, most employers and their staff come into an interview with a set of predetermined questions they believe will give them some insight into a candidate's ability to fit into the position they have open."

"Yeah," Nathan countered, "and a lot of the time when I've been interviewed, most of the questions don't make any sense. I get the feeling sometimes they are just a lot of trick questions."

"You're right," said Michael. "Many times the questions seem like they don't make a lot of sense to candidates, especially open-ended, behavioral-oriented questions like 'Tell me about a time when ...' or 'How would you handle this situation ...?' or 'Give us an example of ...'

"Unfortunately, candidates spend more time trying to look for hidden meanings than they do addressing the question at hand. When they do respond, the candidate comes across as either ill prepared, lacking confidence, or unable to communicate effectively. They seem distant and unable to connect. This almost always destroys any positive connection candidates may have made when first sitting down at the interview table."

"Look, I'm not sure that's my problem," Nathan argued. "It's their hang-up!"

"Well, when you project that kind of attitude it does become your problem, especially when you're dealing with savvy interviewers. Being respectful, prepared, and completely focused are all necessary for survival in today's technical, service-oriented, information-based, and competitive job market."

"Yeah, I get all that garbage, but in the end it's just a mind game that employers play, and I can play that game too," Nathan sarcastically remarked.

"By the way," he added, "Stop referring to me as Nay-Than; just call me Nate, and I'll do the same for you ... Mike! I'm not into this formality stuff. I'm not stupid, insensitive, or ill-mannered, just plain spoken, that's all. From the day I enlisted, and throughout my training and combat experience, I taught myself to be that way in order to survive. The military never gave me what they promised from the get-go! I don't trust anyone who can't keep their promise."

"Well, Nate," Michael continued, "what we are talking about here is not a mind game but rather a mindset, and there's a big difference. You're not in a strategic military ops mode anymore. Employers are not the enemy, and you're not out to destroy them. The civilian employment interview process these days is more diverse, subtle, and sophisticated. It's a relationship-building event.

"The need to establish and maintain rapport and effective communication will be critical to your success from now on. It's important that you get the big picture, and get rid of that chip on your shoulder. Otherwise, you'll continue to self-destruct every time you get into an interview situation. But, as you just so eloquently stated, it is a matter of survival … yours!"

When asked what he thought the problem was, Nate explained in an apologetic tone, "Man, like I really don't know. I've been doing job search since I got out of the military."

"How long ago was that, Nate?"

"I got out about nine months ago. Well, actually, I kicked back for a month or two before I started to get bored and look for a job. But for the last several months something seems to get in the way, once I get to the interview. I'm fairly articulate, I answer employer questions in a straightforward manner, and I feel pretty good about myself when the interview is over. Like I answer every question thrown at me. One thing for sure, I know I'm qualified for the jobs I apply for. My resume and cover letter are on target. As a matter of fact, I've had employers tell me during the interview how well I present myself on paper. They were really impressed with the design and content of my resume and cover letter."

"Okay, Nate, does that tell you anything?"

"I don't know what you are driving at, Mike!"

"Well, employers keep telling you that you present yourself well on paper, but how about during the interview?"

Herein lay the problem presented to Michael during their initial meeting. Nate had contacted him indicating a long line of disappointing interviews for jobs he knew he was well qualified to perform. Michael sensed that Nate might be having difficulty relating to or trusting authority figures. He was also dealing with rejection—not being selected for positions he applied for even though he appeared well qualified on paper.

"So, tell me about when you get to the end of the interview," Michael said.

"I'm not sure what you mean."

"Okay, here's an example, Nate. At the end of an interview, most employers these days ask the candidate whether they have any questions. How do you respond to that?"

"I usually tell them I don't have any that come to mind right now, because they pretty much said it all in their job announcement. Besides, I feel that if I do ask a question, they'll come back with some sort of trick question. It's all part of the mind game thing. That way I stay clear of their trickery and traps to avoid creating any sort of conflict."

Michael sensed the need to be direct. "Nate, what you've told me so far indicates that over the last several months, all of your interviews have not produced a single job offer. So you have amassed a huge debit of apprehension, resentment, lack of trust, and the inability to connect that most employers are able to read like a neon sign: BAD ATTITUDE, TOO AGGRESSIVE, NOT A GOOD FIT! For you it has now become a self-perpetuating drama and a dilemma with no apparent solution or end in sight. So, I want you to think about why you are causing yourself so much pain and disappointment. I also want you to know that you do have the talent, skills, and experience necessary for employment, and we will get you through this barrier. But, be aware your situation is mainly one of your own making."

As their meeting ended that day, Michael again reminded Nate of a number of factors that contribute to a successful interview, one that leads to a job offer. Primarily, a candidate's proper mindset going into an interview determines the desired outcome.

After Nate left his office, Michael thought about what else could be bothering his client. Obviously Nate had a huge chip on his shoulder. Maybe dealing with fear of failure was the culprit. However, Michael had a nagging suspicion that underneath the antagonistic demeanor there might be something else going on. Michael would need more time with Nate before the truth surfaced and change could come about. The challenge he now faced was to get Nate to hang in there long enough to realize the goal of becoming employed.

"Then again," Michael wondered, "do I want to spend a lot of time with a vet who seems destined to destroy his chances for meaningful employment?"

The answer of course, as he reminded himself, was that not all vets were hard chargers—highly motivated with a positive sense of direction. Some were like bicycle tires low on air—unstable, wobbly, and in need of pumping up so they would have an easier and smoother ride to their destination.

"Anyhow," he concluded, "this vet is reaching out for help at a critical point in his life. I've been there myself, so I guess it's time to man-up and attempt to help this guy out."

As he was leaving the office that day, Michael felt stressed over the life circumstances of the vets he was working with. He knew he needed to remain objective and avoid getting sucked into other people's drama, while at the same time remaining compassionate and empathetic toward his fellow vets. Sometimes this seemed like an impossible task that was placed upon the shoulders of many of today's Vet Reps.

Michael set up a time to have a couple of beers with his mentor Vincent, a retired 30-year Command Sergeant Major. He wanted to discuss the issues he was facing with Nate.

After talking for a time, Vincent said to Michael, "After working with vets for many years, I've discovered that when you spend time in a war zone where you witness horrible events and you're trying simply to survive, you spend the rest of your life after deployment trying to recover. Some never do."

"I suspect you are referring to those suffering from PTSD," Michael said.

"It's interesting you should mention that," Vincent remarked. "From my point of view, no soldier is ever unaffected by the experience of war. To be quite upfront about it, I believe that to a greater or lesser degree all of us who have served in combat suffer from PTSD. Some are able to adjust to the non-combative world, but far too many go on looking over their shoulders because they don't have the buddy bond and trust of knowing someone has got their back.

"Most often, PTSD can affect relationship-building, the way you connect and communicate with people when returning to civilian life. In many respects, only a veteran truly understands and can serve an-

other vet. Yeah, there are other well-trained counselors, social workers, and VA specialists who genuinely care about veterans and can do
a good job working with them. But in my opinion, they just don't have
the camaraderie, an almost immediate connection, that all veterans
have for one another, no matter which branch of the military they
served in. The big thing, though, if you want to help another veteran
who is experiencing difficulty making the transition back to civilian
life, it's important to remain objective without losing your compassion
and empathy."

"Wait a minute, Vince. What do you mean about losing your
compassion?"

"Look at it this way, Mike. Compassion is the humane quality of
understanding the suffering of others and wanting to do something
about it. It's okay to provide direction and instruction, but you have
to let the vet begin to do things for himself because he needs to regain
a certain measure of self-confidence while in transition. He needs to
have a little skin in the game by making an effort. It's a little bit like the
tough love some parents need to adopt when they are forced to deal
with a troubled or recalcitrant child. This is not to infer that vets need
to be treated like children, by no means. It's not the person but rather
the behavior and the barriers to meaningful relationships that need to
be dealt with."

"So how do you deal with it?" Michael asked.

"Deep down inside you really care, but if you wear your heart on
your sleeve, then you become subject to emotional manipulation by
the person you are attempting to help. For the Vet Rep it's important to recognize your own vulnerability, and for the vet, it's all about
self-discovery—learning to reconnect with self before being able to
connect with others."

After gaining Vincent's insights, Michael again met with Nathan.
"Nate," he began, "we need to get you to look at the interview process
a little differently than you have in the past. We need to produce the
results you were expecting, and that is getting job offers. Are you up
for it, and are you willing to work with me?"

"Yeah, man, I want to get a job and move on with my life," Nathan said. "So, what do you have in mind?"

"Well, I need you to answer a few questions for me. When we first met you mentioned the military never gave you what they promised from the beginning of your enlistment to the end of it. What did you mean?"

Nate suddenly looked up at the ceiling, as though the thought was coming from above, somewhere out there in the vastness of the universe. Quickly his face darkened and turned somber. Angrily, he said, "Every time I think about it I get totally pissed!"

Nate paused for a second and took a deep breath. Mike asked, "I don't understand, Nate. Why the anger?"

"I let the recruiter know I wanted to get into computers because that's what my test scores indicated I was highly qualified for. Plus the fact that through my junior and senior year of high school I took everything I could that dealt with math, science, and computers. I even started taking college courses as a high school junior. When I graduated, I applied for scholarships, but there were only a limited number available and the competition was very strong. I didn't apply early enough, so I missed out on some great opportunities.

"Is this when you decided to go the military route?" Mike asked.

"Yeah. I heard the Army, if you qualified, would provide you with the training in a field of your choice. Isn't that how it goes, Mike?"

"To the best of my knowledge, that's the way it's supposed to work. But, I also know that generally the Army puts you where they need you and you don't have much choice. It seems unfair, but sometimes that's the way the system works. However, speaking strictly from my point of view, you should be told that up front so you can make an informed decision about whether or not you want to enlist."

"Well, guess what?" Nate remarked. "I told the recruiter that computers were my passion, that I was good with both hardware and software development and if I enlisted in the Army that's what I wanted to be doing.

"The recruiter told me that I first had to successfully complete ASVAB testing, and my scores would determine what I would be doing when I enlisted. I took the ASVAB cold and a series of other tests to determine my MOS. I didn't do any of the recommended study guide stuff. I just sat down and took the test cold."

Mike was studying Nate's behavior. "So what happened?" he asked.

"When I was done, the recruiter told me to go home and wait, that he would call me in a couple of days with my test scores. But the next day he called and told me that I had scored the fourth highest in the nation since the military began using the ASVAB in 1968. So, when I asked the recruiter if I would get computers, he said my MOS test scores indicated I probably had a lock on it, and that with a score like mine I could probably get into any field I wanted.

"So, the same day I went back to the recruiting office and let the recruiter know that I didn't want to go any place like Afghanistan or Iraq. He told me that with my computer skills and test results, I'd most likely get a duty assignment somewhere like Washington, D. C. He said my going to a place like Afghanistan or Iraq wasn't likely because the military was downsizing troops in those areas and retaining those with more experience. But he said all those final assignment decisions would be made only after I successfully completed basic training."

"I still don't quite understand why you're so uptight," Michael said. "It seems to me like you were getting everything you wanted."

"Okay, Mike, it went like this. I reviewed my choices for computer training, and I signed a contract when I enlisted that said I would receive training as an Information Technology Specialist involving program development and maintenance troubleshooting for computer systems. Halfway through basic training they began giving out AIT (Advanced Individual Training) assignments. They told me that I was going for nine weeks of Logistics training at Fort Sam Houston in Texas.

"When I asked my sergeant why I wasn't getting what I signed up for, he said the Army didn't have any current openings in that field. But he said I could wait a year and then put in a request for an MOS change and possibly end up where I wanted to go when I first enlisted. Or I could deliberately screw up while I was in training and get an Entry Level Separation."

"Well, Nate," Michael noted, "since you are here with an Honorable Discharge, it looks like you decided to go with the flow, right?"

"Yeah, I thought I could tough it out for a year and then go for an MOS change, into the computer field. But here's where the Army system of doing things really screwed me over. The day before we were to graduate from AIT they told me I was going to Iraq, even though the recruiter had told me I wouldn't be going to Iraq or Afghanistan. I almost went AWOL, but I kept telling myself that I'm not a quitter.

"So, I'm in Iraq running the transportation of supplies out of Baghdad in a short convoy, and the truck ahead hits an IED and almost disintegrates in front of me. The blowback and impact of that explosion hits my truck. It tore off the front end and rolled me over a few times before landing on its side. I broke my left collarbone, fractured my elbow and knee cap, and broke my left tibia and a couple of ribs. I also got a concussion, only they called it something else. I forget what it was. But now I have bouts of ringing in my ears and migraine headaches.

"At the time I had eleven months in, and I spent the next nine months in the hospital and physical rehabilitation. The last four months I got sent back to Fort Sam Houston for training in Logistics Management. I don't know why in hell the Army sent me to management school. Maybe they were thinking I would re-up or something. I wasn't buying any of it. I just wanted out."

"So what happen when you got out?" Michael asked. "Did you find a job? What have you been doing since you separated from the Army?"

"Well, just prior to my separation they had me scheduled to go through this thing called TAP, or the Transition Assistance Program, so I could learn about job search—writing cover letters and resumes and establishing a network. But I think the worst thing the Army did to me was tell me in TAP not to worry about finding a job because employers were screaming for veterans coming back from deployment.

It was supposed to be a three-day workshop, but I was so fed up with the Army that I only stayed for the first-day orientation and skipped the last two days.

"My First Sergeant wasn't too happy about my not going to the other two days, but he didn't push it. He knew I wanted out because the Army really gave me the shaft. During my last exam at the VA hospital I was diagnosed as having PTSD, so I've filed for an increase in my disability rating. I'm still waiting for an answer from the VA."

"Again, Nate, what have you been doing job-wise since you got out?"

"Like I said before, I just kicked back for a while, maybe a month or two. But during the last couple of months I've been job hunting. I work most of the way through the application process, but when I get into the interview nothing happens. Where are all those jobs they told me about in TAP—about employers wanting to hire vets?"

"Seems to me you do okay until you get to the interview. Then something happens. What do you think it is?"

"You got me," Nate quickly responded. "It's mostly their fault!"

"Am I hearing you right?" Michael asked. "Are you blaming the military because you can't get through an interview successfully?"

"Well, I guess I am. I just don't trust people with power to make good decisions on my behalf anymore."

"That's quite obvious, and what is also quite apparent is I've never seen you act friendly, even when we first met. There is a general sense of gloom and doom about you, like a dark cloud hanging over your head. You seem to be waiting to see what else can possibly go wrong."

"Can you blame me?"

"Nate, you just may be looking too somber when you enter the interview. Are you aware of that? I'm asking because people may not always remember what you say to them, but they will remember how you made them feel. You have to learn to smile once in a while so you don't turn people off."

"Who knows, I might be," Nathan said. "I don't check myself in a mirror before I go into an interview. Look, I'm a pretty intense guy, and the interview is serious business to me!"

"Yeah, I can feel the intensity and that's my point, Nate. So, what could you do to prepare for an interview that might put you in a more positive light?" Michael asked.

Nate just shrugged his shoulders and looked down for a few seconds. Then he looked back up at Michael and sat very still and adamantly silent.

When he didn't say anything, Michael replied, "Nate, I have another vet coming in for a meeting in a few minutes. How about we schedule another meeting for a week from now?"

"That works for me."

The week passed quickly and when they met again, Michael said, "Nate, to start getting you ready for job interviews, we are going to do some role-playing of a basic mock interview." Michael reached down to a lower right-hand drawer of his desk and retrieved a bright red-lacquered box, placing it on top of the desk.

The lighting overhead bounced off the box, giving it a strange but perceptible glow that cast a red tint over the top of the desk. It was about the size and construction of a cigar box with rounded corners. The top of the box was connected to the bottom by two small bright brass hinges at the back. Nate was still wearing that scowling mask on his face as he spoke. "Nice looking little box. What's it for?"

"It's for you, Nate. It holds one of the world's greatest secrets to successful interviewing."

"Are you for real, man? Now you're playing kids games with me, just like the Army with the games they played!"

"To tell you the truth, Nate, you are not in the military any longer, although the military appears to still be in you. That can be a good or a bad thing, depending on how you look at it. As you may remember, the military had to reprogram you—the way you thought and did things—so that you no longer functioned as an individual but rather as a team member. You and your fellow soldiers were taught to perform in unison without questioning the motives and directions of those in positions of authority. In many respects the civilian sector of employment can be similar."

"How's that?" Nate asked.

"The military and many civilian enterprises today continue to promote the hierarchical structure of leadership and management. Unfortunately, and all too often, it fosters what has been defined as the Organizational Man Concept of operation—those at the higher levels of the hierarchy tend to think, say, and do alike, even at the risk of supporting those in error within their ranks. This is known as the Herd Instinct Mentality.

"It's designed to protect the status quo, while those at the lower level of the structure are either ignored, reassigned, or expunged for asking questions like 'Why do you do things this way?' These lower level people are the individuals outside of the group in power, and they have little influence in the decision-making processes of the organization."

"You got that right," Nathan said, "It sounds just like where I came from!"

Michael continued, "Well, Nate, you need to consider the fact that you just re-upped. You enlisted again."

"What!"

"That's right. You just signed up for the real-live, workaday world of job search. It's diverse, competitive, and many times entrenched with the hierarchal structure of management, similar to the military.

"You'll discover that looking for a job will seem like a full-time job. It can be a gut-wrenching, energy-draining, and oftentimes disappointing experience. It involves continual self-motivation and being self-driven to make any progress—you have to be up for it every day. But guess what, there is no 'basic training' or 'boot camp' set up to reprogram you back into the civilian world.

"Actually, I think the military hasn't done a very good job with their three-day TAP program. While the military's intent is laudable, their efforts are out of sync with veteran expectations and needs, especially when it comes to employment. It takes more than a three-day program—and in many instances, more than three months—for most vets to start getting their act together, especially those who served in a combat zone.

"So, Nate, let me ask you again, how long have you been out of the military and out of work?"

"I'm going on close to nine months."

"Do you reasonably think you should have been employed by now?"

"Well, based on the number of interviews I've had, yeah, I think I should have a job by now."

"Regarding your job search, what do you think you are doing that can be classified as a positive approach to the process?"

"Well, I think I write good cover letters and resumes, obviously, since I keep getting invitations to participate in interviews. I have a strong desire to be self-sufficient and self-sustaining. I have experience and training in all of the jobs I applied for. I guess you could say I'm self-motivated because I continue to do job search."

Then Michael asked, "What do you think you aren't doing during the interview that keeps you from getting job offers?"

Nate, slouched in his chair, stared at Michael in silence. His arms were defensively folded across his chest. Finally, he said, "Looks like we're going around in circles here. I told you before that I answer all their questions, especially when they ask me to give examples of the way I handle work and possible operational situations and personal relations on the job."

"So, you think employers are genuinely impressed with the way you handle the interview?"

"Well, I mean, they seem satisfied enough with my answers because they keep nodding their heads like they are agreeing with me. Like I said before, I've been complimented by interviewers on my cover letters and resumes, and that makes me feel like my interviews are okay."

"Nate, during the introduction part of the interview, how do you establish rapport?"

"I'm not sure what you mean by rapport. An introduction is an introduction. You shake hands, say 'Hi, glad to meet ya,' and sit down."

At this point in their discussion, Michael stood up and came around his desk to where Nate was sitting. "Nate, please stand up and role-play a basic interview introduction with me."

Michael, entering his role, introduced himself by saying, "Good morning. I'm Roger Moore, Human Resource Manager for the Brown and Brown Realty Company Inc. Welcome."

Michael extended his hand. Nate shook hands while uttering the words, "Glad to be here." Then he sat down.

Michael, obviously wincing in pain from Nate's viselike grip, let his hand drop to his side. He felt as though his hand had just been slammed in a car door. He flexed his fingers until his hand stopped throbbing.

Then he said, "Wow! Nate, that was some introductory handshake! Do you always shake hands that way when meeting someone for the first time?"

"Well, a handshake is a 'man shake'—that's the way I was brought up!"

"What about in the Army when you were deployed out?"

"Okay, if you were tight with members of your team, the ones who had your back, you would do a grip and hug, a high five, or a fist bump. If you were playing ball and a teammate made a great jump shot or hit a home run, you'd give 'em a pat on the butt or a 'booty bump.'"

"What about an officer or a noncom, maybe the First Shirt, or maybe a nice-looking woman you've been introduced to that you may want to ask out on a date?"

"Nah, man, just a regular handshake."

"Why?"

"Well, because you want to make a good impression!"

"So what is the difference between a man shake and a regular handshake?"

"With the man shake you use a crusher grip, and with a regular handshake you go for just a firm grip."

"Nate, when you are doing an interview introduction, which do you use?"

"Most of the time I use a man shake. As I said, I want to create something memorable."

"Do you suppose that if you used a man shake on a person interviewing you, causing pain like you did with me, that it would result in a favorable hiring decision, as memorable as the hand shake might be? Do you think it might be perceived as overly aggressive or resentful of authority?"

Hesitantly Nate answered, "Maybe."

Studying Nate's reactions to the things he was saying to him, Michael continued by defining the art and the necessity of establishing rapport with interviewers, especially during initial introductions.

"Rapport," he indicated, "is important because it establishes a mutual common bond or trust between individuals—how people relate to each other. What one individual sends out, the other tends to send back. Thus, the ultimate goal of rapport is establishing a comfortable sameness, not submission."

"What do you mean by submission?" Nate challenged.

"Well, the intensity and manner of handshake you used with me was not only painful, but I got the sense it was a show of dominance. I noticed that when we shook hands you rotated your hand ever so slowly over the top of mine.

"Really?" Nate asked.

"Similarly," Michael pointed out, "in the canine world, especially in wolf packs, the leader or the alpha male performs what is called a 'covering movement' by placing his head and neck over the top of the head, neck, and shoulders of another male seeking membership in the pack, to test for submissiveness. Your handshake was more likely to be perceived, subliminally, as unfavorable aggressive behavior by an employer—more like a subtle attempt at intimidation or resentment rather than a gesture of appreciation or a means of developing a common bond."

"Man, you are out to lunch. Are you for real?"

Michael, unfazed by Nate's response, continued, "You want to enter into another person's comfort zone without causing apprehension and resistance. You do this through friendly facial expressions and by making eye contact. You hold that eye contact while shaking hands.

"I noticed that during our role-playing you deliberately looked down for my hand instead of looking for it in your peripheral vision while maintaining eye contact. This could intuitively be interpreted as insincerity on your part, even though you verbalized, 'Glad to be here.' It's called incongruent behavior."

"I didn't realize I was doing anything wrong," Nate said. "It's just the way I am."

"Nate, I'm not trying to play the 'gotcha game' here. I'm trying to get you to realize what it takes to create a favorable first impression. So, was there something missing in the introduction we just did? And if so, what do you think it was?'

"Obviously, something is missing or you wouldn't be asking the question."

"That's right, Nate, but it is important that you recognize what that something is or you'll continue to blow every interview that comes along. It's the one factor that holds the whole process together. It's the secret something that goes into establishing immediate rapport."

Michael pushed the red box toward Nate, who inquisitively leaned forward in his chair to gaze at it.

"Nate," Michael continued, "the secret to establishing immediate rapport and increasing your chances of a successful interview, as I said before, is in this box. But before we get to the box, I want to ask you a few more questions. They may seem a little personal. Is that all right with you?"

"I guess so. You've been doing pretty well with questions so far. I just want to see where you're going with all this."

"Nate, are you currently in a relationship with someone special in your life?"

"Yeah, well, sort of. I mean, we have been dating for a while. I really like her. My mother keeps telling me I don't deserve her because I act so discontented and irascible most of the time, ever since I got out of the Army. She says that unless I change my ways, keeping this girl happy and interested in me will be next to impossible. Mom thinks she will end up leaving me."

"So, what does your father say?"

"Well, he keeps saying I need to get my act together, get a job, get married, have kids, and move on with my life. He's right, and that's what I'm trying to do."

"Have you discussed your interview situation with the person you are dating, and what does she think?"

"Strange you should mention that. She told me a couple of weeks ago that I need to start projecting some positive energy and things will begin to change for me. She said that how I perceive myself is how other will see me. I'm still thinking about that one. All I know is that she always talks straight to me, and I really feel good when I'm around her.

"Okay, Mike," Nate went on. "I'd like to ask you something. What do all these questions have to do with job search, interviews, and building rapport with people?"

"What do you think it means, Nate?" Michael asked.

"I think you're trying to game my mind just to make a point."

"What do you think the point is?"

"That I'm unhappy and fed up with all the bullshit people are always trying to lay on me, and I'm having a problem handling it all!"

"You know what, Nate, you are absolutely right. I was wondering when you would begin to figure it out. That's exactly what I'm doing!"

"Why?"

"Okay, let me demonstrate why. Do you see that metal chair with the straight legs sitting in the corner?"

"Yeah, I see it. So what?"

"Well, Nate, I want you to go over, take hold of that chair from the back, and push it forward across the room to this desk."

"What?"

Hesitantly, Nate did as he was instructed and began to push the chair across the carpeted floor of Michael's office. He moved the chair about two feet when the front legs dug into the carpet. This caused Nate to stop abruptly.

Nate pushed the chair again, about a foot this time, before the front legs of the chair bit into the carpet again, stopping all forward movement. A look of exasperation and defiant determination crossed Nate's face, indicating he was not about to give up. As he began for the third time to push the chair, Michael told him to stop, which Nate gratefully did.

"Nate, now I want you to grab the chair again by the back. This time balance the chair on its back two legs and pull it the rest of the way to the desk."

As Nate pulled the chair it effortlessly glided across the carpet to Michael's desk.

Nate stopped at the desk and Michael said, "If you will notice, I removed the plastic glide blocks from the bottom of the chair legs so that when you aggressively began pushing the chair across the room, it kept digging into the carpet and stopped your forward progress. But when you pulled the chair balanced on its back two legs at an angle leaning toward you, it was easy to move, even though the plastic guide blocks had been removed. Why do you think it was easier to move the chair the second time?"

"Because there was no resistance and because … Oh man! Because I trusted what you said about pulling instead of pushing the chair?"

"Well, that's partly right," Michael said. "But really it's because for just a moment you weren't caught up in your own little universe. You need to understand that the Universe, outside of self, wants you to succeed and loves you, pal. But you haven't been making it easy for anyone or anything to do that. Do you think you are getting some insight here, Nate?"

"Sort of. I'm not exactly sure."

"Okay, Nate, here it is. If you enter an interview room pushing mad out in front of you, even though all of it is internal, people are still picking up on it. They'll be like that carpet and will give you what, Nate?"

"Yeah, man, resistance!"

Mike continued working with the momentum of the moment. "When we were kids, my great grandfather told us, 'If you let your mind carry a heavy burden of the past, you will continue to experience more of the same.'

"Nate, reflecting back on your military experience and recent job search, do you suppose that what my great grandfather said has any relevance to your current situation?"

"I'm not certain of anything anymore. Except, I do know one thing for sure: I don't like getting pushed around, and when I feel I'm being pushed, I want to push back. But it seems the harder I push the less likely I am to accomplish anything. Right now I'm feeling like I can't move forward with my life, and I don't want to move backward either."

There it was. The realization, faintly masked, that Michael had been waiting for as he and Nate sat back down at the desk.

"Nate, are you familiar with the sport of Judo?"

"Yeah, I watched them practicing it a few times while I was in the Army. I thought about doing it myself but then I got deployed and blown up. I'm not sure if I'm up for that right now. What's that got to do with what you're talking about?"

"Just this. My great grandfather, Taso Ishioto, was a Judoka. He was a red belt holding the Judo rank of Kudan or 9th Degree. He had his own Dojo (practice hall) where he taught the martial art. Before he passed on I used to practice with him. I was one of his students, and I eventually got to the rank of San Dan, 3rd Degree Black Belt. He always instilled in us that Judo was not just a sport or martial art but also a way of living.

"As a matter of fact Judo is called the 'Gentle Art.' In the beginning I was always after the win. I was very aggressive on the mat, always pushing and pulling an opponent hard. But I was never too successful in executing a successful throw or technique. I wasn't very gentle. I had a very shameful attitude about wanting to rise up in the Judo ranks, from beginner to Black Belt where I would command respect as a superior Judoka. One day my great grandfather took me aside and told me that I needed to learn how to give way to gain the advantage. He taught me Tomoe Nage, or 'Circle Throw.'

"What's that?" Nate asked.

"If you have ever watched fight scenes in the movies, it's where the good guy is backing up while the bad guy advances or pushes, and the good guy suddenly sits down, puts his foot in the bad guy's stomach, lies back, and at the same time pulls the bad guy over his head, landing him on his back. It's the art of using the other guy's strength against himself. It's acting in a submissive manner, or giving way, in order to gain the advantage. Rather than resist, or pushing back, the pressure or energy being applied to you, it is possible to meld with that flow of force or energy and redirect it to your own advantage."

"Okay, so I get the Judo thing. You never made it to the same rank as your grandfather. What's that got to do with interviews and my getting a job?"

Michael patiently smiled. He knew what was about to happen and explained, "Before my grandfather left this world, he said, 'Michael, I see that you have mastered the art of giving way to gain the advantage. Your Tome Nage is perfection. You have learned not to push so hard in life for something you strongly desire. As I have told you, follow the flow of Universal Energy and what you desire will be yours.' A few weeks later he passed away, and after the burial ceremony, we went out to sea and scattered his ashes over the ocean's surface. When I returned home I found an envelope on top of my dresser next to my great grandfather's picture. It contained one of the many Zen proverbs he was fond of quoting:

"'When you seek it, you cannot find it.
Your hand cannot reach it,
nor your mind exceed it.
When you no longer seek it,
it is always with you.'

"So, here's the last question, Nate. How can you tell when a person is generally happy and appears content with their life situation? What two signs, gestures, or behaviors do they most often outwardly exhibit?"

"I don't have the slightest clue, man!"

"Okay, Nate, here's a clue, and it's the secret to building rapport, having a successful interview, learning to give way to gain the advantage and going with the flow of universal energy that everyone responds to, without exception. This is especially true for children."

Michael lightly pushed the red box toward Nate and said, "Before you raise the lid of this box to discover the secret, I want you to do two things for me."

"What's that?"

"I want you to raise your eyebrows as high as you can, as though you are happily surprised, and give me a big smile!"

"Mike, you got to be kidding. I can't do that. I don't feel like smiling."

"Nate, just this one time fake it till you make it. Trust me. It will change your life for the better."

Michael watched intently as Nate hesitantly reached out for the lid of the box with a nothing-to-lose, Oh-what-the-hell grin on his face. The lid now fully open, the light from inside the box instantly reflected outward, fully illuminating Nate's face. That stupid smile turned into a look of astonishment, the mind and the body struggling to maintain composure.

A muted sound, like an afterthought, of stifled laughter caught in Nate's throat. Then, a moment of frozen silence—an unstoppable stark realization of self-truth. The earth had moved off its axis, wobbling now, fighting the imbalance of emotion taking over. He watched himself in the mirror attached to the inside of the box's cover, tearing up while attempting to regain the smile, more genuine than before. Finally, raucous laughter and weeping. "I get it, man, I get it! It's a kid's thing, but I get it!"

"Yeah, it's sort of a kid's thing, but sometimes it takes the simplicity of a child's belief, imagination, and creativity to function and succeed in the job search environment as a consenting contributor to and participant in your own progress. It's all about doing the simple things in life," replied Michael.

Nate withdrew a hanky from his back pocket, wiped his face, and blew his nose hard, until the pressure in his ears subsided. Then he asked, "Why the mind of a child when I'm an adult?"

"Because," Michael said, "a child's mind hasn't been exposed to and totally corrupted by negative influences and experiences like the minds of adults. A kid's mind is still fresh, pliable, and open to an anything-is-possible world.

"I've discovered that vets progress more quickly toward their employment goals and in their personal lives if they maintain an open, inquisitive, humble, and unfettered mind, like that of a child. Bottom line, we would all do well at times to practice emulating the creativity of a child to resolve some of the conflicts and problems we as adults seem to create for ourselves, as you've just experienced."

Nate took a deep breath and slowly let the air out through pursed lips. Then he asked, "Okay, Mike, where do we go from here?"

They shook hands. Nate was smiling and shaking his head in apparent wonder. They both started laughing.

"That was really unexpected," Nate offered.

"No, it wasn't," Mike answered. "Today you just got a whole lot closer to getting hired, but we still have a little ways to go. Hang in there, pal. You're almost there."

The following week Michael reviewed with Nate the critical need for being logistically and psychologically prepared for the interview. He began by defining these terms:

Logistical Preparation – The ability to manage the details of an undertaking or self-initiated function or event as it applies to job search and the interview. (**Example**: doing employer research; composing and sending out a cover letter and resume; familiarizing yourself with the date, time, and location of the interview; remembering to compose and bring questions to ask the employer; reviewing the job description in order to answer employer questions intelligently; selecting clothes to be worn, etc.)

Psychological Preparation – The ability to develop and maintain the proper mental attitude or enhancing/supportive thoughts that elevate or preserve self-esteem, confidence, and enthusiasm for generating a positive outcome.

(**Example**: seeing yourself entering the interview room and getting through the introduction with an impressive, warm smile; solid eye contact and a glad-to-be-here handshake; responding to interview questions in a manner that impresses the employer; hearing the words, "When can you start?")

Nate commented, "It seems like a lot of extra steps just to get an interview, to say nothing of getting through one that results in a job offer. But then again, I had no idea that there was more to interviewing than just showing up, and I guess getting lucky."

"Well, Nate, just so you know, completing a successful interview that results in a job offer has nothing to do with luck. It all has to do with being prepared. Think about what brought you here in the first place and the major barrier you broke last week. What do you believe that was all about? Was that luck?" Michael asked.

There was a long pause as Nate digested the question. The extended silence became a deafening roar in his ears, forcing him to finally speak. "I guess I was mad at the world and resisted the fact that I'm responsible for how things will turn out in my life."

Michael continued, "Nate, your willingness to look inside yourself and recognize the need for change will serve you well as you move forward on your job search journey. I've dealt with a number of vets who resist making the necessary changes to move on with their lives. A lot of them are still out there doing job search. Their biggest obstacle is a self-destructive indifference. They're still asking questions like, 'What's the big deal about preparing for an interview?'

"Human nature being what it is, we have a tendency to follow the path of least resistance when it comes to the process of preparing for an interview. I can't count the number of times I've heard the comment, 'It's only a job.' Well, the big deal is this: if it's just another JOB, and that's all you want, fine. But, if you are after a career or a real opportunity that will make a difference in your life, then it is not just another JOB. It's your future, and your ATTITUDE determines the outcome."

Nate interrupted, "Yeah, but suppose you do have negative thoughts like that? We all have them from time to time. I should know; I've had a few. Nobody can tell what you are thinking."

"Don't fool yourself, Nate. Even if you don't say it out loud, but you think 'It's no big deal, I'll find a JOB sooner or later,' that kind of attitude eventually will reflect your demeanor—give you away. As I believe you are beginning to realize, a job offer could be coming a lot later rather than sooner if you continue the way you have in the past.

"Just keep in mind that if you are mentally unprepared, most employers and HR people will know. These people who do interviews for a living are very quick to pick up on body language, general attitude, the way you answer questions, and the tone of your voice—they can read you like a book. This is especially true if you habitually bring emotional baggage with you into the interview."

"Well, that's kind of hard to avoid sometimes, don't you think?"

"Making a habit of preparing yourself logistically and psychologically for every interview you go to ensures that more often than not you will be in the *zone*. Just "*clearing the mechanism*" and focusing on the objective in front of you, eliminating all intervening and distracting thoughts that might keep you from doing what you need to do.

"Planning ahead means developing focus and being prepared to address three basic questions generally on every employer's mind, even though they may never verbalize them: 'Why should we hire you?', 'What can you do for us?' and 'Will you fit in?'"

"Wait a minute," Nate interrupted again. "What do you mean by 'being in the zone' and 'clearing the mechanism'?"

"Nate, have you ever watched the 1999 movie *For Love of the Game*? It stared Kevin Costner as Billy Chapel, the pitcher for the

Detroit Tigers, and he's pitching the last series of games for the season in Yankee Stadium."

"I'm not sure," Nate said. "Is that the movie about the guy who has all those problems with his girlfriend and her daughter, and he cuts himself with a skill saw and screws up his pitching hand and his arm, and he's in pain all the time and is thinking about ending his twenty-year baseball career?"

"You got it; that's the one," Michael acknowledged. "Well, it's the bottom of the ninth inning, with two outs with a man at bat. But throughout the game he has been reflecting about the problems he has with his girlfriend, his aching arm, and the fact that he is probably pitching his last game. His team wants to end the game with a shutout, yet he's been dragging his personal baggage with him all afternoon into early evening, even into the dugout between innings.

"Billy doesn't realize it, but in spite of the baggage he's been pitching a perfect game. Everyone on the team is aware of it except Billy. It's the one shining moment of a very marginal and dismal season for the Detroit Tigers. Billy's friend, the catcher Gus Sinski, calls time-out, walks to the mound, and says to Billy, 'The boys are all here for you, we'll back you up, we'll be there 'cause, Billy, we don't stink right now. We're the best team in baseball right now, right this minute, because of you. You're the reason. We're not going to screw that up. We're going be awesome for you right now. Just throw!'

"In the background, Yankee fans are booing as Billy begins to toe the rubber and catches himself again with his mind not in the game. He steps back, plagued by competing thoughts and the pain in his shoulder and arm. We hear him thinking to himself, 'God, I always said I would never bother you about baseball because always seemed silly. But if you could make this pain in my shoulder stop for ten minutes ...' This is Billy's trick for concentration, to 'be in the zone, clear the mechanism.' And after that he delivers three strikes in a row for a perfect game."

When Michael finished, Nate smiled and said, "Looks like I've never totally been in the game—in the *zone*, so to speak—and *clearing the mechanism* means I need to forget about the past and concentrate on and prepare for what's in front of me now."

Michael told Nate he had finally arrived. "Everything you have done thus far in your job search has all been focused upon accomplishing one major function, or outcome: completing an interview resulting in a job offer. This also entails considering the answers to a number of critical questions you ask yourself that ultimately will determine the outcome of your interviews in the future."

Michael provided Nate with the list of following questions, which they reviewed together:

1. Did I research the employer I'm interviewing with? What do I know about the product or service the employer provides?

2. If I'm inexperienced, out of practice, or discover that I have the wrong attitude about the interviewing process, did I research available self-help texts and/or seek advice or counseling from a qualified person about how to interview and what to expect?

3. Am I open to practicing my interview skills with someone interested in helping me to succeed (e.g. participate in mock interviews)? If I am unable to find someone to practice interviewing with, am I willing to watch interview training scenarios such as those presented on YouTube or on the Internet?

4. Am I familiar with some of the following different types of interview questions being used by both private and government employers?

   - **Credential verification questions** – If you have academic training, this type of question might include "What was your GPA?" or "How long were you at (name of school)?" Also known as resume verification questions. Its purpose is to objectively verify the depth of knowledge of the credentials or experience in your background.

   - **Experience verification questions** – This type of question includes "What did you learn in your previous job?" or

"What were your responsibilities in that position?" Its purpose is to subjectively evaluate features of your background.

- **Opinion questions** – This type of question includes "What would you do in this situation?" or "What are your strengths and weaknesses?" Its purpose is to subjectively analyze how you would respond in a work-oriented situation.

- **Behavioral questions** – This type of question includes "Would you please provide an example of how you did that?" or "What were the steps you took to accomplish the task and what was the outcome?" Its purpose is to objectively measure past behaviors as a predictor of future results.

- **Competency questions** – This type of question includes "Can you give me a specific example of your leadership skills?" or "Explain a way in which you sought a creative solution to a problem." Its purpose is to review past behaviors that reveal your competency for the position you have applied for.

- **Brainteaser questions** –This type of question includes anything from "What is 1000 divided by 73?" to "How many ping pong balls could fit in a Volkswagen?" to complex algorithms. Its purpose is to evaluate not only your mental math calculation skills but also your ability to create the mathematical formula necessary to provide an answer (or estimate, as may be the case).

- **Case questions** – This category includes problem-solving questions ranging from: "How many gas stations are there in Europe?" to "What is your estimate of the global online retail market for books?" Its purpose is to evaluate your problem-solving abilities and to show how you analyze and work through potential case situations.

- **Dumb questions** – This type of question includes "What kind of animal would you like to be?" and "What color best describes you?" Its purpose is to get past your pre-programmed answers to find out if you are capable of an original thought. There is not a right or wrong answer, since it is used primarily to test your ability to think on your feet.

5. Am I confident I can meet the employer's expectations of performance? In other words, have I thoroughly reviewed the employer's job description, required qualifications, and expectations for performance?

6. If the job description was sparse, and I am in doubt as to what is required to perform the job, have I taken the time to research job titles and descriptors using U.S. Department of Labor online references such as OOH (Occupational Outlook Handbook), O' Net (Occupational Information Network) and SOC (Standard Occupational Classification System)? Or did I bother to make contact with people who actually do the work in order to become better informed?

7. Do I rely on my cover letter and resume as the primary source of applying for the job, rather than recognizing them for what they really are—a marketing and advertising tool designed to generate employer interest in offering an interview? Do I fully understand that a job offer doesn't usually occur until the interview?

8. A day or two before the interview, did I contact the employer to confirm the date and time of the interview?

9. Did I take the time and trouble to determine exactly where (the physical location) the interview will be conducted? Does the time I'm planning for the commute and parking allow me to arrive at least fifteen minutes before the interview?

10. Did I develop a few focused questions to ask the employer that demonstrate my desire to become an asset to and a contributing member of the organization?

Once they completed reviewing the list, Michael scheduled Nate for their next meeting. "Nate," he said, "I think you are about ready to return to the real world of job search. We have maybe one or two meetings left, but I just want you to know you've made great progress, pal, and you ought to be proud of yourself. We'll see you next week."

A few days later, Michael met with his partner, Local Veterans Employment Representative Sam Flowers, and they decided to get Nate involved in doing a mock interview.

They contacted Richard Fellows, HR Manager for Regional Logistics Inc., whom they had used before to do mock interviews with other veterans. Since Nate had a background in the handling and transportation of materials and manpower, they felt it was an ideal fit for him.

Nate came in for his scheduled meeting. Michael advised him that it would be beneficial to practice utilizing some of the interviewing and demeanor skills he had been exposed to over the past few weeks. For that reason, Michael had arranged for Nate to attend a mock interview with a local employer on Friday morning.

Nate, a little taken aback by his mentor's surprise announcement, asked, "Hey, Mike, how many of these mock interviews do I have to do before I get to do the real thing?"

"Nate, just get through this one. Let me know what happens and we'll go from there. Actually, as far as the real thing goes, I think you're ready to fly on your own, but before you do I'm thinking a little practice wouldn't hurt.

"As a matter of fact, most successful candidates I know have practiced before an interview, even if it was just sitting quietly and visualizing the interview as it plays out, including being offered a job. It's all part of the interview preparation process."

Michael concluded by saying, "So, give me a call after the interview and let me know how you think it went."

On Friday afternoon, when Michael had not had any word from Nate, he called Richard Fellows. "Richard, this is Michael. I'm just calling to find out how Nathan Stores did in the mock interview you had with him this morning. He hasn't called me yet to let me know how things turned out."

"I'm not surprised," Fellows replied. "I think he was in somewhat of a state of shock when he left here this morning, although he tried hard not to show it."

"What are you talking about? Was he rude? Did he lose his temper?" Michael anxiously inquired.

"Quite the contrary," Fellows replied. "He aced the interview. He was fifteen minutes early and dressed to the nines: spit-shined shoes, white shirt, tie, clean shaven and all. For a mock interview your man was over the top, especially with his winning smile, his firm but very businesslike handshake, and his eye contact. It gave us a sense of his sincerity. He answered all our questions regarding logistics operations and how closely our operations matched his background and training. And he asked a few very pointed questions about opportunities for making contributions to our organization. He also asked for a tour of our facilities, which really impressed us."

"Outstanding," Michael said.

Mr. Fellows continued, "One of our interview panel members asked Nathan if he thought he was a bit overdressed for a semi-professional job, that of managing a team of warehouse workers in a challenging work environment. We were blown away by his answer. He said, 'I just wanted to show that I was prepared, but most of all I dressed like this to show respect for the employer who took time out of his busy day to discuss with me the possibilities of employment with his company.'"

"Incredible," Michael said. "Just totally, unexpectedly incredible!"

Richard Fellows ended their conversation by saying, "Although this was supposed to be a mock interview, you need to know that the company has been in the planning stages of creating a new position, Coordinator of Logistics Operations, to handle our company's continuous growth.

"We hadn't considered recruiting for the position yet, but Nathan's positive attitude and on-target suggestions of how we might improve our operations and meet our clients demand for increased services provided us with an opportunity we just could not afford to pass up. So, we offered him the job, and he accepted. He starts next Monday."

VOYAGER BASICIS

In many instances veterans, as well as their nonveteran counterparts in the civilian world, believe that an interview is just another perfunctory step in the job search process and preparation for it isn't critical. Yes, and very often they all bring with them real or imagined emotional baggage that tends to impede their progress as a viable and worthy candidate. Just know that the harboring of past failures, fears, and resentment most certainly can negatively impact a candidate's interview outcome.

So, if the mind carries a heavy burden of negative experiences, one can expect to receive more of the same, usually perpetuated by a lack of awareness and preparation. Therefore a person needs clarity of thought to determine what life situation, if any, is presently (OCCURING RIGHT NOW, THIS MOMENT IN TIME) a barrier to a successful interview.

Note that taking time to prepare for an interview can lead to considerable mental "what if-ing." Most candidates don't enjoy being interviewed—there's a genuine fear of self-disclosure, which, after all, is what an interview is all about.

Preparing for something you're afraid of can be a daunting, difficult, and debilitating task. However, the wisdom of an old Chinese proverb may have some merit when it comes to overcoming interview anxiety: "Do that which you fear the most and you will no longer fear it."

In this regard, the value of mock interviews cannot be overstated or overrated, even for the more experienced candidate.

Generally speaking, this is one of the reasons for the illusion that good resumes get jobs—people would like to place their hopes on the resume rather than the interview. Sending out a resume isn't as frightening as sitting down with an interviewer face-to-face.

BUT ... good resumes are a crucial element of interview preparation —they are designed to get an interview, not to replace it.

Contrary to what many candidates believe, it's not the length and amount of time involved in preparing for an interview but rather the focus, quality of thought, and activity engaged in that determines the outcome.

The following considerations will help you to be well prepared for a successful interview:

1. The primary and most critical factor many employers look for in candidates during an interview is not previous experience, outstanding skills, or academic accomplishment. Yes, those all contribute to getting a candidate to the interview. But being totally prepared can only be accomplished if a candidate approaches the interview with the right attitude or mindset. It's the one characteristic employers instinctively pursue and value the most that distinguishes one candidate from another.

2. The best way for a candidate to demonstrate preparedness and a winning attitude is to include words and phrases that are inclusive, such as, "Our team," "We organized," "Accomplished," "Assisted others," "Demonstrated a willingness to," etc. Being prepared requires giving examples of making an effort to go beyond what generally is expected (e.g. contributing to and/or making improvements in a process or procedure, or beating a deadline).

3. There will be times when a candidate has conducted some basic or preliminary research of an organization or employer prior to the interview, and is of the belief they are now prepared. However, such belief may be farther from the truth than the candidate realizes. Thorough research of an organization leads to a better interview outcome.

4. It is important for the candidate to understand that if they are after their "dream job," then no amount of focused preparation

is too much. And it doesn't matter if it's an entry-level ("a foot in the door") career opportunity or a career-advancing move. One of the best sources of interview preparation information will be someone who is an insider—someone already working for the company or organization the candidate is applying to. Locating someone a candidate can connect with is an important element of the interview preparation process.

Preferably, your contact should be at your approximate level of skill and experience. Such a person understands the challenges you might face in the position for which you have applied, and can help as you prepare for the interview and the job.

5. An ideal starting place for finding a contact is your own network of friends, fellow veterans you have served with, or other business acquaintances—taking the time to seek out and ask if they know anyone employed at the prospective employer's place of business can pay big dividends.

6. In instances where personal network referrals are not possible, the candidate should consider some in-depth employer research as to company history. Become familiar with products or services offered, company officials and types of specialists in various fields, departments and divisions of the organization.

7. An excellent source of organizational information is the annual report. It may contain a comment or two from the chief executive officer or the company's president regarding recent accomplishments and future plans.

8. Other good sources of information are the local chamber of commerce, the local office of economic and community development, various local business-promoting organizations, colleges, and the Internet.

9. Again, this whole process of seeking out information about an employer, a business or organization, or anyone or any subject

is called research. And, any applicant or candidate for interview who desires to become successful in the job search process (e.g., interview preparation) must be willing to do the research.

10. The source, amount, and quality of the research conducted is limited only by the candidate's imagination, ingenuity, and creativity. If the research is thorough enough, the applicant might even be considered an insider at the interview. Having knowledge that only a small percentage of the business community knows, and that an even smaller percentage of other candidates and company employees are aware of, could prove to be a distinct advantage over the competition.

11. Regardless of what method is used to identify and locate a company contact, an applicant needs to consider doing the following:

- Identify and contact a potential company insider far enough in advance of the interview to allow time for scheduling and preparation.

- Ensure that enough research has been done so the contact person will not have to provide all the minor details about the company the applicant should already know.

- Generate questions about the person or individuals who usually conduct interviews to ascertain their likes and dislikes and what piques their interest and what turns them off.

- Inquire about the company and its primary focus or method of doing business, profitability issues, quality control, operational improvements, the status of the company in the global and domestic marketplace, and the personal development of its employees.

- Ask about the interview process itself—the basic steps involved.

• See yourself proceeding through the interview—addressing questions put to you by the interviewer is the art of preparation known as visualization. The process of seeing yourself in such a positive light is an important element in developing and maintaining the right mental attitude while preparing for and continuing throughout the entire interview process.

12. Rehearsing in your mind beforehand what you will say and do is preparatory to successfully performing it. In many instances, once we have trained ourselves to visualize beforehand what we intend to do, it becomes an instinctive and intuitive process—applicable to just about any life situation leading to a successful outcome.

Such practice when done in conjunction with a mock interview really can put a candidate in a position of advantage over competitors. Even without a mock interview, visualization stands alone as one of the most powerful tools in man's quest for success.

There are many examples throughout history of man's endeavors that speak to this very powerful tool. A very revealing example involves a martial arts master who was famous for de-horning fighting bulls and killing them in the bull ring with nothing but his bare hands.

When asked what the secret was to his skill and strength, he indicated he had rehearsed the event many times in his head before actually doing it. He remarked, "And when it was time to face the beast, at the moment of truth, I saw myself doing the act an instant before it was done. It is as though I have already completed the task."

Every interview candidate has access to this tool and the ability to use it to his or her advantage, but only if they will take time to consider it.

13. There is tremendous power to be gained once candidates are able to understand the way they mentally approach confronta-

tional and challenging life situations. It can positively or negatively limit the content of what they think about themselves preparing for and going into an interview.

The very process of preparation in a step-by-step manner can become an internalizing self-image builder focused on success.

As those who study human behavior tell us, there is often a difference between how we see ourselves, how we perceive others see us, and how we really are.

This dichotomy of self-imagery can change once a candidate realizes they are capable of developing and presenting an acceptable view of themselves through the validation of others.

Once a candidate generates an idea about how things should be, and when that idea is supported by others, it is as though the candidate is able to predict and determine a positive outcome. Bottom line, as a candidate changes his or her self-image and beliefs, so changes the results.

As a side note, it is important to understand, in this author's opinion, there is a distinct difference between an applicant and a candidate. Although these terms have been used interchangeably by HR managers and recruiters for decades, they tend to generate some confusion among job seekers regarding their status as it applies to being considered for employment.

For clarity's sake, an applicant is someone attempting to get the attention of an employer through the submission of a document of application or resume, with a more distant scope and limited proximity of influence that involves a larger field of undetermined qualified competitors, requiring preparation.

A candidate is someone selected to participate in a limited and closer proximity of influence among a narrower field of highly qualified competitors, called an interview, requiring more intense preparation.

Therefore, when preparing for an interview, a candidate should consider selecting someone willing to provide strategic constructive criticism and vocalizing support, such as in a post-mock interview analysis that indicates the candidate is qualified and the best person for the job.

By using this approach it is anticipated the candidate will come to accept it and more likely to visualize themselves in a very positive light.

Note: One of the secrets to successfully preparing for an interview is seeking the support of others as you work to become focused and confident.

14. Adequate preparation can also provide candidates with the ability to convince an employer that they are the right individual for the position. Belief in oneself is crucial to the selling of oneself during the interview.

15. The only way for a candidate to really be articulate and convincing is through practice. The ideal practice involves a mock interview with a person skilled in the interview process, such as a career counselor or a job search development/placement specialist. With the continued advancement of a rapidly changing job market, counselors have become busy people who are always in demand.

    Note: When making an appointment, the candidate preparing for an interview must be willing to adjust their schedule to fit that of the counselor's, especially when a counselor is willing to work with a candidate free of charge.

    Many counselors and career coaches, when conducting mock interviews, use videotaping of the process as a self-instructional learning aid for the candidate.

    Videotaping enables the candidate to experience immediate feedback, revealing strong and weak interviewing skills. It allows for more than just one opinion about what actually occurred during the process—that of the interviewer and that of the person interviewed, each with a different view of how the interview went.

Quite often there's a big difference between how a candidate thinks they came off during an interview and how they actually appeared. It's not usual for a candidate viewing their performance on tape for the first time to respond with, "I can't believe I said and did that!" This is the best way to improve your interview performance—by reviewing both what you did wrong and what you did right, and then implementing necessary changes.

When time permits, repeated videotaping can bring out the best in any candidate who is willing to learn, to be objective, and most of all to invest the time. But, whether or not a videotape is used, there is still real value to be obtained from even one mock interview.

A candidate would do well to consider that the real difference between a successful interview and a mediocre one is the amount of practice or review that precedes a job interview. Conducting mock interviews, especially with a professional, always pays huge dividends.

16. For today's veteran, professional career counselors and job search specialists are as close as your local American Job Center.
    Note: For veterans, your local AJC is the place where counselors specifically trained to serve veterans are located. The big plus here is that most of these counselors are veterans themselves, and most are able to quickly make that all-important positive connection in providing meaningful assistance to a veteran.

17. An alternative to actual participation in a mock interview is reviewing the mock interviews of others online. The drawback is that you can't get personal feedback; still, the value of viewing others being interviewed is undeniable.

    Go to any web browser, like Google, and enter the following: *Mock Interview Training and Review YouTube.*

    The point is that some kind of practice or dress rehearsal should always be performed in preparation for the reality of an employment interview. Without it, a veteran candidate has a high probability of going into an interview and performing in a cold and stiff manner. Think of interview practice as preparation for running a race—all long-distance runners know that failure to warm up and stretch before a race begins significantly decreases their chances of being competitive, and increases the probability of injury and the inability to complete the event.

18. Most of the books written on the interview process usually provide a list of the types of questions that may be asked, along with suggested answers that might be given in response. While it can prove beneficial to review and understand such questions and answers, keep in mind that many employers are primarily interested in whether or not a candidate can adequately address the following four basic concerns:
    - Are you qualified and/or can you learn to do the job?
    - Why should I hire you over other qualified or willing candidates?
    - Will you fit in?
    - Are you dependable?

Q&A CONSIDERATIONS

Employers tend to follow a specific pattern of inquiry, and a candidate's responses to those questions help the employer determine whether the candidate will genuinely be a fit for their organization. The questions help employers become acquainted with the job performance, personality, and character of the candidate. They include behavioral questions and "off-the-wall," stress-loaded questions which are often unscripted. The following are but a few examples of questions and answers that require only a short response or moderate summarization:

Q: "Tell me (us) about yourself."

A: *The employer does not want to know about your family tree or your whole employment history, but do provide enough information to keep the interviewer interested. For example: "With over seven years* *of marketing-related experience in designing and conducting public re-lations and business promotions events, I am confident I can hit the ground running and make [our] marketing program very profitable."*

Q: "What do you think is the most valuable contribution you can make to our organization (program)?"

A: *"My whole focus is to accomplish whatever task is assigned. Although I'm no workaholic, I do bring with me a work ethic that fo-cuses on a willingness to do whatever it takes to get the job done, in-cluding collaborative efforts with members in my department and organization-wide."*

Q: "Why do you want to work for this company?"

A: *With this kind of question, the employer wants to know if you are merely looking for a job, or if you are really interested in a career oppor-tunity with the company where you can make valuable contributions. A focused response is required: "I have been very selective in choosing a company in which [we] share common values and work ethic principles. Your company is one of my top choices."*

Q: "Where do you see yourself in the next three to five years?"

A: *With this inquiry, the employer wants to determine whether you are capable of setting goals for yourself. Also, if the employer is to make an investment in your training and advancement, he wants to know whether you intend to stick around for a while. So, consider respond-ing this way: "My immediate goal is to obtain a career opportunity that promotes both business and professional growth. My long-term goal will depend upon where this company is in the next three to five years. My primary focus is on becoming a contributing member of the company through projects and assignments with increasing responsibilities and trust."*

Q: What kind of work satisfies you the most?"

A: *The employer in this instance is interested in a candidate's mo-tivation—identifying what it is that gets you excited enough to deliver above-average performance consistently. A candidate faced with this* *kind of behavioral question should consider providing an example of an identified work-related problem using the STAR Method:*

- *S [Situation] – Describe the situation you were involved in or the task that you needed to accomplish. You should describe a specific event or situation; do not generalize about what you've done in the past. Be sure to provide enough detail for the interviewer to understand. The situation can be from a previous job, from a volunteer experience, or any relevant event.*

- *T [Task] – What goal were you working toward? What needed to occur for you to be successful?*

- *A [Action taken] – Describe what action you initiated. Be sure to focus on what you did and how it impacted efforts of the team, if one was involved. Avoid indicating what you might do; explain what you did do.*

- *R [Results achieved] – What was the outcome? How did the event end? Describe what you accomplished and what you learned from your experience.*

Q: "What do you think makes you stand out from the other candidates we've interviewed?"

A: *With this kind of question, the employer is looking to determine how you perceive your own capabilities. Here you will need to quickly present in a concise and convincing manner your experience, skills, and abilities as they apply to the position for which you are interviewing.*

Example: "I have what I consider to be critical technical knowledge and skills, as well as the ability to connect with people very quickly. I simplify technical information into easy-to-digest portions for others. I encourage questions from others in order to establish an ongoing exchange of ideas and information. This allows me to learn something new."

Q: "If you were a chef, what kind of meal would you prepare that best exemplifies who you are?"

A: *This question is designed to help the employer determine how adaptive and creative you are—how well you think on your feet. Can you respond intelligently and remain on target with your answer? Are you focused?*

So, consider the following response: "I enjoy fancy dishes occasionally, but really, I'm a meat-and-potatoes kind of person. The simpler and more basic it is, the more I enjoy the meal."

Keep in mind that with this kind of question, there is no correct or ideal answer. It's how you see yourself in connection with what it takes to get the job done.

Q: "What do you think your previous employers will have to say about you?"

A: *An employer asking this question is seeking confirmation of your ability to get along with superiors and be a top performer.*

This is the time for you to demonstrate how you feel about your own capabilities, accomplishments, and relationship-building skills that have helped you earn the respect of fellow workers and ranking members of your unit or department.

This is the time to "beat your own drum" and "toot your own horn," but in a positive and pleasing manner.

Example: "They will tell you that whenever I've been involved in a project or given a specific work assignment, it has always been completed according to specifications and ahead of schedule." Or ...

"My previous employer will say that I left my department in better shape than I found it in when I first started." Or ...

"My supervisor will say I'm easy to approach, I get along with everyone, I'm good at asking work-related questions, and I have a good sense of humor—that I was serious about doing a good job but didn't take myself too seriously."

Q: "What are your salary expectations?"

A: *Salary or wage considerations are almost always reserved for the final stages of the hiring process. Sometimes discussed in a second in-*

terview or in a separate negotiation meeting, this subject is most often broached during an initial interview as it nears its conclusion.

Salary should always be initiated by the employer. Keep in mind that a candidate will have the advantage if he or she can get the employer to provide a salary range first.

Since the name of the game is Interview Preparation, a veteran candidate should already have a good idea of what someone in the applied-for position is paid by doing the research first. Candidates have the advantage when they come to an interview knowing what they would be willing to accept salary-wise, should they want to negotiate with the employer when the subject comes up.

When there is no offer of employment on the table, the following responses, or something similar, should be considered:

A) "To give you a figure that we can both agree upon, I'd like to ask, what do you generally pay someone with my skills and background?" Or ...

B) "Is this a new position, and what did you have in mind salary-wise when it was created?" Or ...

C) "Are you making an offer of employment providing we can agree upon a beginning salary?" Or ...

D) If the employer does initially state a figure and it is below the bottom figure you were willing to accept, the following response may be very appropriate: "Based upon my background and experience, I had a figure in mind between (give the low and the high amount). I believe I'm a good fit for the position, and it's the kind of career opportunity I've been looking for." Or ...

"I'm open to accepting your offer, but with the understanding that after three to six months, when you've had an opportunity to see how I perform, the door is left open for further salary consideration."

E) Consider another scenario: You apply for an entry-level position even though your experience, training, and education exceed the *requirements. The employer recognizes you are overqualified, but he is locked into a beginning salary and doesn't want to negotiate. However, you still view the job as a viable opportunity. The following response may be considered as a means of getting your foot in the front door:*

"To be truthful, I considered my qualifications when I applied, but the way I look at it is, either I'm qualified or I'm not. While income is an important factor, my focus right now is on career-building and not just on a JOB. I want to learn and make valuable contributions that result in a long-term commitment to a company where I can find opportunities for advancement and personal growth."

CAUTION!!! *Do not get into this kind of response when interviewing with an employer if you are unwilling to accept a lower salary and/or you are unwilling to make long-term commitments.*

Q: "Before we conclude this interview, do you have any questions you want to ask?"

A: *Please take note, there are three basic rules that successful candidates follow in response to this question:*

Rule #1 – Never say "No." Always be prepared to ask a few questions.

Rule #2 – Never ask about salary or benefits if it has not been put on the table for discussion.

Rule #3 – Never offer more than three or four questions, due to possible interviewer time constraints, but do ask the right ones.

Once the employer has opened the door, walk through it boldly and really shine with the kind of quality questions that give the employer a reason to hire you.

Remember, although a candidate may be one of several to be considered for hire, the advantage goes to the candidate who asks presumptive questions—acting as though a job offer is imminent or has already been made (e.g. acting as if he or she is already on the job), by using inclusive terms like "we," "us," "our," "team," and "collaborative effort," etc.

This approach can quickly make a positive impression on the employer by showcasing a candidate's self-confidence and genuine interest in the employer's organization.

Note: There is a difference between being "presumptive" (providing reasonable grounds for belief) and being "presumptuous" (acting too bold or forward, taking too much for granted).

The following are examples of the type of questions that might be asked by a candidate (within the three to four questions limit):

Q: "What kind of training and support can I expect to receive as an employee?"

This kind of question lets the employer know you are interested in growing into the job, enabling you to make contributions to the employer's business or the organization's operations.

Q: "What are you looking for in the way of performance from the person you select to fill this position?"

A question like this will help to solidify expectations of performance beyond what has been covered in a job announcement or statement of required qualifications. It lets the employer know of your sincerity about doing a good job.

Q: "What is the most significant attribute you look for in an employee in carrying out the responsibilities of this position?"

As a worthy candidate, you are saying to the employer, "I'm very interested in knowing what it takes to succeed and get the job done."

Q: "Could you describe the other members of the team (or department) I'd be working with?"

With this question the candidate lets the employer know he or she is a team player and knows how to get along with others—more commonly referred to as "making a good fit."

Q: "Would it be possible for me to get a tour of your business operation (or facility)?"

In this instance the candidate is showing the employer they would be a "hands-on" employee. Again, the candidate is demonstrating an interest in the employer's business, beyond it being merely just another JOB.

Because it is an investment in time and effort to give a candidate a tour and to introduce him or her to various employees, an employer's willingness to do so may indicate a high interest in the candidate. The candidate can know they have a higher probability of being hired.

Q: "When can I expect to hear from you regarding a hiring decision?"

This question serves to remind the employer not to delay in making an offer if you are seriously being considered. Employers (e.g. hiring managers) know that most savvy candidates will continue to conduct a job search until there is a bona fide offer of employment on the table. It's all a matter of common courtesy and of making decisions in a timely manner.

Q: "When would you like me to start?"

NOTE: This question requires some boldness, and some risk, on the part of the candidate. But when used properly and strategically, it puts the employer on notice that you are serious and eager to become part of the organization. However, to achieve its maximum effect this question has to be staged—like the delivery of a punch line when telling a joke or humorous story. To receive the desired response, it's all a matter of timing.

After asking a few questions and receiving favorable responses that indicate interest, the candidate should thank the employer for the interview—giving the impression the candidate is through asking questions and concluding the interview.

Then, after a pause of a second or two, as the candidate is preparing to stand up, shake hands with the employer, and exit the interview, the following scenario can be played out:

Candidate: "I do have one other question."

Employer: "Yes, what is it?"

Candidate: "I'm ready. When would you like me to start?"

Please note: This approach is used only when the candidate is certain the employer is genuinely interested and he or she has had an outstanding interview. In many instances, when there are a considerable number of candidates being interviewed, this tactic has resulted in the candidate being hired on the spot, with the interview ending as follows:

Employer: "When can you start?"

Candidate: "Now!" or "Would tomorrow morning be good?"

9

THE NECESSITY, VALUE, AND METHOD OF SAYING THANK YOU

The Key to Continuing Employer Rapport.

Their words weren't exactly hostile or hurtful, but they were intense. It was a good thing she closed her office door, as the exchange of words was getting louder.

"Listen, Randy," Grace insisted, "there is a reason you send a thank you note following an interview, and it's not to ingratiate yourself with the employer."

"Okay, then," Randy countered, "if it's not to gain favor with the employer and to make yourself noticed, then why would you do it?"

"Well, Randy, can you think of any other reason you might send a thank you card to an employer, or to anyone else who had a connection with your interview?"

"I can't think of any. I just don't see the advantage in saying thank you to an employer, or to anyone else, for that matter. Besides, I don't even know if I got the job yet or ... didn't get it. So why should I think about saying thank you?"

Grace lowered her voice and said emphatically, "When I first separated from the military, I was a little stifled in my outlook on how things were done in the civilian sector. After eight years of following orders, there weren't a lot of words of thanks going around. It was all about doing your job, of surviving and getting out."

"How long were you out of work before you were employed?" Randy asked.

"After I separated from the military, it took me six months to get my first job. It was just a J.O.B. to get by until I decided what direction I wanted to go career-wise. I worked as a computer data analyst for the electronics company my dad retired from.

"It was a lot like being in the military, very impersonal and mission-driven. So I stayed with it for about two years while I finished a bachelor's degree in Human Development and Counseling. After graduation I contacted a Vet Rep at my American Job Center. We worked together to get me into a social services job. I thought I was doing okay in the interviews, but for some reason I just wasn't making the connection. My Vet Rep asked me if I was sending out thank you cards after each interview to employers and anyone connected with my interviews. When I said no and mentioned similar views to what you just expressed to me, he sat me down and opened my eyes and my heart to the real world of getting what you want out of life, and being of service to others. Long story short, I spent about three years in social services counseling, but in the back of my mind I was always intrigued and very much influenced by what my Vet Rep shared with me about saying thank you, which is part of the reason I became a Vet Rep. I've been one for the last twelve years."

Prompted by Grace's personal story, Randy asked, "So, what did your Vet Rep tell you about the 'thank you' thing?"

"He said far too many candidates fail to consider that we live in a society whose members are sometimes impolite and ungrateful. Their focus tends to be more oriented toward getting rather than giving. And if you have learned anything about job search, especially the interview process, it's all about attitude. For example, some vets coming out of the military have a false sense of entitlement regarding employment. They tend not to move beyond their perception of what it takes to establish meaningful rapport with a prospective employer, and so the WIIFM attitude prevails."

"What's a WIIFM?"

"It means What's In It For Me," Grace said. "Unfortunately, this 'getting' attitude indicates an impatience and a hurry-up mentality to acquiring what is erroneously believed to be the important things in life, It's a 'me first' focus on life."

"Sorry, Grace, but I don't see anything wrong with promoting yourself. That's the way the world works. If you don't speak for yourself, who will?"

"Randy, it's not a matter of just speaking up for yourself. It's how you do it and what you say that count."

Grace could sense by the puzzled look on Randy's face that he was in his own world and used to his own counsel.

Grace continued in the hope that he would catch on to the message she was delivering. "Sometimes when a person's view is narrowly focused on 'What's In It For Me,' they neglect to think about such things as the social graces and common courtesy. But the way the world really works, based upon Universal Principles that have been in force since time began, suggests the getting what we want in life is generally preceded by the act of giving first. Let me put it another way. Giving —in this case, saying thank you—is offered for its own sake, to show gratitude without expecting anything in return."

"Well," Randy said, "suppose I went to an interview and didn't get the job. Why would I even bother sending out a thank you card? It doesn't make any sense."

"I understand your reluctance but consider this," Grace said. "Some of the vets I've worked with over the years, when notified they weren't selected, experienced a dark cloud of disappointment, a feeling of personal rejection and failure. So, when the act of saying thank you is mentioned, they routinely dismiss it as useless and a waste of time because they didn't get what they wanted."

"You got that right. Like I said, it's a waste of time and it doesn't make sense. It's like I'm thanking someone for not hiring me. So, what's your point, Grace?"

"Hear me out, Randy," she said. "I've worked with some very astute vets who have sent out thank you cards in spite of their disappointment. When I asked them why, they said because it made them feel better. Some call it 'grace under pressure.' It helped them keep a positive outlook while continuing to do their job search."

The reflective tone in Grace's voice as she spoke, yet undetected by Randy, indicated a subtle strategy in the making.

As they ended their meeting, Randy said, "I'll give what you said some thought."

"We'll talk about it next time we meet up," she said. "Right now I have to get ready for an appointment with an employer I'm working with."

The meeting ended that day with Randy feeling somewhat vindicated. He had made his point, or so he thought. Yet, there was something nagging at him. His head told him he had reached safe ground, but his gut feeling left him a little uneasy. He asked himself, "Was it a matter of being right, or did everything come down to doing the right thing, according to someone else?"

The week evaporated quickly, and he was back at the American Job Center. As he walked into Grace's office, she was the first to speak. "Randy, I want you to meet Ed Racine. He is the CEO of Future Electronics. I've known Ed for a number of years and have sent several veterans to him to explore employment opportunities. You might want to listen to what he has to say about saying thank you following an interview."

Caught unaware, Randy's first thought was that he been set up. But he decided it was probably a good idea to sit and listen, since he was actually at a loss for words right then.

After the two men shook hands and were seated, Ed remarked, "Look, I can't speak for all employers, so I'm only referring to my own experience. As Grace said, we have worked together putting vets to work for a number of years. Yes, not all vets we've hired bothered to say thank you after an interview. Looking back, I suspect that our HR department hired vets solely based on their documented qualifications.

"Some of them never made it past their probationary period because they turned out not to be a good fit for our upbeat and enthusiastic work environment. The truth is, we generally hire for personality and demonstrated drive and train for competency."

Ed went on to tell about the first time he got involved with hiring a veteran. "Seems I had arranged an out-of-town workshop for members of my HR staff to attend, and had already paid up front for their training. We were more or less committed to sending personnel.

"At the same time we posted a job announcement for a new public relations position we badly needed filled because of recent subsidiary company expansion. There was some urgency in bringing the new person aboard as soon as possible."

"So, there I was, saddled with the task of facilitating interviews and ultimately making the hiring decision. I had picked several members of the operations team to make up the interview panel, but the hiring decision was mine alone to make. We had twenty-five applicants that we narrowed down to seven top candidates to be called in for an interview. They all seemed equally qualified."

Ed continued, "A few days later, I'm in the conference room where we had the interviews, cover letters, resumes, and Q&A interview answer sheets scattered out in front of me. I'm rummaging through and rereading all these documents on the table before me, and I notice this small envelope with FUTURE ELECTRONICS and my name printed neatly across the front. Curious, thinking it was some sort of invitation that had gotten mixed with other documents on the table, I opened it and pulled out a folded card that said THANK YOU in big bold letters across the face of the card."

Ed told Randy that the message inside read as follows:

Dear Mr. Racine:

Just a few words of appreciation for the time you took out of a busy day to meet with me and discuss employment opportunities with Future Electronics.

As a veteran in search of the opportunity to make a contribution to a new employer and its community I really had a strong sense of support – thanks for making me feel at home.

An opportunity to become a member of your team would be a highlight of my career.

Sincerely yours,
Shirley McAllister

"Wow," Randy blurted out, "I never realized people expressed themselves like that to employers!"

Ed Racine smiled and remarked, "Neither did I until I read that note. I vaguely remembered the name I had seen on a cover letter and resume. So I searched the pile on the table until I located the cover letter, resume, and Q&A sheet of Shirley McAllister.

"After I reread her material a few times, I came to the conclusion that she wasn't much more qualified than the rest of the candidates we interviewed. But I decided to offer her the job, and my decision was based on the fact that no one else had bothered to say thank you. She exhibited the kind of considerate heart we needed that would be the bedrock of a caring and sharing Public Relations Program Representative. Although Future Electronics is a high-tech producer, we are also a human-factor facilitator. I never wanted to lose sight of that concept."

After Ed Racine left her office, Grace asked Randy, "Does any of what he said make sense to you?"

Randy was somewhat in awe, and yet at the same time he was convinced that Shirley McAllister's hiring was a fluke, a lucky happenstance. He shrugged his shoulders and muttered, "I'm not sure. I'll have to think about it. Besides, guys don't talk like that!"

"Well, how do they talk, Randy?"

Still in his midtwenties, and still very much influenced by the military's "get it done" attitude, his response was not totally unexpected: "Okay, man, just give me the damn shovel and let me start digging!"

"Really?" Grace questioned. "Are you telling me women in the military act and talk different than guys in the military when it comes to performing?"

Randy looked at his watch. "Geez, Grace, I almost forgot. I have to meet someone, and I'm going be late if I don't leave now. I'll call you later to set up another meeting."

Several weeks passed before Randy finally contacted Grace. "Sorry about not calling you sooner," he said, "but I've been busy with my job search and a couple of interviews. It's been a week and I still have not heard back from the last two employers I interviewed with. Can't figure it out. I know I was qualified for both of those jobs. In fact, the last employer said he would call me with a decision in a day or two. I thought I had it made."

That experience, again, failed to remind Randy of what might be lacking in his efforts to get a job. He obligingly sat down in front of Grace, whining his tale of woe.

Grace chose her remarks carefully. "You know, Randy, what Ed Racine was saying a couple of weeks ago was no fairy tale. He told you what impressed him most about the candidate he hired for his new public relations position—it was the fact that she showed consideration and appreciation. Saying thank you is a key rapport-building and rapport-maintenance factor in many business operations these days."

She offered Randy this final piece of wisdom: "Thank you cards aren't duties but gifts—they are designed to create goodwill, and goodwill creates opportunity. They make a recipient feel valued, leaving a little happiness in their wake. Just know that personal notes build personal relationships."

Their meeting ended that day with Grace providing some instruction on how to develop and write a thank you card. Randy agreed to experiment with the thank you card process, even though he wasn't convinced it had any chance of working for him.

A week later, while job searching on the Internet, he had to do a double take at the following job announcement:

> **Wanted: Veteran with Avionics and Electronics experience. Certification required. This is a ground-floor opportunity for advancement with a startup company, excellent pay and benefits provided from day one.**
>
> **Please submit your cover letter, resume, references, and copy of A/P Certification to: Attention: HR Director, Keystone AvTech & Electronics 1848 Industrial Blvd. Seattle, WA 98199. Note: those candidates selected for an interview will be involved in a group process, with an emphasis on troubleshooting and correcting avionics & electronics problems.**

Randy couldn't believe his good fortune. The job announcement just about covered all his qualifications. He was pumped. A few days after applying, he was notified that he was a competitive candidate and was provided with interview specifics. He hadn't felt this good in a long time. This job was made for him. He had a couple of concerns, though.

He did the research and discovered that a group interview process involved multiple candidates being interviewed at the same time to see who stands out, how well candidates function in a group of people they do not know, and if candidates can show teamwork attributes needed to complete a task.

"Well, that's no problem," he decided. "It's what the military is all about."

The second issue he faced was one of major concern. Would this be the time to experiment with a thank you card?

The day arrived. All six finalists were seated at the conference table, waiting for the interview to begin. There was the cacophony of their voices and collective energy, like Formula-1 racing cars at the Ultimate Grand Prix starting line, engines revving up while waiting for the race to begin. Their loud chatter was followed suddenly by silence as two interviewers walked through the door.

"Good morning, everyone," one of them said. "This is Eva Marcone, HR Director, and I'm Ed Racine, owner and CEO of Keystone AvTech & Electronics, a subsidiary of our parent company, Future Electronics Corporation. Welcome..."

VOYAGER BASICS

A candidate needs to remember that sending a thank you card following an interview, whether it was successful or not, is crucial to establishing and maintaining future employer rapport and support. Why?

Because the negative and energy-draining feelings associated with imagined or perceived rejection (not getting a job offer) can destroy personal incentive and drive—a necessity for continuing to conduct a job search in an expectant and positive manner.

From a more practical viewpoint, writing a thank you note could create a positive connection with an employer who may present other future employment opportunities, which is more commonly referred to as learning not to burn your bridges behind you!

NOTE: Nowhere in the job search process is having the right attitude more important that when an employer advises that you have not been selected for hire.

For a candidate, showing consideration and gratitude with a thank you note after an interview—even though you may not have been hired—is crucial to generating the initiative to continue on to the next interview, and ultimately to an offer of employment.

You do it—not only because it's the right thing to do, but because it is the first step in learning to overcome adversity. Saying thank you identifies the individual as a class act—not only in the mind of the employer but, more importantly, in the applicant's own mind.

Within every adversity is the seed of an equivalent benefit, but attempting to find it is another matter. The barrier that many applicants and candidates face most of the time is that they become so immersed in a negative situation, often of their own making, that they don't take the time to look for that seed. Saying thank you helps an individual to remember to take the time … to look!

The idea of sending out a simple thank you card requires a candidate to consider the following:

- Saying thank you shouldn't be done with the expectation that the favor will be returned, or that perchance in some way it makes the employer feel obligated. Unfortunately, many candidates do think in this manner. Realistically, it doesn't work that way—the act of saying thank you is one of respect and sincerity. Either you believe in the value of expressing your appreciation and/or gratitude, or you don't. However, if you are a believer, bear in mind that writing a thank you note shouldn't be put off until you find it convenient. Do it right away. Just remember that the closer to the interview you send the note, the greater the chance of a positive response or outcome.

- Remember, there are no guarantees that come with expressing your thanks—it's a matter of extending a common courtesy.

Saying thank you could be the one influential factor that turns a hiring decision in your favor. Look at it this way: if you don't believe in expressing thanks, then perhaps the employer may not believe in you, especially if the position you interviewed for in some way involves customer services, human/public relations, teaching, assuming a leadership role, or functioning as a team member.

- Saying thank you is an indication that you do believe in yourself. Employers generally hire those candidates who demonstrate initiative and a sense of confidence in their ability and a willingness to do the job. The only true guarantee a candidate can get from saying thank you is the one gained through self-belief.

- Once a candidate has made an affirmative decision to say thank you, the best and only way to go about it is to ensure the gesture is one of simplicity, in its construction and delivery. This is the key that unlocks the door to employer acceptance—simplicity.

The following suggestions will help you write a simple yet meaningful thank you note after an interview:

1. Once a candidate decides who they will send a thank you card to, it should be done in a timely manner—ideally immediately following the interview but no later than 24 hours afterward.

2. Candidates don't always remember who they had contact with during an interview because they are dealing with nervousness and are focused on making a good first impression.

   To ensure the accurate collection and recording of important names, the candidate should bring a small pad and pen for jotting down notes and names when the opportunity arises. Or …

   Just bring the notepad and pen to serve as a reminder to stop and ask the secretary or receptionist for names and contact information on the way out of the employer's business following the interview.

3. The submission of a form letter has traditionally been used to say thank you following an interview, and it certainly is an appropriate method still used by many candidates, provided it is short and to the point. However, in far too many instances, zealous candidates tend to make it too obvious they are attempting to market themselves, often overdoing the "I'm the best qualified person for the job."

   This approach is more commonly referred to as high pressure or the hard sell which, more often than not, most employers resent.

   NOTE: Candidates attempting to continue to market and sell themselves in a thank you letter should understand that more is not always better—putting too much spice in the stew makes it unpalatable.

But when just the right amount is added to subtly tease the taste buds, the experience is enjoyable and the recipient is ready for a second helping. Forget the letter; send a thank you card!

4. Use of a thank you card becomes an extension of any positive rapport established during the interview. This simple gesture, although viewed by some as insignificant, can pay BIG DIVIDENDS when candidates with similar qualifications are being considered.

5. Maintaining simplicity begins with the selection of the card. Make sure the card has a white or beige background and is blank on all sides except the front which should have the words THANK YOU (in capital letters and bold print) across the face of it.

6. Forget cards that have borders decorated with flowers, little animals, or cartoon characters—they diminish the effect of a simple THANK YOU.

7. The inside of the card should be completely blank. Only the bottom half of the card is used to convey a brief, concise message— this eliminates the possibility of becoming verbose (too wordy).
   EXAMPLE of the interior message:

   Date: Month/Day/Year

   Dear Mr. Alexander:

   Just a few words of appreciation for the time you took out of a busy schedule to interview me.

   Your professional manner, openness about company operations, inquiry about my qualifications and background, and the questions you allowed me to ask really made me feel welcome and at home.

   The opportunity to become a contributing member of the Alexander team would be the highlight of my career.

   Sincerely,

8. For maximum effect, be sure the card is inserted the proper way in the envelope—that is, position the card so the words THANK YOU are facing the recipient as the card is removed from the envelope.

9. The envelope also requires a little proper staging. Place only the employer's name, business name, and address on the front of the envelope, establishing an expectation of something special—different from the usual #10 business envelope. For the last phase of staging the envelope, write the candidate's address only (excluding the name) on the back flap. This creates a little mystery—the employer's curiosity as to who sent the card won't be satisfied until the envelope is opened and the card read.

10. Before attempting to hand-generate a thank you message on the card, practice printing or writing (cursive style) what you want to say on a separate sheet of paper. Practicing will help you clarify your message and will also help you check for grammatical, spelling, and punctuation errors before composing the card and sending it to the employer.

    NOTE: Once an invitation to an interview has been received, a candidate can initiate a different approach to the use of a thank you card—sending one to thank the employer for the opportunity to participate in an interview.

    EXAMPLE of a pre-interview THANK YOU card:

    Date: Month/Day/Year

    Dear Mr. Marsh:

    Your interview invitation arrived today and I am honored to participate in the process.

    Recent research of Marsh International revealed that your organization is considered one of the premier U.S. operations in the field of fiber optics.

    The opportunity you present to determine if my qualifications are a match to your needs, and becoming part of the operations team, are things dreams are made of.

Again, thank you for this opportunity to interview.
Sincerely,

NOTE: First, this method should only be implemented via the U.S. Mail, using the same staging process previously explained. Such a note should only be sent when there's sufficient time (four to five days) before the interview is scheduled to take place, and when the identification of the employer or person facilitating or conducting the interview is known.

Second, to create an out-of-the-box impression after the interview, send a follow-up thank you card. Refrain from any mention of the first card but do indicate that the interview far exceeded your expectations, and it's one of the reasons you want to become part of the employer's organization.

11. Without exception, every candidate who sends a thank you card needs to remember this one basic principle: Never ever ask the employer or recipient if they received the card. Failure to observe this rule will in all likelihood ruin any opportunity a candidate may have had for an offer of employment or second interview.

   Just be aware that the act of saying thank you has always been accepted as a gesture of sincerity and courtesy. It is a sign of respect and appreciation of another's kindness or generosity and shows that you hold them in high esteem.

   It's something that is genuine and comes from the heart. It should never be used as a means of manipulation (i.e., seeking recognition.) Making an inquiry as to the receipt of the thank you card will appear as though the candidate were saying to the employer, "Look, I sent you a thank you card; the least you could do is say thank you in return!" Such an attitude, once perceived by an employer, can label a person both insincere and insecure—two traits that employers shy away from like bad breath.

12. Any follow-up contact with an employer should focus only on determining your status as a candidate. Sending a thank you card is like planting a seed. Sometimes it germinates and produces the flower of success, and sometimes nothing happens. Then you move on to planting the next seed in more fertile ground. Keep in mind, no one ever goes back and digs up the seed to determine why it didn't produce the results hoped for.

13. If during a follow-up contact the employer does mention the thank you card, it's safe to assume that it is being acknowledged and accepted in the spirit for which it was intended. Once it has been mentioned, you simply respond, "You are very welcome," and continue to move forward with determining your status as a candidate. If you are offered employment or a second interview, great! The seed of appreciation you planted has blossomed. If not, the door remains open to ask the employer for a referral and/or request consideration for future similar positions.

    Having established rapport with the employer, it is far more likely that you and your thank you card will be remembered in a positive light.

14. Showing appreciation to an employer for the opportunity to interview is more likely than not to be worth the time invested. However, expressing thank you is no guarantee it will result in a job offer.

    The only reward candidates can be assured of is the one they give themselves—the satisfaction of having acknowledged to the employer a measure of gratitude for having been considered for employment in the first place.

15. When a candidate and employer are in sync with one another, then expressing thank you becomes an extension of any rapport established during the interview. Unfortunately, if a candidate is not in the habit of conveying thanks to anyone, for

anything, at any time, seldom will mutual rapport take place either during or after the interview.

16. When composing thank you card messages for more than one person connected with your interview, avoid sending the same message to everyone.

17. Save all previously developed messages for future interview follow-up with other employers.

18. Consider sending a thank you card to anyone who assisted you in any way with obtaining an interview. The more people you express thanks to, the more positive energy the act is likely to generate—the greater the desire, the greater the input, the greater the outcome. The Roman philosopher Seneca said, "Let the man, who would be grateful, think of repaying a kindness, even while receiving it."

19. Sometimes it becomes necessary for an applicant to establish himself as a candidate in order to obtain an interview.

    If an applicant has not had a response from an employer within seven (7) to ten (10) business days following the submission of a cover letter and resume and/or application, consider the following scenario:

    - Call the employer, introduce yourself, and make an inquiry. "Good morning. This is Jason Brown. Seven days ago I submitted a cover letter and resume for the IT Tech position. Did you receive those documents?"

    - If the answer is yes, then ask, "Could you please tell me what my status is as a candidate?"
      Note: Regardless of the answer—unless it is, "We have already filled the position"—proceed to the next question:

    - "What is the next step I should take to get an interview?"
    The results of using this approach are mixed but … nothing ventured, nothing gained.

10

EPILOGUE

Manifesting Success is a Never-ending Journey.

As the introduction suggests, most life events of the individuals presented in **VOYAGER/VETERAN** are gleaned from my own personal experience assisting veterans who struggled to find their way through a maze of unfortunate circumstances, disappointment, self-doubt, and confusion—many times situations of their own making, and oftentimes matters beyond their control.

Much of what I have accomplished with veterans is a result of learning how to ask pertinent questions, as well as learning how and being willing to listen patiently as they struggled with issues of self-doubt and self-disclosure. Most had much to share regarding the personal and traumatic events that impacted their development and their attainment of career, employment, and life goals. To be sure, such issues were not easily revealed or resolved within 30 or 60 minutes of first-time, face-to-face meetings.

Often, several meetings had to occur before a vet would be open and trusting enough to provide in-depth personal information that would allow him or her to receive the kind of assistance needed to move forward with his or her life and career.

Over time, such emotion-laden personal commentary became a learning experience for me, and provided the kind of background and anecdotal material worth sharing with other veterans and those who serve them. It became a journey of mutual benefit, the premise upon which **VOYAGER/VETERAN** is based.

Concepts introduced throughout this journey, while at times appearing unconventional, were designed to encourage veterans to embark upon an experimental voyage of creative and intuitive job search while accepting and becoming facilitators of change in their own lives.

For the Vet Rep, establishing and maintaining ongoing dialogue with veteran clients represents a paradigm shift away from the way things were accomplished in the past, transitioning into the light of self-discovery and learning—comparing what you thought you knew about conducting job search, to the reality of what you need to know for the veteran to be competitive and productive.

In summary, **VOYAGER/VETERAN** endeavors to promote the reality of change as the one constant in today's job search process for veterans, Vet Reps, and allied professionals alike. It offers a variety of paths to be considered on the journey to employment—advancing from only one way of doing things (traditionalism) to an out-of-the-box adaptive model for progress. It gives the veteran applicant permission to consider and/or create alternative options to achieving top candidate status, leading to offers of employment, sustainability, and self-sufficiency.

The signs of change are all around us, all the time. And, what is with you, around you, and in you, generally tends to remain the same most of the time. But what needs to change is our perception of the creative variables possible—we can chose to recognize them as learning and life-enhancing opportunities or decide to ignore them and experience disappointment.

Take time to value and enjoy the voyage. Learning is a journey that never ends.

Best wishes,

P.D. Pritchard, DVOP

To help us continue to learn, improve, and provide essential support to our veterans, your comments and criticisms about **VOYAGER/ VETERAN** are encouraged.

Please send all inquiries, comments or, criticisms to:

peter.pritchard@comcast.net

NOTATIONS

DISCLAIMER

It should be noted there are thousands of books and websites available that provide job search guidance, written by individuals with varied degrees of education, expertise, and training in the job search and career development field—the latest of their publications of which is usually considered to be the best and latest invention since sliced bread. So please take note, **VOYAGER/VETERAN:** *The Journey to a Successful Job Search Mindset* is not the end-all answer to contemporary job search for veterans. But, what it is intended to provide is a basic model or foundation for engagement with an ever-changing job market. It is also a means to building a diversified set of job search skills relative to the changing needs of the veteran.

VOYAGER/VETERAN DEFINED

VOYAGER/VETERAN is an anecdotal presentation and guide designed to promote the right mindset for the veteran, young and seasoned alike, as an aid to conducting a simple but meaningful and successful job search in a very competitive job market.

DVOP (Vet Rep)

A Disabled Veteran Outreach Program representative is a veteran who specializes in developing job and training opportunities for veterans—with special emphasis on veterans with service-connected disabilities and/or other related barriers to employment. The DVOP specialist offers services to veterans enabling them to be competitive in the labor market—linking them to employers, veteran organizations, the Department of Veterans Affairs, and community-based organizations in an effort to find appropriate jobs and training opportunities once they are determined to be job-ready. Additionally, the DVOP serves as a Case Manager for veterans enrolled in federally funded training programs such as DAV's Vocational Rehabilitation Program. United States Department of Labor (Veteran's Employment & Training Service, 12/2018).

www.dol.gov/vets/programs/fact/Employmentservicesfs01.htm

LVER (Vet Rep)

A Local Veterans Employment Representative is a veteran who works in collaboration with a DVOP to determine that a veteran is job-ready and to assist with connecting them with employers. In short, a LVER is a Veteran's Advocate. They conduct outreach activities such as facilitating job fairs and conducting seminars and workshops for employers to successfully recruit veterans. They also help veterans translate their military experience into civilian occupations by assessing the veteran's interests and skills, conducting job search workshops, and establishing job search groups. LVERs have special responsibilities in helping federal contractors identify veteran candidates for their open positions (Workforce Training & Education Coordinating Board, 12/2018).

www.wtb.wagov/LocalVetsEmployReDir.asp

Note: Although DVOPs and LVERs have special and defined major responsibilities, the services they provide are so closely related they tend to overlap and are interchangeable depending upon the particular service needs of their clients and the U.S. region they serve in. This ensures priority and quality service for all qualified veterans.

About the National Veterans Training Institute (NVTI)

For more than 30 years, NVTI has trained a variety of veteran's employment and training professionals, including employment service personnel, veterans service organization leaders, federal and state staff, Department of Defense personnel, Native American groups that work with veterans, county service representatives, and others.

NVTI was established in November, 1968 and authorized in 1988 by P.L. 100-323. The Employment and Training Reporter, Volume 18, from 1986 reported DOL VETS was piloting courses for DVOP specialists and LVER staff. The courses were held the week of November 30, 1986, and the week of December 14, 1986, respectively. Under Title 38, Sec. 4109 USC, NVTI does not work directly with veterans; it trains the personnel who help veterans find and retain gainful employment.

NVTI programs are funded by the U.S. Department of Labor/ Veteran's Employment and Training Service, and administered by Management Concepts, with training conducted in Dallas, Texas, and selected regional sites. The Institute is the only one of its kind in the United States.

VSO (Vet Rep)

Every state provides Veterans Service Officers. They are specifically trained to assist veterans with Veterans Administration (VA) claims and to help identify veteran benefits available through local, state, and federal governments, usually based upon military service. The most recognized veteran organizations that also have their own VSOs include:

- Veterans of Foreign Wars (VFW) – https://www.vfw.org/NVS
- American Veterans (Amvets) – https://amvetsnsf.org/nso
- Vietnam Veterans of America (VVA) https://www.vvaorg/servicereps.html
- Disabled American Veterans (DAV) www.dav.org/veterans/NSOfficers.aspx
- Paralyzed Veterans of America (PVA)

www.pva.org/find-a-national-service-office-or-chapter

- American Legion (AL) – www.legion.org/serviceofficers
- Military Order of The Purple Heart (MOPH)
  www.purpleheart.org/ServiceProgram/Officerlocations.aspx
- National Veterans Foundation, 12/2018
  https://nvf.org/veteran-service-officers

VET REP

A common/generalized term used by veteran clients and the general public at large—a terminology most often used in referring to any governmental or veterans organization representative providing services to veterans.

VOYAGER

Starship USS Enterprise, Star Trek, Gene Rodenberry, Author via Wikipedia.org/wiki/USS Enterprise_(NCC-1701).

1 – DEALING WITH THE PAST:

Readability Monitor (Keeping Track of Readable Language)

From: The Average Sentence Length
By: Nirmaldasan, Via Google http://strainindex.worpress.com/2008/07/28/the-average-sentence-length

Wikipedia, 2014

(28) – Plutarch, The life of Lycurgus, 22.2

(29) – Plutarch, Moralia, Sayings of Spartan Women, 24.1

(30) – Miller, William Ian (2002) The Mystery of Courage, Harvard University Press, 2002, ISBN 978-0-674-00826-7.

Biographical of Mgy/Sgt John J. Valdez

Staff Non Commission Officer in charge,
American Embassy Saigon, R South Vietnam

"Last off the roof of the embassy during the fall of Saigon."
[Leatherneck Magazine May, 1975, USMC]

Fragging: When Soldiers In Vietnam Revolted Against Their Officers, Murdering Them With Grenades

By: Gina Dimuro, February, 17, 2019

http://allthatsinteresting.com/fragging-vietnamwar

Fragging- Wikipedia

http://en.wikipedia.org/wiki/fragging

Vietnam War Body Count Controversy – Wikipedia

http://en.wikipedia.org/wiki/vietnam_war_body_count_contrversy

Zen Tea

A collection of Zen stories, Posted July 11, 2012

Via Google search:

http://endofthegame.net/2012/07/11/a-collection-of-zen-stories

The Mammalian Diving Reflex

Dartmouth Undergraduate Journal of Science

Posted by DUJS/ In Winter 2012/March 11, 2012

Via Google search: http://dujsdartmouth.edu/winter-2012the-mammaliandivingreflex.VQMeRY7F9yw

The Muddy Road

A collection of Zen stories, Posted July 11, 2012

Via Google search: http://endofthegame.
net/2012/07/11/a-collection-of-zen-stories

What Is the Socratic Method?

Excerpted from Socrates Café' by Christopher Phillips

Via Google search: http://philosopher.org/socratic_method.html

Forgiving One Another

What does the Bible say about "forgiving one another?"

51 Bible Verses about Forgiving One Another

Via Google search: www.openbible.infotopics/forgiving_one_another

2 – SHORTCUTS:

3-S TANGO

S_ _t, Shower & Shave

Gedunk

Marine / Navy slang for snacks, candy bar, associated with the canteen or snack bar of a large vessel of the United States Navy or United States Marine Corps. The term in this sense was first recorded in *Leatherneck Magazine*, 1931.

Wikipedia Search: https://er.wikipedia.org/wiki/Gedunk_bar

"There Are No Shortcuts to Success"

Dan Waldschmidt, Author of EDGY Conversations, A blog, February 19, 2010, www.danwaldschmidt.com

"4 Reasons Why There Are No Shortcuts to Success"

Asif Premji, General Manager at Okotoks Honda dealership in Calgary, Alberta, Canada, June 13, 2017,
https://ca.linkedin.com/in/asifpremji

Luckily, There Are No Shortcuts

Kris Heap, Professional Dentist & Blogger, Author of "Successfully Create a Life You're Proud Of," krisheap@successify.net

3 – PREPARING FOR THE FUTURE BY ACCEPTING CHANGE:

Average Is Over

Tyler Cowan, "Powering America Beyond the Age of The Great Stagnation," Plum Publishing, 2014.

4 – THE VALUE OF LEARNING TO NETWORK:

JAG Corps

Reference via www.jag.navy.mil/careers_/navy_navyparalegals.htm
The U.S. Navy JAG Corps has legal careers for attorneys & paralegals:

- Judge Advocate General's (JAG) Corps open to law school graduates & law school students who are within two years of graduation.

- Paralegal specialist positions called (Legalman) are available for those without degrees.
  https://www.navy.com/careers/attorney-legalsupport

Naval Paralegals

United States Navy: Judge Advocate General's Corps, 2015, Legalman (LN) Rating Accession. Conversion Procedures – JAGINST 14440.1E
www.jag.navy.mil/careers_/navy_paralegals.htm

Guru

In Hinduism & Buddhism, a spiritual teacher, especially one who imparts initiation. A tutor, sage, counselor mentor, an influential teacher or popular expert.
www.google.com/guru
See also: www.urbandictionar/define.php?term=guru

Bindi

The Bindi is a colored dot, usually red, worn in the center of the fore-head, originally worn by Hindus & Jains from the Indian subcontinent. The dot is representative of the point at which creation begins, and may become unity.

https://en.wikipedia.org/wiki/Bindi_(Decoration)

National Defense Reserve Fleet (NDFR)=(Mothball Fleet), 06/15/2015

https://en.wikipedia.org/wiki/national_defense_reserve_fleet

Networking

"The Intersection of Purpose, Passion and Communication," Career Transition Group, April, 2015, Peabody Career Center, Vanderbilt University, adapted from:

www.alumni.hbs.edu/careers/networking.html

"The Truth About Using Social Media to Find a Job,"

by DavevOdegard, *Primer Magazine*, 2013,

www.primermagazine.com

"Why Face-To-Face Networking Is Beneficial for Job Search,"

by Deborah Shane, May 22, 2013, www.careerealism.com

"Top Ten People You Must Have In Your Network to Find a Job,"

by Tai Goodwin, February 2, 2015, www.careerealism.com

"Three Rules for Job Networking,"

by Kelly Crigger, May 18, 2018, www.Military.com

5 –THE APPLICATION CHALLENGE:

"Drill Instructor"

www.wickipedia.org/wiki/Drill_Instructor

"U.S. Marine Corps Jobs for Women"

What Does the USMC Have to Offer Women? 08/01/2015
www.usmc.net/usmc_jobs_for_women

"Marine Corps Nursing Careers,"

08/01/2015,www.usmilitary.com/3229/marine-corps-nursing-careers

Y.O.U. Job Search Guide, "Thirteen Steps to Your Employment Success,"

by P.D. Pritchard, 07/2007, Author's Corner, LLC Nashville, TN
www.authors-corner.com & www.youjobsearch.com

"The Book of U.S. Government Jobs, Where They Are, What's Available and How to Complete a Federal Resume,"

chapter 6, 11th Edition, by Dennis V. Camp, Bookhaven Press, LLC, 2011.

"Ten Steps to a Federal Job for Veterans,"

by Kathryn Troutman, author of veteran job search books & curriculum, 12/13/2016. www.military.com

6 – THE FEDERAL APPLICATION PROCESS:

"The Book of U.S. Government Jobs, Where Are They, What's Available and How to Complete a Federal Resume,"

11th edition, by Dennis V. Damp, Bookhaven Press, LLC, 2011.

7 – THE REALITY OF RESUMES AND COVER LETTERS:

The Book of Government Jobs,
11th edition, by Dennis V. Damp, Bookhaven Press, LLC, McKees Rocks, PA, 2011. www.info@bookhavenpress.com

Y.O.U. Job Search Guide, "Thirteen Steps To Your Employment Success,"
by P.D. Pritchard, 07/2007, Author's Corner, LLC Nashville, TN www.auther-corner.com & www.youjobsearchguide.com

The Muse,
"Powerful Verbs That Will Make Your Resume Awesome," 06/19/2017, www.themuse.com

Cover Letter Etiquette,
04/19/2017, www.military.com

Why You Should Encourage Veterans to Submit a Cover Letter,
by Linda Citroen, 2017, www.military.com

7 Steps to an Amazing Cover Letter,
by Jim Sweeney, 09/20/2018, jimmy@careerjimmy.comhttps://connect.efinity.com/appsuite/v=7.8.4-27.20180612.093120/print.html?print_1537443893635

Red Letter Resumes,
03/29/2017, www.redletterresumes.com

How to Write an Effective Resume,
2017 by Colonel John C. Buckley (Retired) U.S. Army, Career Coach & Mentor. www.military.com

20 Tips to Make Your Resume Stand Out,
by Linda Citroen, 2017 www.military.com

5 Resume Blunders to Avoid,
by Linda Citroen, 2017, www.military.com

Why White Space On Your Resume Is a Good Thing,
by Melissah Misquitta, 01/15/2015. https://empoweringstrengths.com

Resumes 101,
"White Space Is Your Friend," 06/14/2013. http://pilotonline.com

Resume Must-Haves,
"Relevance & White Space," by Liz Ryan, 05/12/2010. www.glassdoor.com

8 – PREPARING FOR AND PARTICIPATING IN THE INTERVIEW:

The Suck Less Job Search,
by Adam Reiter, Chief Jobs Officer, The Suck Less Job Search, Portland, OR, www.sucklessjobsearch.com, www.adam@sucklessjob-search.com , www.info@sucklessjobsearch.com

The Magic of Conflict,
by Thomas F. Crum, with introduction by John Denver, Simon & Schuster Publishers, New York, 1987.

Present Yourself With Impact,
by Caryl Winter, Ballantine Books, New York, 1983.

The Power of Now,
by Eckhart Tolle, September, 2001, New World Library, Novato, CA.

For The Love of The Game (film),

1999, by Michael Shaara (1991), starring Kevin Costner [as Billy Chapel] ("Clear the Mechanism," Gotta Stay In the Zone.") Wikipedia, 06/18/2018.

RAPPORT

is the close and harmonious relationship in which people or groups concerned are "in sync" with each other, understand each other's feelings or ideas, and communicate smoothly. Wikipedia, 04/16/2018. https://en.wikipedia.org/wiki/Rapport

ASVAB for Dummies,

(Armed Services Vocational Aptitude Battery), 03/10/2018, by Rod Powers & Jennifer Lawler, www.military.com/join-armed-forces/asvab

When Military Recruiting Goes Bad,

03/04/18,www.thebalance.com/top-lies-some-recruiters-tell-3354054

Lies They Tell Transitioning Veterans,

"Your MOS Is Your Destiny," by Peter A. Gudmundsson (a former Marine artillery officer & CEO of Recruit Military), www.military.com,09/19/2018,
www.military.com/veteran-jobs/career-advice/military-transition/lies-transitioning-veterans-mos-is-yourdestiny-html

United States Army Basic Training,

Wikipedia, 03/10/2018
https://en.wikipedia.org/wiki/United_States_Army_Basic_Traning

The Eight Types of Interview Questions,

05/28/2018
https://collegegrad.com/mastering-the- interview/the-eight-types-of -interview-questions/

The Organization Man,
by William H. Whyte, NY: Simon & Schuster, 1956.

What "The Organization Man" Can Tell about Inequity Today,
by Gary Sernovitz, *The New Yorker,* December, 29, 2016.

Behavioral Questions,
"Please Don't Tell Me About Yourself," 03/25/2018, by: Mark Murphy, author of *Hiring for Attitude*, McGraw-Hill, 2011.
https://hiring.monster.com/jr/hr-beswtpractices/recruiting-hiring-advice/interviewing-candidates/behavioral-questions.aspx

Behavioral Interview Techniques,
"The STAR Approach," 06/15/2018, Career Services, Wayne State University, 1001F/AB.
www.quintcareers.com/STAR_interviewing.html

How To Behave in a Behavior-based Interview,
0615/2018, Career Services, Wayne State University, F/AB.
www.quintcareers.com/behavioral_interviewing.html

How Do I Prepare for a Behavior Interview?,
06/15/2018, Career Services, Wayne State University, 1001F/AB.
www.quintcareers.com/behavioral_interviewing.html

Behavioral Interview Questions and Answers,
"Everyday Interview Tips," 06/02/2017.
https://everydayinterviewtips.com/questions-and-answers/behavioral-interview-questions-and-answers

Top Ten Behavioral Interview Questions and Answers,
"The Balance," by Alison Doyle, 02/04/2017.
https://thebalance.com/top-behavior-interview-questions-2069618

The Importance of a Positive Attitude during an Interview Process,

https://www.dwsimpson.com/9317/
the-importance-of-a-positive-attitude-during-an-interview-process

How Dragon-slaying Stories Will Help You Get The Job,

Forbes/Leadership/ "If I Only Knew," by Liz Ryan, contributor,
03/07/2017.

www.forbes.com/sites/lizryan/2017/03/07/
how-drago-slaying-stories-will-help-you-get-the-job

3 Biggest Interview Mistakes,

You'll Want To Avoid These At All Costs," by J.T. O'Donnell, Inc.
Magazine, 08/08/2017.

www.msm.com/enmoney/jobs/3-biggest-job-interview-mistakes-

you'll-want-to-avaoid-these-at-all-costs

The Seven Best Questions to Ask at an Interview,

by Hudson, Australia, 0/15/2015, http://au.hudson.
com/latest-thinking/latest-thinking-blog/postid175/
the-7-best-questions-to-ask-at-an-interview-rp

What to Do When You Hear You Are Overqualified,

"Your Next Mission, a Personal Branding Guide For The Military-to-
civilian transition," by Lida Citroen, 2017, Military.com.
lida@lida360.com

9 – THE NECESSITY, VALUE, AND METHOD OF SAYING THANK YOU:

Y.O.U. Job Search Guide,

"Thirteen Steps to Your Employment Success," by P.D. Pritchard, July
7, 2007, Author's Corner, Publisher, 07/05/2007, Nashville, TN.
books@authors-corner.com

Interview Etiquette,

"Is the Handwritten Thank You Note Outdated?" Learn vest, Forbes Magazine, 12/2018, by Molly Triffin, June, 2014.
https://www.forbes.com/sites/learnvest/2014/06/09/interviews-etuquette-is-the-handwritten-thank-you-note-outdated-472k-Cached-Similarpages

ABOUT THE AUTHOR

P.D. Pritchard

Pete has a diverse background spanning the width of several careers and decades of employment, educational, and community service experiences. They have contributed to his knowledge and understanding of what does and doesn't work for individuals conducting contemporary job search in today's competitive job market.

His fifty plus years of experience include assignments as a U.S. Air Force instructor and trainer; police department policy/procedure R&D analyst, inter-governmental ombudsman and police recruiting and training coordinator; vocational rehabilitation consultant and job placement specialist; JTPA placement and job coach, staffing agency manager, and his current assignment as a Disabled Veterans Outreach Program specialist with the Tennessee Department of Labor.

Much of his energies these days are directed at assisting veterans with significant barriers to employment to develop and marshal the self-motivational skills needed to continually move forward with their lives after serving their country.

Pete is the first to admit that his approach is not always the end-all answer to every job search issue that comes up in today' s evolving job market but, what he does offer veterans in his latest book, *VOYAGER/ VETERAN*, is the development of a mindset upon which to build a basic foundation for securing meaningful employment.

He has also worked as a drug and alcohol abuse prevention counselor in an Alaskan native school system, and wrote a monthly newspaper column chronicling his experiences working with Inupiaq students and communities in the Arctic.

As a Director of Career Services and Community Relations and, as a Campus Chief Administrator for a proprietary business school, he was responsible for resolving student retention and employment issues—advising at-risk and non-traditional students providing counseling and guidance on how to identify and establish career and occupational goals that lead to self-sufficiency, independence, solid employment opportunities, and on-the-job success.

Pete, a Certified GCDF (Global Career Development Facilitator), is a graduate of the Lila Atchison School of Community Service and Public Affairs, at the University of Oregon in Eugene, Oregon, achieving Master and Bachelor Degrees, and an Associate Degree in Criminal Justice Disciplines from Shasta Junior College in Redding, California. He has completed additional post-graduate work in the teaching of at-risk students, communications, educational and in-structional disciplines and curriculum/lesson plan development through the University of Oregon, University of Alaska, and Western Michigan University. He is a graduate of the National Radio Institute (NRI) School of Nonfiction Writing, a subsidiary of McGraw-Hill Publishing, in Washington, D.C., and the National Veterans Training Institute (NVTI) in Denver, Colorado. His unique style of developing and conducting job search training materials and counseling make it a worthwhile, productive, and creative learning experience for the veterans he serves.